Mount Washington and the Presidential Range Trail Guide

7th Edition

Mount Washington and the Presidential Range Trail Guide

7th Edition

Compiled and edited by
Gene Daniell and Steven D. Smith

APPALACHIAN MOUNTAIN CLUB BOOKS
BOSTON, MASSACHUSETTS

Cover Photographs: Robert Kozlow, and Jerry and Marcy Monkman
Cover Design: Brandy Polay
Book Design: Dede Cummings Designs
Cartography: Larry Garland

© 2003 Appalachian Mountain Club. All rights reserved.

Distributed by The Globe Pequot Press, Inc., Guilford, CT.

Published by the Appalachian Mountain Club. No part of this publication may be reproduced or transmitted in any form or by any means, electronic or mechanical, including photocopying and recording, or by an information storage or retrieval system, except as may be expressly permitted by the 1976 Copyright Act or in writing from the publisher. Request for permission should be addressed in writing to Appalachian Mountain Club Books, 5 Joy Street, Boston, MA 02108.

Library of Congress Cataloging-in-Publication Data

Mount Washington and the Presidential Range trail guide / compiled and edited by Gene Daniell & Steven D. Smith.—7th ed.
p. cm.
Rev. ed. of: Hiking guide to Mount Washington and the Presidential Range. 6th ed. c1998.
ISBN 1-929173-25-3 (alk. paper)
1. Hiking—New Hampshire—Washington, Mount—Guidebooks. 2. Hiking—New Hampshire—Presidential Range—Guidebooks. 3. Washington, Mount (N.H.)—Guidebooks. 4. Presidential Range (N.H.)—Guidebooks. I. Daniell, Gene. II. Smith, Steven D., 1953- III. Appalachian Mountain Club. IV. Hiking guide to Mount Washington and the Presidential Range.

GV199.42.N42W374 2003
917.42'20444—dc21

2003006964

The paper used in this publication meets the minimum requirements of the American National Standard of Information Sciences—Permanence of Paper for Printed Library materials, ANSI Z39.48-1984.

Due to changes in conditions, use of the information in this book is at the sole risk of the user

Printed on chlorine-free recycled paper using soy-content inks. ♲

Printed in the United States of America.

10 9 8 7 6 5 4 3 2 1   03   04   05   06   0

Contents

ACKNOWLEDGMENTS vii
INTRODUCTION viii
   About This Guide viii
   The Presidential Range viii
   White Mountain National Forest ix
   Appalachian Mountain Club Trails xi
BEFORE YOU GO xii
   Weather and Climate xii
   Trip Planning xii
   Following Trails xiii
   What to Carry xv
   Backcountry Hazards xvi
   Brook Crossings xxi
   Drinking Water xxi
   Camping xxii
   Winter Climbing xxv
   Protecting the Beauty of the Mountains xxvii
   A Final Note xxviii
HOW TO USE THIS GUIDE xxx
   Suggested Hikes xxx
   Trail Descriptions xxxi
   Distances, Times, and Elevation Gains xxxii
   Maps xxxiii
   Abbreviations xxxv

Contents

1. **MOUNT WASHINGTON AND THE SOUTHERN RIDGES** .. 1
   - Mountain Safety 2
   - Summit Buildings 5
   - Mount Washington Observatory 6
   - Mount Washington Auto Road 6
   - Mount Washington Cog Railway 7
   - Skiing in the Mount Washington Area 8
   - Geography 10
   - Huts 16
   - Camping 19
   - Trail Descriptions 21
2. **THE NORTHERN PEAKS AND THE GREAT GULF** 72
   - Geography 76
   - Huts 79
   - Camping 79
   - Trail Descriptions 81
3. **A BRIEF HISTORY OF THE WHITE MOUNTAINS** 145
   - Early Exploration and Settlement 147
   - The Era of the Grand Hotels 156
   - The Era of the Logging Barons 161
   - The Twentieth Century 163
4. **NATURAL HISTORY** 169
   - Geology 169
   - Climate 173
   - Plants and Animals 174

APPENDIX A: FOUR THOUSAND FOOTERS 184
APPENDIX B: ACCIDENT REPORT 189
INDEX 193
ABOUT THE AMC 200
LEAVE NO TRACE 201

Acknowledgments

Properly recognizing everyone, past and present, who made some contribution to this book would require a small book of its own, but the editors would like to recognize a few people whose contributions were especially indispensable.

First we would like to thank our families and particularly our wives, Debi Clark and Carol Smith. Their contributions to this book, though not outwardly visible, were immense. Without their constant assistance, encouragement and support, as well as companionship on many hikes, we would never have been able to give this book the time and energy it deserved. Therefore we dedicate our part of the life of this book to them, with love and gratitude.

Among the others who made unusually important contributions to this book, we wish to recognize the following:

First we want to thank the AMC Books staff: Beth Krusi, Belinda Thresher, Blake Maher, and Laurie O'Reilly. Not only did they assume all the myriad (and frequently tedious) professional responsibilities of publishing this book so that we could concentrate on preparing the text, they managed to cope with the eccentricities and frailties of the editors without complaint, giving generous support and assistance even when we made their jobs harder.

Also, we want to thank Larry Garland, who turned our fantasy of bright, beautiful new computer-generated maps into a reality. His obsession with making things right is at least equal to our own, and as a result he has managed to digest a staggering amount of detail and overcome many difficulties inherent to such a pioneering effort in order to produce maps that will actually help hikers plan their trips and complete them successfully. Larry deserves more appreciation than we will ever be able to give him.

We want to thank those who made other contributions to this book, including those individuals from the trail-maintaining organizations and other individuals who provided information, suggestions, corrections, and advice: Rebecca Oreskes, Don Muise, Dave Neeley, Dave Govatski, and Roger Collins of the WMNF, Andrew Norkin of AMC Trails, Doug Mayer, Jack Stewart, Mike Micucci and Dave Salisbury of the RMC, Mohammed Ellozy, Richard Curry, Carl Schildkraut, Roy Schweiker, Roioli Schweiker, Dave and Marita Wright, and Ken and Ann Stampfer—as well as all the others, too numerous to mention, who helped in some way to make this a better, more accurate book.

Introduction

ABOUT THIS GUIDE

This book aims for complete coverage of hiking trails located in the Presidential Range of the White Mountain National Forest in New Hampshire, an area consisting of Mount Washington, the high Northern Peaks, and the several ridges that run to the south. This area is bordered on the east by NH 16, on the north by US 2, on the west by the Jefferson Notch Road, and on the southwest and south by US 302.

THE PRESIDENTIAL RANGE

The Presidential Range lies somewhat north of the center of the White Mountains. The main ridge extends for more than 14 miles from northeast to southwest and consists of eleven peaks, with Mt. Washington, the highest at 6288 ft., roughly in the center. To the north of Mt. Washington are the Northern Peaks—Mts. Clay (5533 ft.), Jefferson (5716 ft.), Adams (5799 ft.), and Madison (5366 ft.). The Southern Peaks consist of Mts. Monroe (5372 ft.), Franklin (5001 ft.), Eisenhower (4760 ft.), Pierce (or Clinton) (4312 ft.), Jackson (4052 ft.), and Webster (3910 ft.). The five highest peaks in the range—Washington, Adams, Jefferson, Monroe, and Madison (Clay being generally regarded as a shoulder of Washington)—are the five highest in the northeastern United States. There are several subsidiary ridges, of which the longest, the Montalban Ridge, extends southward from Mt. Washington over Boott Spur (5502 ft.) for about 15 miles. Several of the peaks on this ridge offer exceptional views, including Mt. Isolation (4003 ft.), Mt. Davis (3819 ft.), Stairs Mtn. (3463 ft.), Mt. Crawford (3119 ft.), Mt. Resolution (3415 ft.), Mt. Parker (3004 ft.), Mt. Pickering (1930 ft.), and Mt. Stanton (1716 ft.).

There are many interesting features of the range other than the peaks, of which perhaps the most striking are the great ravines, technically called glacial cirques, that cut into the sides of the range. The largest of these, the Great Gulf, lies to the northeast of Mt. Washington and is enclosed by Mts. Washington, Clay, Jefferson, Adams, and Madison. There are several cirques on the Northern Peaks, the most prominent of which is King Ravine, which lies on the north side of Mt. Adams. On Mt. Washington's east face lie Tuckerman Ravine and Huntington Ravine, famous respectively for alpine skiing and rock and ice climbing. To the south are the Gulf of Slides, also a skiers' attraction, and Oakes Gulf at the head of Dry River. There are numerous waterfalls on the steep mountain brooks that drain the slopes of the range.

WHITE MOUNTAIN NATIONAL FOREST

Most of the higher peaks of the White Mtns. are within the White Mountain National Forest (WMNF), which was established under the Weeks Act and now comprises about 770,000 acres, of which about 47,000 acres are in Maine and the rest in New Hampshire. It is important to understand that this is not a national park, but a national forest; parks are established primarily for preservation and recreation, while national forests are managed for multiple use. In the administration of national forests, the following objectives are considered: recreation management, timber production, watershed protection, and wildlife habitat management. It is the policy of the USFS to manage logging operations so that trails, streams, camping places, and other spots of public interest are protected. Mountain recreation has been identified as the most important resource in the WMNF. The boundaries of the WMNF are usually marked wherever they cross roads or trails, usually by red-painted corner posts and blazes. Hunting and fishing are permitted in the WMNF under the state laws; state licenses are required. Organized groups, including those sponsored by nonprofit organizations, must apply for an Outfitter-Guide Permit if they conduct trips on WMNF land for which they charge any kind of fee; contact any WMNF office for details. Much informational literature has been published by the WMNF and is available free of charge at the forest supervisor's office at PO Box 638, Laconia, NH 03247, 603-528-8721 (TDD for hearing impaired: 603-528-8722), and other information centers.

Wilderness Areas: The National Wilderness Preservation System, which included the Great Gulf, was established in 1964 with passage of the Wilderness Act. The Presidential Range–Dry River Wilderness, the Pemigewasset Wilderness, the Sandwich Range Wilderness, and the Caribou–Speckled Mtn. Wilderness have since been added to the system, making a total of about 115,000 acres of designated Wilderness in the WMNF—about 15 percent of its area. Regulations for these areas prohibit logging and road building, as well as any use of mechanized equipment or vehicles, including bicycles. It should be noted that Wilderness Areas are established by an act of Congress, not simply by USFS administrative action, though the recommendations of the USFS are a critical part of the process of selecting areas for congressional designation. Management of these areas in accordance with guidelines contained in the Wilderness Act is entrusted to the USFS. Most important is the protection of the natural environment, and among other qualities that the USFS is charged with preserving is the opportunity for visitors to enjoy solitude and challenge within this natural environment. As a consequence, for example, "structures for user convenience" such as shelters are not permitted in Wilderness Areas.

In general, Wilderness visitors should look forward to a rougher, wilder, more primitive experience than in other parts of the WMNF, and should expect USFS regulations to emphasize the preservation of Wilderness qualities even when substantial inconvenience to hikers results. Those who are mainly looking for a pleasant hiking experience in scenic surroundings, perhaps with a group of cherished friends, would do well to look elsewhere—there are many wild, beautiful places outside of designated Wilderness. It is one of the ironies of Wilderness protection that such designation often draws crowds of people who imagine they can enjoy a true wilderness experience simply by visiting a piece of land with this official certification, and as a result the wildness that caused the area to be designated as Wilderness is severely compromised.

Scenic Areas: The USFS has also established ten Scenic Areas in the WMNF to preserve lands of outstanding or unique natural beauty, three of which are in the Presidential Range: Gibbs Brook, Pinkham Notch, and Snyder Brook. Furthermore, camping is restricted in many areas under the Forest Protection Area (FPA) program to protect vulnerable areas from damage. To preserve the rare alpine plants of the Mt. Washington Range and other significant and uncommon ecosystems within the entire WMNF, rules prohibit removal of any tree, shrub, or plant without written permission. Cultural sites and artifacts on public lands are also protected by federal law. If you discover such remains, please leave them undisturbed.

Trailhead Parking Fees: By a program initiated in 1997, the WMNF requires the purchase of a recreational permit for visitors who wish to park vehicles on WMNF land (including roadsides and other areas in addition to official trailheads). These permits are available for a day, a week or a year. There are self-pay stations at most affected trailheads where hikers can purchase a one-day permit; because the one-day fee is $3 and no change can be made, hikers intending to buy a one-day pass should make sure they have the correct change. Many important trailheads are located just outside the WMNF and are thus not subject to the fee, and there is some doubt about other trailheads, but signs notifying visitors about the permit program are posted at most of the trailheads at the beginning of the roadside areas where the permits are required. Because of uncertainty as to the status of some trailheads, and because the AMC does not wish to encourage overuse of free parking areas by those wishing to avoid the permit fee (which may cause serious parking problems in some places), no attempt has been made in this book to indicate which trailheads or other areas are subject to the permit requirement.

APPALACHIAN MOUNTAIN CLUB TRAILS

As a well-known and respected authority on hiking trails, the AMC works cooperatively with many federal, state, and local agencies, corporate and private landowners, and numerous other trail clubs and outdoor organizations.

AMC trails are maintained through the coordinated efforts of many people who volunteer their labor or contribute financial support, and the Trails Program staff and seasonal crew. Most of the difficult major construction projects are handled by the AMC trail crew, based in the White Mountains, which began operations in 1917 and is probably the oldest professional crew in the nation. Hikers who have benefited from the trails can help maintain them by donating their time for various projects and regularly scheduled volunteer trips with the AMC chapters. For hikers who are willing to assume a responsibility for regular light maintenance of a trail, there is an Adopt-a-Trail Program.

The AMC Volunteer Trails Program is active throughout the AMC's chapters and maintains control over 1,200 miles of trails, including 350 miles of the Appalachian Trail. Under the supervision of experienced leaders, hundreds of volunteers spend from one afternoon to two weeks working on trail projects.

For more information on any aspect of the club's trail and shelter efforts, contact AMC Trails Program, Pinkham Notch Visitor Center, Box 298, Gorham, NH 03581, or AMC Trails Program, 5 Joy St., Boston, MA 02108. Comments on the AMC's trail work and information on problems you encounter when hiking or camping are always welcome.

Before You Go

WEATHER AND CLIMATE

The descriptions in this book are intended to apply in the conditions that are usually encountered during the normal hiking season, which runs approximately from Memorial Day to Columbus Day. In some years ice or snowdrifts may remain at higher elevations until the early part of June—or even longer—and possibly much later than that in some of the major ravines, on north-facing slopes, and in other sheltered places. Such conditions vary greatly from year to year and place to place; one year most trails may be fairly clear by mid-May, but the next year hikers may find icy patches and even significant drifts well into June. When snow or ice are present, trails are often far more difficult to follow, and usually far more arduous, or even dangerous, to hike on.

Winterlike conditions can occur above treeline in any month of the year. Even on sunny days in midsummer, hikers above treeline should always be prepared for cold weather with at least a minimum of a wool or synthetic fleece, sweater, hat, mittens, and a wind parka, which will give comfort on sunny but cool days and protection against sudden storms. Spring and fall are particularly difficult seasons in the mountains, since the weather may be pleasant in the valleys and brutal on the summits and ridges. A great number of the serious incidents in the mountains occur in spring and fall, when hikers, deceived by mild conditions at home or even at trailheads, may find themselves facing unanticipated severe, perhaps life-threatening, hazards.

TRIP PLANNING

Plan your trip schedule with safety in mind. Consider the strength of your party and the general strenuousness of the trip: the overall distance, the amount of climbing, and the roughness of the terrain. Get a weather report, but be aware of the fact that most forecasts are not intended to apply to the mountain region; a day that is sunny and pleasant in the lowlands may well be inclement in the mountains. The National Weather Service in Gray ME issues a recreational forecast for the White Mountain region and broadcasts it on its radio station each morning approximately from 5 a.m. to 10 a.m.; the forecast from the

Mount Washington Observatory is posted at Pinkham Notch Camp at about 8 a.m., and is also carried on the National Weather Service telephone line (603-225-5191). Mountain weather information is also available on the AMC website (www.outdoors.org).

Plan to finish your hike with daylight to spare (remember that days grow shorter rapidly in late summer and fall). Hiking after dark, even with flashlights (which frequently fail), makes finding trails more difficult and crossing streams hazardous. Let someone else know where you will be hiking, and avoid letting people get separated from the group, especially inexperienced ones. Many unpaved roads are not passable until about Memorial Day, and from November to May the WMNF closes with locked gates many of its roads that are normally open during the summer season; many trips are much longer when the roads are not open.

FOLLOWING TRAILS

Maps: Hikers should always carry a map and compass and carefully keep track of their approximate location on the map. The maps included with this guide are topographic maps (maps with the shape of the terrain represented by contour lines). They are designed as an aid to planning trips and following well-established trails, and for determining a reasonable course of action in an emergency. They therefore cover fairly large areas, which necessarily limits the amount of detail that can be shown on them. In particular, on trails that closely follow streams, it is often difficult to show accurately the number and location of crossings; the text of the trail's description should also be consulted for this information. Due to this limited detail, these maps are not generally suitable for following obscure trails or for bushwhacks (planned trips away from trails). Maps with more detail (which necessarily cover much smaller areas) are published by the US Geological Survey.

Compass: The best compass for hiking is the protractor type: a circular, liquid-filled compass that turns on a rectangular base made of clear plastic. Excellent compasses of this type, with leaflets that give ample instructions for their use, are available for about $10. Such a compass is easily set to the bearing you wish to follow, and then it is a simple matter of keeping the compass needle aligned to north and following the arrow on the base. More sophisticated and expensive compasses have features designed for special applications that are often not useful in the woods; they are normally harder to use and apt to cause confusion in an emergency situation. Directions of the compass given in the text are based on true north instead of magnetic north, unless otherwise specified. There is a deviation of 16° to 17° between true north and magnetic north in the White Mountains. This means that true north will be about 17° to the right of (clockwise from) the compass's north needle. If you take a bearing from a map, you should add 17° to the bearing when you set your compass. On the maps included with this guide, the black lines that run from bottom to top are aligned with true north and south.

Trail Markings: In general, trails are maintained to provide a clear pathway while protecting the environment by minimizing erosion and other damage. Some may offer rough and difficult passage. Trails in officially designated Wilderness Areas, by policy, are managed to provide a more primitive experience and thus are maintained to a lower standard and sparsely marked and signed. Hikers entering Wilderness must be prepared to make a greater effort to follow their chosen route. Most hiking trails are marked with paint on trees or rocks, though a few still only have ax blazes cut into trees. The trails that compose the Appalachian Trail (AT) through the White Mountains are marked with vertical rectangular white paint blazes throughout. Side trails off the AT are usually marked with blue paint. Other trails are marked in other colors, the most popular being yellow. Except for the AT and its side trails, the color of blazing has no significance and may change without notice; therefore blazing color is not a reliable means of distinguishing particular trails from intersecting ones. Above timberline, cairns (piles of rocks) mark the trails. The treadway is usually visible except when it is covered by snow or fallen leaves. In winter, signs at trailheads and intersections and blazes also are often covered by snow. Trails following or crossing logging roads require special care at intersections in order to distinguish the trail from diverging roads, particularly since blazing is usually very sparse while the trail follows the road. Around shelters or campsites, beaten paths may lead in all directions, so look for signs and paint blazes.

If You're Lost: If you lose a trail and it is not visible to either side, it is usually best to backtrack right away to the last mark seen and look again from there; this will be made much easier if you carefully note each trail marking and keep track of where and how long ago you saw the most recent one. Even when the trail cannot be immediately found, it is a serious but not desperate situation. Few people become truly lost in the White Mountains; a moment's reflection and five minutes with the map will show that you probably know at least your approximate location and the direction to the nearest road, if nothing else. Most cases in which a person has become lost for any length of time involve panic and aimless wandering, so the most important first step is to stop and take a break, make an inventory of useful information, decide on a course of action, and stick to it. (The caution against allowing inexperienced persons to become separated from a group should be emphasized here, since they are most likely to panic and wander aimlessly. Make sure also that all party members are familiar with the route of the trip and the names of the trails to be used, so that if they do become separated they will have some prospect of rejoining the group.) If you have carefully kept track of your location on the map, it will usually be possible to find a nearby stream, trail, or road to which a compass course may be followed. Most distances are short enough that it is possible, in the absence of alternatives, to reach a highway in half a day, or at most in a whole day, simply by going downhill, carefully avoiding any dangerous cliffs (which will normally be found in areas where the map's contour lines are unusually close together), until you come upon a river or brook. The stream should then be followed downward.

WHAT TO CARRY

Adequate equipment for a hike in the White Mountains varies greatly according to the length of the trip and the difficulty of getting to the nearest trailhead if trouble arises. If you are only strolling in to a pond or waterfall a mile or so from the road in good weather, then perhaps a light jacket, a candy bar, and a bottle of water will suffice. If, however, you are going above treeline and are not inclined to turn back at the first sign of questionable weather, you will need a good pack filled with plenty of warm clothing and food for emergency use, and other equipment. No determination of what one needs to take along can be made without considering the length of a trip and the hazards of the terrain it will cross.

Essential Gear: Good things to have in your pack for an ordinary summer day hike in the White Mountains include guidebook, maps, at least 2 quarts of water per person, compass, knife (good-quality stainless steel, since ordinary steel rusts very quickly), rain gear, windbreaker, wool or synthetic sweater(s), hat and mittens, waterproof matches, enough food for your usual needs plus extra high-energy foods in reserve (such as dried fruit or candy), first-aid supplies (including personal medicines; a nonprescription painkiller such as aspirin, acetaminophen, or ibuprofen; adhesive bandages; gauze; surgical gloves; and antiseptic), needle and thread, safety pins, nylon cord, trash bag, toilet paper, and a (small) flashlight with extra batteries and a spare bulb.

Clothing: Blue jeans, sweatshirts, and other cotton clothes are popular but, once wet, dry very slowly and may be uncomfortable; in adverse weather conditions they often seriously drain a cold and tired hiker's heat reserves. While such clothes are worn by many hikers on summer trips, those people who are planning to travel to remote places or above treeline should seriously consider wearing (or at least carrying) wool or synthetics instead. Wool keeps much of its insulation value even when wet, and it (or one of several modern synthetic materials) is indispensable for hikers who want to visit places from which return to civilization might require substantial time and effort if conditions turn bad. Not only do hats, mittens, and other such gear provide safety in adverse conditions, but they also allow one to enjoy the summits in comfort on those occasional crisp, clear days when the views are particularly fine, when the other hikers who snickered at one's bulging pack are driven from the magnificent vistas with terse greetings forced through chattering teeth.

Boots: Wear comfortable hiking boots. Lightweight boots, somewhat more sturdy than sneakers, are popular these days. Experienced hikers can often wear sneakers quite safely and comfortably on easy to moderate hikes. Unfortunately, most of the people who actually do wear sneakers on the trails are inexperienced and not accustomed to walking on rough trails, and have legs and ankles that are not trail-toughened. As a result, many leg injuries occur on short, relatively easy trails because of the large numbers of inexperienced hikers who wear sneakers when they need the support of boots.

BACKCOUNTRY HAZARDS

In emergencies call 911 or the toll-free New Hampshire State Police number (800-525-5555) or Pinkham Notch Camp (603-466-2727).

Hypothermia: The most serious danger to hikers in the White Mountains is hypothermia, the loss of ability to preserve body heat because of injury, exhaustion, lack of sufficient food, and inadequate or wet clothing. Most of the dozens of deaths on Mt. Washington have resulted from hypothermia. It is important to understand that the victim does not "freeze to death," since death occurs at a body temperature of about 80° F. Many cases occur in temperatures above freezing; the most dangerous weather conditions involve rain, with wind, with temperatures below 50° F. The symptoms include uncontrolled shivering, impaired speech and movement, lowered body temperature, and drowsiness. The result is death, unless the victim (who will not understand the situation, due to impaired mental function) is rewarmed. In mild cases the victim should be given dry clothing and placed in a sleeping bag, then quick-energy food and something warm (not hot) to drink. In severe cases only prompt hospitalization offers reasonable hope for recovery. It is not unusual for a victim to resist treatment and even combat rescuers. It should therefore be obvious that prevention of hypothermia is the only truly practical course. Uncontrollable shivering should be regarded as a sure sign of hypothermia; this shivering will eventually cease on its own, but that is merely the sign that the body has given up the struggle and is sinking toward death.

Much has been written about hypothermia, and some of the advice has been confusing, largely because a victim in an advanced state of hypothermia requires radically different treatment from one in the early stages of the illness. Basically, chronic hypothermia—the form usually encountered in hiking situations— develops over the course of several hours when a person loses body heat faster than it can be generated. The body uses a number of means to prevent the temperature of vital organs from dropping to a level where proper functioning will be impaired; most important of these defensive actions is the withdrawal of blood supply from the extremities of the body into the core. This is the reason that poor coordination of hands and legs is an important sign of a developing problem. As the situation becomes more serious, the body goes into violent shivering, which produces a substantial amount of heat but consumes the body's last remaining energy reserves very rapidly. At this point rapid and decisive application of the treatments mentioned above may still save the victim's life. (Unfortunately, an exhausted hiker, or one who has not been eating or drinking properly, may not possess the energy reserves for violent shivering.) Violent shivering is the body's last response; once the shivering ceases the body has no more weapons to use and the descent toward death is quite rapid. This is profound hypothermia; and profound hypothermia cannot be treated in the field, since it requires advanced techniques such as circulating warm water through the abdominal cavity to rewarm the victim from the body core outward. Any attempt to rewarm such a person in the field will cause cold blood from the extremities to return to the heart, almost certainly causing death from heart failure. Extreme care must also be used in attempting to transport such a person to a trailhead, since even a slight jar can bring on heart failure. Since successful rescue of a profoundly hypothermic person from the backcountry is so difficult, the need for prevention or early detection must be obvious. In almost all cases, the advent of hypothermia is fairly slow, and in cold weather all members of a hiking group must be aware of the signs of developing hypothermia and pay constant attention to the first appearance of such signs—which may be fairly subtle—in all fellow party members, so as to detect the condition in one of their companions well before it becomes a serious matter. Those who do not pay attention to the well-being of their companions may well have the experience of standing by helplessly while a friend dies.

In sum, a person who is shivering violently must be treated for hypothermia immediately and aggressively. Since victims do not always exhibit violent shivering, as a general rule it is safe to render this sort of treatment to anyone who is able to eat or drink voluntarily, perhaps with minor assistance. Once violent shivering has ceased, or when a victim is unable to eat or drink without exceptional assistance, the existence of a state of profound hypothermia must be assumed. The victim should be protected from further heat loss as much as possible and handled with extreme gentleness, and trained rescue personnel should be called for assistance unless the party is capable of providing an advanced litter evacuation themselves.

For those interested in more information, a thorough treatment of the subject is contained in *The Basic Essentials of Hypothermia* (2nd ed., 1999) by William W. Forgey, M.D., published by The Globe Pequot Press, PO Box 480, Guilford, CT 06437, www.globe-pequot.com.

Lightning: Lightning is another serious hazard, particularly on the Presidential and Franconia Ranges and on any bare ridge or summit. In other mountain ranges throughout the world, where thunderstorms are more common and shelter often much farther away, fairly elaborate advice is often provided for finding the least unsafe place to sit out a storm. In the White Mountains the best course of action is to avoid the dangerous places when thunderstorms are likely, and to go down the mountain to shelter in thick woods as quickly as possible if an unexpected "thumper" is detected. Most thunderstorms occur when a cold front passes, or on very warm days; those produced by cold fronts are typically more sudden and violent. Weather forecasts that mention cold fronts or predict temperatures much above 80° F in the lowlands and valleys should arouse concern.

Animals and Insects: The most risky part of hiking in the White Mountains, in the opinion of many people, has always been the drive to the trailhead, and the recent rapid increase in New Hampshire's moose population has added a significant new hazard. During the first nine months of one recent year, for example, collisions between moose and automobiles caused the deaths of four people and more than 160 moose. The great majority of these collisions occurs in the period from early May to the middle of July, when the moose leave the woods to avoid the black flies and seek out the road salt that has accumulated in ditches near highways. Motorists need to be aware of the seriousness of the problem, particularly at night when these huge, dark-colored animals are both active and very difficult to see. Instinct often causes them to face an auto rather than run from it, and they are also apt to cross the road unpredictably as a car approaches. It is thus safest to assume that moose will behave in the most inconvenient manner possible. Otherwise they probably constitute little threat to hikers on foot, though it would be wise to give bulls a wide berth during the fall mating season.

Bears are common but tend to keep well out of sight. The last known case of a human killed by a bear in New Hampshire was in 1784—a 10-year-old boy in the town of Londonderry—and since that time many thousands of bears have perished from attacks by humans or their automobiles. Nevertheless, the bear is a large and unpredictable animal that must be treated with respect, though not fear. Several recent serious incidents have been unnecessarily provoked by deliberate feeding of bears, or by harassment by a dog leading to an attack on people nearby. Bears live mostly on nuts, berries, and other plants, and dead animals, and rarely kill anything larger than a mouse. Since the closing of many of the town dumps in the White Mountain region, where some bears routinely foraged for food, bears have become a nuisance and even a hazard at some popular campsites; any bear that has lost its natural fear of humans and gotten used to living off us is extremely dangerous.

The philosophy of dealing with bears has undergone some modification in recent years. Formerly the usual advice was that, if approached by a bear, one should throw down one's pack and back away slowly. This advice works, but unfortunately it teaches the bear that people have food and that very little effort and risk is required to make them part with it. The result is a bear that is likely to be more aggressive toward the next visitor, which may result in injury to the human (who may be you) and frequently results in a death sentence for the bear. Most hikers regard bears as an indispensable feature of wild country in New England, and preservation of the bears requires us to make sure that they remain wild, so feeding them either deliberately or through carelessness should be regarded as tantamount to bringing about their execution. Thus the current advice is that a hiker confronted by a bear should attempt to appear neither threatening nor frightened, and should back off slowly but not abandon food unless the bear appears irresistibly aggressive. A loud noise, such as one made by a whistle or by banging metal pots, is often useful. Careful protection of food at campsites is mandatory; it must never be kept overnight in a tent, but should be hung between trees well off the ground.

Deer-hunting season (with rifles) is in November, when you'll probably see many more hunters than deer. Seasons involving muzzle-loader and bow-and-arrow hunters extend from mid-October through mid-December. Most hunters usually stay fairly close to roads, and, in general, the harder it would be to haul a deer out of a given area, the lower the probability that a hiker will encounter hunters there. In any case, avoid wearing brown or anything that might give a hunter the impression of the white flash of a white-tailed deer running away. Wearing hunter's-orange clothing is strongly recommended.

There are no poisonous snakes in the White Mountains. Mosquitoes and black flies are the woodland residents most frequently encountered by hikers. Mosquitoes are worst throughout the summer in low, wet areas, and black flies are most bloodthirsty in June and early July; at times these winged pests can make life in the woods virtually unbearable. Fishermen's head nets can be useful. The most effective repellents are based on the active ingredient diethyl-metatoluamide, generally known as "DEET," but there are growing doubts about its safety. Hikers should probably apply repellents with DEET to clothing rather than skin where possible, and avoid using them on small children. There are other effective repellents available. There is also a good deal of folklore and tradition on the subject: people who seek true solitude in the woods often employ the traditional creosote-scented recipes, reasoning that anything that repels fellow humans might have the same effect on insects.

Ticks have been an increasing problem in recent years, becoming common in woods and grassy or brushy areas at lower elevations, especially in oak forests. At present the most feared tick (the tiny, easily overlooked deer tick, which can transmit Lyme disease, a potentially very serious illness that may be difficult to diagnose if the characteristic "bull's-eye" rash does not develop) is not yet common in the White Mountains, though its range seems to be steadily increasing. The common tick in the White Mountains is the larger wood tick (also known as the dog tick), which can also carry serious diseases such as Rocky Mountain spotted fever. Countermeasures include using insect repellent, wearing light-colored long pants tucked into your socks, and frequent visual checks of clothing and skin. Ticks wander for several hours before settling on a spot to bite, so they can be removed easily if found promptly. Once a tick is embedded, care must be taken to remove the whole animal; the head detaches easily and may remain in the skin, possibly producing infection.

Theft: Cars parked at White Mountain trailheads are frequently targets of break-ins, so valuables or expensive equipment should never be left in cars while you are off hiking, particularly overnight.

BROOK CROSSINGS

Rivers and brooks are often crossed without bridges, and it is usually possible to jump from rock to rock; a hiking staff or stick is a great aid to balance. *Use caution*; several fatalities have resulted from hikers (particularly solo hikers) falling on slippery rocks and suffering an injury that rendered them unconscious, causing them to drown in relatively shallow streams.

• If you need to wade across (often the safer course), wearing boots, but not necessarily socks, is recommended. Note that many crossings that may only be a nuisance in summer may be a serious obstacle in cold weather when one's feet and boots must be kept dry.

• Avoid trails with potentially dangerous stream crossings during high-water periods. Higher waters, which can turn innocuous brooks into virtually uncrossable torrents, come in spring as snow melts, or after heavy rainstorms, particularly in fall when trees drop their leaves and take up less water. Avoid trails with potentially dangerous stream crossings during these high-water periods.

• If you are cut off from roads by swollen streams, it is better to make a long detour, even if you need to wait and spend a night in the woods. Rushing current can make wading extremely hazardous, and several deaths have resulted. Floodwaters may subside within a few hours, especially in small brooks. It is particularly important not to camp on the far side of a brook from your exit point if the crossing is difficult and heavy rain is predicted.

DRINKING WATER

The pleasure of quaffing a cup of water fresh from a pure mountain spring is one of the traditional attractions of the mountains. Unfortunately, in many mountain regions, including the White Mtns., the presence of cysts of the intestinal parasite *Giardia lamblia* in water sources is thought to be common, though difficult to prove. It is impossible to be completely sure whether a given source is safe, no matter how clear the water or remote the location.

• *Carry Your Own Water:* The safest course is for day-hikers to carry their own water, and for those who use sources in the woods to treat the water before drinking it.

• *Filters:* There are also various kinds of filters available, which are constantly becoming less bulky and expensive and more effective; they also remove impurities from water, often making it look and taste better, so that sources that are unappealing in the untreated state can be made to produce drinkable water.

• ***Boiling:*** Water may also be boiled for five minutes or disinfected with an iodine-based disinfectant.

• ***Chemical Treatment:*** Chlorine-based products, such as Halazone, are ineffective in water that contains organic impurities, and all water-purification chemicals tend to deteriorate quickly in the pack. Remember to allow extra contact time (and use twice as many tablets) if the water is very cold.

The symptoms of giardiasis are severe intestinal distress and diarrhea, but such discomforts can have many other causes, making the disease difficult to diagnose accurately. The principal cause of the spread of this noxious ailment in the woods is probably careless disposal of human waste. Keep it at least 200 ft. away from water sources. If there are no toilets nearby, dig a hole 6 to 8 in. deep (but not below the organic layer of the soil) for a latrine and cover it completely after use. The bacteria in the organic layer of the soil will then decompose the waste naturally. Many people unknowingly carry the Giardia parasites, which have sometimes been present in municipal water supplies and frequently do not produce symptoms. Some authorities feel that the disease is more likely to be spread by party members to each other than by contaminated water. For this reason it would be advisable to be scrupulous about washing hands after answering calls of nature.

CAMPING

Those who camp overnight in the backcountry tend to have more of an impact on the land than day-hikers. In the past some popular sites suffered misuse and began to resemble disaster areas as campers left piles of trash and devastated the surrounding trees by stripping them for firewood. For this reason backpacking hikers should take great care to minimize their effect on the mountains by practicing low-impact camping and making conscious efforts to preserve the natural forest. If available on your chosen trip route, the best alternative is to use formally designated campsites to concentrate impact and minimize damage to vegetation. Many popular campsites and shelters have caretakers. In other areas, choose previously established campsites to minimize the impact caused by the creation and proliferation of new campsites. When selecting an established campsite, choose the ones that are farther away from surface water to protect the water quality for future and downstream users. Several websites (including www.LNT.org) are now devoted to encouraging "Leave No Trace" principles.

Shelters and Tentsites: There are more than 50 backcountry shelters and tentsites in the White Mountain area, open on a first-come, first-served basis. Some sites have summer caretakers who provide trail and shelter maintenance, educate hikers on low-impact camping methods, and oversee the environmentally sound disposal of human waste. An overnight fee is charged at these sites to help defray expenses. Most sites have shelters, a few have only tent platforms, and some have both. Shelters are intended as overnight accommodations for persons carrying their own bedding and cooking supplies. The more popular shelters are often full, so be prepared to camp at a legal site off-trail with tents or tarps. Make yourself aware of regulations and restrictions prior to your trip. Unless one plans carefully, it is quite possible to find oneself far from any legal, practical campsite with night swiftly approaching.

Trailside Camping Regulations: Trailside camping is really practical only within the WMNF, with a few limited exceptions, such as the established campsites on the Appalachian Trail. The laws of the states of Maine and New Hampshire require that permission be obtained from the owner to camp on private land, and that permits be obtained to build campfires anywhere outside the WMNF, except at officially designated campsites. Camping and campfires are not permitted in New Hampshire state parks except in campgrounds.

Overnight camping is permitted in almost all of the WMNF. To limit or prevent some of the adverse impacts of concentrated, uncontrolled camping, the USFS has adopted regulations for a number of areas in the WMNF that are threatened by overuse and misuse. The objective of the Forest Protection Area (FPA) program (formerly called the Restricted Use Area program) is not to hinder backpackers and campers, but to disperse their use of the land so that people can enjoy themselves in a clean and attractive environment without causing deterioration of natural resources. By protecting the plants, water, soil, and wildlife of the White Mountains, these restrictions should help provide a higher-quality experience for all visitors. Because hikers and backpackers have cooperated with FPA rules, many areas once designated as FPAs have recovered and are no longer under formal restrictions. However, common sense and self-imposed restrictions are still necessary to prevent damage.

Stated briefly, the 2002 FPA rules prohibit camping and wood or charcoal fires above timberline (where trees are less than 8 ft. in height), or within a specified distance of certain roads, trails, streams, and other locations, except at designated sites. Some of these restrictions are in force throughout the year and others only from May 1 to November 1. Because the list of restricted areas changes from year to year, however, hikers should get current information from the USFS in Laconia, NH, (603-524-6450), AMC at Pinkham Notch Visitor Center (603-466-2725), or any ranger district office for up-to-date information estimate.

Fire Regulations: Campfire permits are no longer required in the WMNF, but hikers who build fires are still legally responsible for any damage they may cause. Fires are not permitted on state lands except at explicitly designated sites, and on private land the owner's permission is required. During periods when there is a high risk of forest fires, the forest supervisor may temporarily close the entire WMNF against public entry. Such general closures apply only as long as the dangerous conditions prevail. Other forestlands throughout New Hampshire or Maine may be closed during similar periods through proclamation by the governors. These special closures are given wide publicity so that local residents and visitors alike may realize the danger of fires in the woods.

Low-impact Camping: In addition to following the camping regulations established by the USFS, you should practice low-impact camping.

• If you camp away from established sites, look for a spot more than 200 ft. from the trail and from any surface water, and observe Forest Service camping regulations for the area.

• Bring all needed shelter, including whatever poles, stakes, ground insulation, and cord are required. Try to choose a clear, level site for pitching your tent.

• Use a compass, and check landmarks carefully to find your way to and from your campsite.

• Do not cut boughs or branches for bedding.

• Avoid clearing vegetation, and never make a ditch around the tent.

• Wash your dishes and yourself well away from streams, ponds, and springs.

• Heed the rules of neatness, sanitation, and fire prevention, and carry out everything—food, paper, glass, cans, etc.—that you carry in (and whatever trash less thoughtful campers may have left). Food should not be kept in your tent; if possible, hang it from a tree—well down from a high, sturdy branch and well away from the tree trunk—to protect it from raccoons and bears.

In some camping areas, a "human browse line" where people have gathered firewood over the years is quite evident: limbs are gone from trees, the ground is devoid of dead wood, and vegetation has been trampled as people scoured the area for the smallest burnable twig. The use of portable stoves is often mandatory in popular areas, and is encouraged elsewhere to prevent damage to vegetation. Operate stoves with great caution—fuels can be explosive. Wood campfires should not be made unless there is ample dead and down wood available near your site; never cut green trees. Such fires must be made in safe, sheltered places and not in leaves or rotten wood or against logs, trees, or stumps. Before you build a fire, clear a space at least 5 ft. in radius of all flammable materials down to the mineral soil. Under no circumstances should a fire be left unattended. All fires must be completely extinguished with earth or water before you leave a campsite, even temporarily. Campers should restore the campfire site to as natural an appearance as possible before leaving the campsite.

Roadside Campgrounds: The WMNF operates a number of roadside campgrounds with limited facilities; fees are charged, and several of these campgrounds are now managed by private concessionaires. Consult the WMNF offices for details. Many of these campgrounds are full on summer weekends. Reservations for sites at some WMNF campgrounds can be made through MISTIX (800-280-CAMP). Several New Hampshire state parks also have campgrounds located conveniently for hikers in the White Mountains and other parts of the state. Reservations can now be made at all state campgrounds (603-271-3628, weekdays). For details on state parks and campgrounds, contact the Office of Vacation Travel, Box 856, Concord, NH 03301 (603-271-2665). Brochures on state parks and state and private campgrounds are usually available at New Hampshire highway rest areas throughout the normal camping season.

WINTER CLIMBING

Snowshoeing and cross-country skiing on White Mtn. trails and peaks have steadily become more popular in the last decade. Increasing numbers of hikers have discovered the beauty of the woods in winter, and advances in clothing and equipment have made it possible for experienced winter travelers to enjoy great comfort and safety. The greatest danger is that it begins to look too easy and too safe, while snow, ice, and weather conditions are constantly changing, and a relatively trivial error of judgment may have grave, even fatal, consequences. Conditions can vary greatly from day to day, and from trail to trail; therefore, much more experience is required to foresee and avoid dangerous situations in winter than in summer. Days are very short, particularly in early winter when darkness falls shortly after 4 P.M. Trails are frequently difficult or impossible to follow, and navigation skills are hard to learn in adverse weather conditions (as anyone who has tried to read a map in a blizzard can attest). Breaking trail on snowshoes through new snow can be strenuous and exhausting work. Some trails go through areas that may pose a severe avalanche hazard. In a whiteout above treeline, it may be almost impossible to tell the ground from the sky, and hikers frequently become disoriented.

Winter on the lower trails in the White Mtns. often requires only snowshoes or skis and some warm clothing. Even so, summer hiking boots are usually inadequate, flashlight batteries fail quickly (a headlamp with battery pack works better), and water in canteens freezes unless carried in an insulated container or wrapped in a sock or sweater. The winter hiker needs good physical conditioning from regular exercise, and must dress carefully in order to avoid overheating and excessive perspiration, which soaks clothing and soon leads to chilling. Cotton clothes are useful only as long as they can be kept perfectly dry (an impossible task, thus the winter climbers' maxim "cotton kills"); only wool and some of the newer synthetics retain their insulating values when wet. Fluid intake must increase, as dehydration can be a serious problem in the dry winter air.

Above timberline, conditions often require specialized equipment, and also skills and experience of a different magnitude. The conditions on the Presidential Range in winter are as severe as any in North America south of the great mountains of Alaska and the Yukon Territory. On the summit of Mt. Washington in winter, winds average 44 mph and daily high temperatures, 15° F. There are few calm days, and even on an average day conditions will probably be too severe for any but the most experienced and well-equipped climbers. The Mt. Washington Observatory routinely records wind velocities in excess of 100 mph, and temperatures are often far below zero. The combination of high wind and low temperature has such a cooling effect that the worst conditions on Mt. Washington are approximately equal to the worst reported from Antarctica, despite the much greater cold in the latter region. Extremely severe storms can develop suddenly and unexpectedly. But the most dangerous aspect of winter in the White Mtns. is the extreme variability of the weather: it is not unusual for a cold, penetrating, wind-driven rain to be followed within a few hours by a cold front that brings below-zero temperatures and high winds.

No book can begin to impart all the knowledge necessary to cope safely with the potential for such brutal conditions, but helpful information can be found in *Winterwise: A Backpacker's Guide* by John M. Dunn (1996, Adirondack Mountain Club) and the *AMC Guide to Winter Camping* by Stephen Gorman (2nd ed., 1999, AMC Books), which—despite their titles—are also quite useful for those primarily interested in day-hiking. Hikers who are interested in extending their activities into the winter season are strongly advised to seek out organized parties with leaders who have extensive winter experience. The AMC and several of its chapters also sponsor numerous evening and weekend workshops, in addition to introductory winter hikes and regular winter schedules through which participants can gain experience. Information on such activities can be obtained from the AMC information center at 5 Joy St., Boston, MA 02108 (617-523-0636; www.outdoors.org).

PROTECTING THE BEAUTY OF THE MOUNTAINS

Please use special care above timberline. Extreme weather and a short growing season make the vegetation in these areas especially fragile. Mere footsteps can destroy the toughest natural cover, so please try to stay on the trail or walk on rocks. And, of course, don't camp above timberline—it is illegal and very damaging to alpine vegetation.

Once every campsite had a dump, and many trails became unsightly with litter. Now visitors are asked to bring trash bags and carry out everything—food, paper, glass, cans—they carry in. Cooperation with the "carry in/carry out" program has been outstanding, resulting in a great decrease in trailside litter over the past few years, and the concept has grown to "carry out more than you carried in." We hope you will join in the effort. Your fellow backcountry users will appreciate it.

The Appalachian Mountain Club is also a national education partner of Leave No Trace, a nonprofit organization dedicated to promoting and inspiring responsible outdoor recreation through education, research, and partnerships. The Leave No Trace Program seeks to develop wildland ethics—ways in which people think and act in the outdoors to minimize the impact they have in the areas they visit and to protect our natural resources for future enjoyment.

The Leave No Trace ethic is guided by these seven principles:

- Plan ahead and prepare
- Travel and camp on durable surfaces
- Dispose of waste properly
- Leave what you find
- Minimize campfire impacts
- Respect wildlife
- Be considerate of other visitors

For more information and material contact Leave No Trace, PO Box 997, Boulder, CO 80306, or visit www.LNT.org.

A FINAL NOTE

Hiking is a sport of self-reliance. Its high potential for adventure and relatively low level of regulation have been made possible by the dedication of most hikers to the values of prudence and independence. This tradition of self-reliance imposes an obligation on each of us: at any time we may have to rely on our own ingenuity and judgment, aided by map and compass, to reach our goals or even make a timely exit from the woods. While the penalty for error rarely exceeds an unplanned and uncomfortable night in the woods, more serious consequences are possible. Most hikers find a high degree of satisfaction in obtaining the knowledge and skills that free them from blind dependence on the next blaze or trail sign and enable them to walk in the woods with confidence and assurance. Those who learn the skills of getting about in the woods, the habits of studious acquisition of information before the trip and careful observation while in the woods, soon find that they have earned "the Freedom of the Hills."

In recent years the cellular phone has begun to appear on the trails in great numbers. Properly used, it can contribute to hiker safety; improperly used, it can lead to unnecessary rescues and eventually to loss of life. Please remember that good reception (which unfortunately seems to require more and more ugly towers on many of our hills) does not exist in many parts of the mountains, particularly in deep, remote valleys, and that both phones and their batteries can fail, often at particularly inconvenient times. Cell phone use may be deeply unwelcome by fellow hikers who are trying to get away from it all. It takes a fair amount of time to organize rescue parties, which often require volunteers to leave their regular jobs; in addition, an unnecessary rescue mission may leave no resources to be called on if a real emergency occurs. Please make sure that there really is an emergency situation before you call for help. All such operations are expensive—someone has to pay—and they frequently put good people at risk. It is crucial to make sure there really is an emergency situation before calling for help. No one should expect a cell phone to bail them out from the consequences of foolish decisions. In the state of New Hampshire, hikers who are deemed to have acted in a foolish manner will be charged for the expense of their rescue. The least risky course is to act as if you do not have a cell phone until a situation develops where its use becomes unavoidable.

The AMC earnestly requests that those who use the trails, shelters, and campsites heed the rules (especially those having to do with camping) of the WMNF, NHDP, and SPNHF. The same consideration should be shown to private landowners. In many cases the privileges enjoyed by hikers today could be withdrawn if rules and conditions are not observed. Trails must not be cut in the WMNF without the approval of the forest supervisor, nor elsewhere without consent of the owners and definite provision for maintenance.

The trails that we use and enjoy are only in part the product of government agencies and public nonprofit organizations; there is ultimately no "they" responsible for providing the hiking public with a full variety of interesting, convenient, well-maintained trails. Many trails are cared for by one dedicated person, or a small group. Funds for trail work are scarce, and unless hikers contribute both time and money to this purpose, the diversity of trails available to the public is almost certain to experience a sad decline. Every hiker can make some contribution to the improvement of the trails, if nothing more than pushing a blowdown off the trail rather than walking around it. They are our trails, and without our participation in their care they will languish. (Contact AMC Trails, Pinkham Notch Visitor Center, Box 298, Gorham, NH 03581 [603-466-2725], for more information regarding volunteer trail-maintenance activities, or see the AMC website, www.outdoors.org.)

How to Use This Guide

SUGGESTED HIKES

In our continued effort to make the *Mount Washington and the Presidential Range Trail Guide* more useful and helpful to readers, a feature called "Suggested Hikes" has been relocated in this edition. At the end of each section of this guide is a list of suggested hikes designed to supply readers with a number of options for easy, moderate, and strenuous hikes within a region. While there are no strict criteria for these classifications, in general a short (easy) hike can be completed in about two hours or less by an average hiker, a moderate hike in a half a day, and a longer (strenuous) hike in a full day of seven or eight hours. The numbers in brackets indicate distance, elevation gain, and time calculated by the formula of a half an hour for each mile of distance or 1000 ft. of elevation gain (see explanation on page xxxii); "ow," "rt," and "lp" mean "one way," "round trip," and "loop" respectively. It should be repeated that the time allowances are merely a rough estimate—many parties will require more time, and many will require less—and they do not include time for extensive stops for scenery appreciation or rest.

When choosing a hike, readers should consider distance, elevation gain, time required, and special factors such as brook crossings and rough footing. A six-mile hike on easy terrain will require considerably less effort, though perhaps more time, than a three-mile hike over rocky trails with 1500 ft. of elevation gain. A hike should be tailored to the amount of time (and daylight) available, and to the experience, fitness, and ambition of the group. Larger groups will generally move at a slower pace.

A list like this provides for a certain number of challenges. Many trails that were obvious candidates for inclusion on this list already attract large numbers of people, and many hikers who visit one of them would likely find a beautiful spot simply too crowded for them to enjoy. Therefore, one of the most important criteria used in choosing these suggested hikes has been whether the places, and the trails that lead to them, can withstand any likely increase in use. All of us should be thoroughly aware of our role in protecting the beauty of the land we pass through—the capacity of the land increases when we walk through it lightly and quietly.

TRAIL DESCRIPTIONS

The Presidential Range is supplied with an extensive network of trails. The Appalachian Trail, running between Georgia and Maine, makes use of this network to cross the range (although it misses several of the summits), passing the AMC Mizpah, Lakes of the Clouds, and Madison huts. In each section of this guide through which the AT passes, its route through the section is described in a separate paragraph near the beginning.

While trails vary greatly in the amount of use they receive and the ease with which they can usually be followed, it cannot be emphasized too strongly that there is almost no trail that might not be closed unexpectedly or suddenly become obscure or hazardous under certain conditions. Trails can be rerouted or abandoned or closed by landowners. Signs are stolen or fall from their posts. Storms may cause blowdowns or landslides, which can obliterate a trail for an entire climbing season or longer. Trails may not be cleared of fallen trees and brush until late summer, and not all trails are cleared every year. Logging operations can cover trails with slash and add a bewildering network of new roads. In addition, even momentary inattention to trail markers, particularly arrows at sharp turns or signs at junctions, or misinterpretation of signs or guidebook descriptions, can cause hikers to become separated from all but the most heavily traveled paths—or at least lead them into what may be a much longer or more difficult route. So please remember that this book is an aid to planning, not a substitute for observation and judgment.

As a consequence, all the trail-maintaining organizations, including the AMC, reserve the right to discontinue any trail without notice and expressly disclaim any legal responsibility for the condition of any trail. Most organizations give priority to heavily used trails, so lightly used trails quite often do not receive their share of attention and following them may require great care.

The Ice Storm of 1998: A major ice storm in January 1998 caused great damage to woodlands in many parts of New Hampshire and Maine. Some areas and trails were practically untouched by this unusually destructive storm, but others suffered severely from the ice that snapped off many branches—and frequently even the upper parts of whole trees. The greatest part of the damage occurred in low- and medium-elevation, predominantly hardwood forests—in general the upper limit of the severe damage was about 2500 ft. Among the areas hardest hit were the south slopes of the Sandwich Range, the Randolph Valley, the Kilkenny region, and parts of the Evans Notch area. Affected trails were mostly cleared within a year or two, but in the heavily damaged areas the loss of the forest canopy has generated a great proliferation of undergrowth. On some trails in these areas the footway may be obscured by fast-growing vegetation during the summer months, particularly later in the season when shrubs and berry bushes reach their maximum growth.

Updating Trail Descriptions: We request your help in keeping the AMC *Mount Washington and the Presidential Range Trail Guide* accurate. New editions are published at intervals of about four or five years. This book belongs to the entire hiking community, not just to the AMC and the people who produce it. If you encounter a problem with a trail, or with a map or description in this book, please let us know. The comments of a person who is inexperienced or unfamiliar with a trail are often particularly useful. Any comments or corrections can be sent to the AMC *Mount Washington and the Presidential Range Trail Guide*, AMC, 5 Joy St., Boston, MA 02108.

DISTANCES, TIMES, AND ELEVATION GAINS

The distances, times, and elevation gains that appear in the tables at the end of trail descriptions are cumulative from the starting point at the head of each table. Elevation gains are given for the reverse direction only when they are significant, and are not cumulative—they apply only to the interval between the current entry and the next one (which will be the entry before the current one in the list). Reverse elevation gains are not given for trails that have summaries in both directions. All trails in this book have been measured with a surveyor's wheel within the past few years. Minor inconsistencies sometimes occur when measured distances are rounded, and the distances given often differ from those on trail signs. Elevation gains are estimated and rounded to the nearest 50 ft.; some elevation gains can be determined almost to the foot, while others (such as where several minor ups and downs are traversed) are only roughly accurate. Elevations of places are estimated as closely as possible when not given precisely by our source maps. The USGS maps are used as the basis for all such information except for the area covered by Bradford Washburn's map of the Presidential Range, where that map supersedes the USGS maps.

There is no reliable method for predicting how much time a particular hiker or group of hikers will actually take to complete a particular hike on a particular day. The factors that influence the speed of an individual hiker or hiking group are simply too numerous and too complex. Most hikers will observe that their own individual speed varies from day to day, often by a significant amount, depending on a number of factors, many of which—such as fatigue, weight of pack, or weather conditions—are fairly easy to identify. (Hikers often forget to consider that a given segment of trail will usually require more time—perhaps much more—when encountered at the end of a strenuous day compared to what it might have required if encountered at the start of the day.)

However, in order to give inexperienced hikers a rough basis for planning, estimated times have been calculated for this book by allowing half an hour for each mile of distance or 1000 ft. of climbing. No attempt has been made to adjust these times for the difficulties of specific trails, since fine-tuning an inherently limited method would probably only lead to greater unjustified reliance on it. In many cases, as hikers gain experience, they find that they usually require a fairly predictable percentage of book time to hike most trails, but eventually they are almost certain to encounter a significant exception. Therefore, all hikers using this book should be well aware of the limitations of the time-estimating formula, and should always regard book times with a critical eye and check each trail description thoroughly for trail conditions that might render the given times misleading; these times may be very inadequate for steep or rough trails, for hikers with heavy packs, or for large groups, particularly with inexperienced hikers. Average descent times vary even more greatly, with agility and the condition of the hiker's knees being the principal factors; times for descending are given in this book only for segments of ridgecrest trails that have substantial descents in both directions. In winter, times are even less predictable: on a packed trail, travel may be faster than in summer, but with heavy packs or in deep snow it may take two or three times the summer estimate.

MAPS

This 7th edition of the AMC *Mount Washington and the Presidential Range Trail Guide* features a new map that was designed on a computer, using a variety of digital data. The most valuable source of data comes from global positioning system (GPS) technology. Every mile of trail in the Presidential Range (except the trails surveyed by Bradford Washburn in the 1980s) was hiked and electronically recorded with GPS technology. The resulting maps accurately depict trail locations. All previous maps, including USGS quadrangle maps, relied on less precise techniques to determine a trail's location. The map featured in this guidebook now provides complete coverage of this area. Universal Transverse Mercator (UTM) grid coordinates are included on the map sheets to facilitate the use of GPS receivers in the field. Additionally, a mileage scale runs around the outer frame of each map to help users estimate distance.

Digital technology also allows the maps to be printed with five colors, making them easier to read. All WMNF lands are shown in green, with designated Scenic and Wilderness Areas highlighted in darker shades. The hiker and backcountry user should be aware that certain regulations may apply to any lands within the WMNF. It is the responsibility of the individual to be aware of landuse restrictions for both public and private land.

Although the original GPS data are very exact, certain features (including roads, streams, and trails) may have been approximated and/or exaggerated in order to show their proper relationships at map scale. We would appreciate your assistance by reporting corrections to: AMC Mount Washington and the Presidential Range Trail Guide Committee, Appalachian Mountain Club, 5 Joy St., Boston, MA 02108.

Extra copies of waterproof Tyvek AMC maps may be purchased at the AMC's Boston and Pinkham Notch offices and at many book and outdoor-equipment stores, as well as on the web at www.outdoors.org.

Detailed maps are available from the US Geological Survey for most of the United States, including all of New Hampshire and Maine. They are published in rectangles of several standard sizes called quadrangles (quads). Most areas in the regions covered in this guide are now covered by the recent, more detailed 7.5-minute quads—some in metric format—which have largely replaced the old 15-minute quads. Although topography on the newer maps is excellent, some recent maps are very inaccurate in showing the location of some trails. These maps can be obtained at a number of local outlets and from USGS Map Sales, Federal Center, Box 25286, Denver, CO 80255 (800-USA-MAPS, www.usgs.gov). Index maps showing the available USGS quads in any state and an informative pamphlet titled Topographic Maps are available free on request from the USGS. USGS maps are now also available on compact disc from a number of sources, including TOPO! and Maptech. It is possible to purchase map sets covering all of New Hampshire, all of the White Mountain National Forest, or even the entire New England–New York region.

The entire Presidential Range area is covered by the new (2002) National Geographic Trails Illustrated Map: Presidential Range/Gorham (#741), which was produced in partnership with the AMC. Some other maps of specific areas of the White Mountains are mentioned in this guide, but there are now so many maps covering various sections of the mountains—with more appearing each year—that it would take too much space to list them all.

ABBREVIATIONS

The following abbreviations are used in trail descriptions.

hr.	hour(s)
min.	minutes(s)
mi.	mile(s)
mph	miles per hour
in.	inch(es)
ft.	foot, feet
km.	kilometer(s)
yd.	yard(s)
est.	estimated
AMC	Appalachian Mountain Club
ASNH	Audubon Society of New Hampshire
AT	Appalachian Trail
CMC	Chocorua Mountain Club
CTA	Chatham Trails Association
CU	Camp Union
DOC	Dartmouth Outing Club
FR	Forest Road (WMNF)
HA	Hutmen's Association
JCC	Jackson Conservation Commission
LCC	Littleton Conservation Commission
MBPL	Maine Bureau of Public Lands
NC	Nature Conservancy
NHDP	New Hampshire Department of Resources and Economic Development Division of Parks and Recreation
PEAOC	Phillips Exeter Academy Outing Club
RMC	Randolph Mountain Club
RTC	Rivendell Trail Council
SLA	Squam Lakes Association
SPNHF	Society for the Protection of New Hampshire Forests
SSOC	Sub Sig Outing Club
TCTA	The Cohos Trail Association
USFS	United States Forest Service
USGS	United States Geological Survey
WMNF	White Mountain National Forest
WODC	Wonalancet Out Door Club
WVAIA	Waterville Valley Athletic and Improvement Association

Section 1

Mount Washington and the Southern Ridges

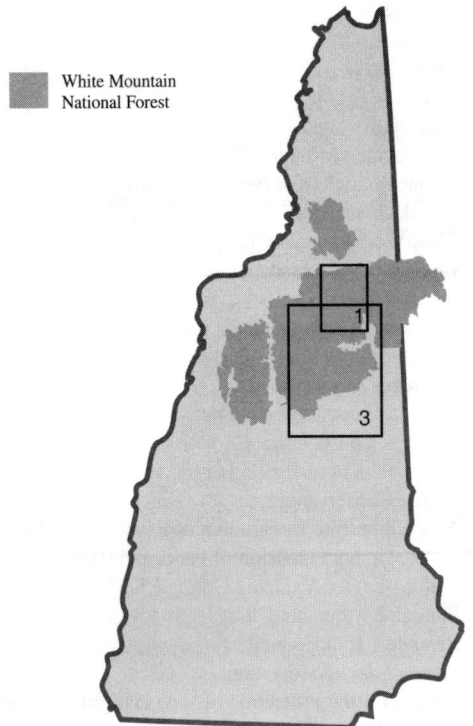

■ White Mountain National Forest

Introduction 2
Trail Descriptions 21
Suggested Hikes 69

LIST OF TRAILS

Trails to Mount Washington from Pinkham Notch

Tuckerman Ravine Trail 21
Lion Head Trail 24
Huntington Ravine Trail 25
Nelson Crag Trail 26
Boott Spur Trail 27
Boott Spur Link 28
Gulf of Slides Ski Trail 29
Glen Boulder Trail 29
The Direttissima 31

Trails on the Upper Cone of Mount Washington

Alpine Garden Trail 31
Southside Trail 32
Tuckerman Crossover 32
Lawn Cutoff 33
Camel Trail 33
Westside Trail 34
Trinity Heights Connector 34

Trails North of Pinkham Notch Visitor Center

Raymond Path 35
Old Jackson Road 35
Crew-Cut Trail 36
George's Gorge Trail 37
Liebeskind's Loop 37

Trails on the Main Ridge of the Southern Peaks

Crawford Path 38
Mount Eisenhower Loop 43
Mount Monroe Loop 44

Trails to the Southern Peaks from the West and South

Ammonoosuc Ravine Trail 44
Edmands Path 45
Webster-Jackson Trail 46
Webster Cliff Trail 48
Mizpah Cutoff 49
Sam Willey Trail 50
Saco River Trail 50
Saco Lake Trail 51

Trails of the Dry River Valley

Dry River Trail 51
Mount Clinton Trail 53
Mount Eisenhower Trail 54
Dry River Cutoff 55

Trails of the Montalban Ridge

Davis Path 56
Stairs Col Trail 59
Rocky Branch Trail 59
Isolation Trail 61
Mount Langdon Trail 63
Mount Parker Trail 64
Mount Stanton Trail 65
Cave Mountain Path 66

Trails of the Jackson Area

Winniweta Falls Trail 66
Iron Mountain Trail 67

This section includes the summit of Mt. Washington and the major ridges that run south from it, which constitute the southern portion of the Presidential Range. It is bounded on the north approximately by the line formed by the Mt. Washington Cog Railway and the Mt. Washington Auto Rd., on the east by NH 16, on the south by US 302, and on the west by US 302 and the Base Rd. The northern portion of the Presidential Range, including Mts. Clay, Jefferson, Adams, and Madison, and the Great Gulf, is covered in Section 2 of this book. Many of the trails described in Section 2 also provide routes to Mt. Washington.

The AMC Presidential Range map (map 1) covers this entire section except for the Iron Mountain Trail and several trails in the southern Montalban region in the south part of the section and a portion of the Davis Path. For those few trails not covered by map 1, the corresponding AMC map number is given. (AMC maps are available from the AMC; see the section on maps in "How to Use This Guide".)

Note: No hotel or overnight lodging for the public is available on the summit of Mt. Washington. No camping is permitted above treeline in summer. In winter, above-treeline camping is permitted in places where there is at least 2 ft. of snow cover on the ground, but not on frozen bodies of water nor on the east face of Mt. Washington's summit cone (the area above Tuckerman and Huntington Ravines and the Alpine Garden, running up to the summit).

In this section the Appalachian Trail follows the entire Webster Cliff Trail from Crawford Notch to its intersection with the Crawford Path near the summit of Mt. Pierce, then follows the Crawford Path to the summit of Mt. Washington. On the way it also crosses the summits of Mts. Webster, Jackson, and Pierce, and passes near Mts. Eisenhower, Franklin, and Monroe. From Mt. Washington, it descends to the Gulfside Trail (see Section 2) via the Trinity Heights Connector. Then, after passing over the ridge of the Northern Peaks (although missing most of the summits) and through the Great Gulf—areas also covered in Section 2— it returns to Section 1 at the Mt. Washington Auto Rd. and follows the Old Jackson Road to Pinkham Notch Visitor Center and NH 16.

MOUNTAIN SAFETY

Caution: Mt. Washington has a well-earned reputation as the most dangerous small mountain in the world. Storms increase in violence with great rapidity toward the summit. The highest wind velocity ever recorded at any surface weather station (231 mph on April 12, 1934) was attained on Mt. Washington. Judged by the windchill temperatures, the worst conditions on Mt. Washington are approximately equal to the worst reported from Antarctica, although actual temperatures on Mt. Washington are not as low. If you begin to experience difficulty from weather conditions, remember that the worst is yet to come, and turn back, without shame, before it is too late. (This warning applies as well to all peaks above timberline, particularly the Northern Peaks.) Each hiker should carry, as a bare minimum, a good rain suit with a hood (or equivalent outfit) that will also protect from wind, an extra sweater, a wool hat, and mittens. Cotton clothes, and blue jeans in particular, while popular and generally suitable for summer ascents of lower mountains, become a threat to survival in bad conditions above treeline due to cotton's propensity for promoting rapid heat loss when wet, which therefore contributes greatly to the development of hypothermia.

Ascents of the mountain in winter are sometimes easy enough to deceive inexperienced hikers into false confidence, but the worst conditions are inconceivably brutal and can materialize with little warning. Safe ascent of the mountain in winter requires much warm clothing, some special equipment such as crampons and an ice ax, and experienced leadership. From Columbus Day to Memorial Day, no building is open to provide shelter or refuge to hikers.

Inexperienced hikers sometimes misjudge the difficulty of climbing Mt. Washington by placing too much emphasis on the relatively short distance from the trailheads to the summit. To a person used to walking around the neighborhood, the trail distance of 4 mi. or so sounds rather tame. But the most important factor in the difficulty of the trip is the altitude gain of around 4000 ft. from base to summit, give or take a few hundred feet depending on the route chosen. To a person unused to mountain trails or in less than excellent physical condition, this unrelenting uphill grind can be grueling and intensely discouraging. If you are not an experienced hiker or a trained athlete, you will almost certainly enjoy the ascent of Mt. Washington a great deal more if you build up to it with easier climbs in areas with less exposure to potentially severe weather.

Visitors ascending the mountain on foot should carry a compass and should take care to stay on the trails. If you are forced to travel in conditions of reduced visibility, favor the main trails with their large yellow-topped cairns over the lesser-used connecting trails that are often far less clearly marked. The hiker who becomes lost from the trails above treeline in dense fog or a whiteout, particularly if the weather is rapidly deteriorating, is in a grave predicament. There is no completely satisfactory course of action in this situation, since the objective is to get below treeline as quickly as possible—with or without a trail—but the weather exposure is generally worse to the west while cliffs are more prevalent in the ravines to the east. If you know where the nearest major trail should be, then it is probably best to try to find it. If you have adequate clothing, it may be best to find a scrub patch and shelter yourself in it. In the absence of alternatives, take note that the Cog Railway on the western slope and the Mt. Washington Auto Rd. on the eastern slope make a line, although a rather crooked one, from west to east. These landmarks are difficult to miss in even the darkest night or the thickest fog, except in winter conditions when they may be concealed by snowdrifts. Remember which side of the mountain you are on, and travel clockwise or counterclockwise to the closer of the two, skirting the tops of the ravines; sooner or later you will reach one or the other. Given a choice, aim for the Auto Rd., as the railroad is on the side of the mountain that faces the prevailing winds.

Whether, as is often stated, Mt. Washington has the worst weather in the world, or at least in North America, is subject to debate. But the dozens of people who have died on its slopes in the last century furnish adequate proof that the weather is vicious enough to kill those who are foolish enough to challenge the mountain at its worst. This appalling and needless loss of life has been due, almost without exception, to the failure of robust but incautious hikers to realize that winterlike storms of incredible violence occur frequently, even during the summer months. Winds of hurricane force exhaust even the strongest hiker, and cold rain driven horizontally by the wind penetrates clothing and drains heat from the body. Temperatures in the 30s and low 40s can be even more dangerous than those below freezing, since rain penetrates and soaks clothing much more rapidly than snow, although at colder temperatures sleet and freezing rain on rocks can further obstruct a belated attempt to return to safety.

As the victim's body temperature falls, brain function quickly deteriorates; this is one of the first, and most insidious, effects of excessive heat loss (hypothermia). Eventually the victim loses coordination, staggers, and then falls, numb and dazed, never to rise again. At this point, any form of first aid in the field is likely to do more harm than good, and even immediate access to the best medical treatment obtainable will not assure the victim's survival. Prevention is the only sure cure. It is true that those who misjudge conditions and their own endurance almost always get away with their mistakes, and thus many hikers are lulled into overconfidence. The mountain spares most of those who underestimate it, including many who are guilty of the most grievous foolishness, but now and then it suddenly claims one or two (who may have been guilty of only minor errors of judgment, or even just of inexperience) without warning, or mercy.

All water sources in this heavily used area should be suspected of being unfit to drink; the safest course is to avoid drinking from trailside sources (for more information about drinking water and safety see p. xxi). Water is available at the Sherman Adams summit building during the months in which it is open, roughly from Memorial Day to Columbus Day.

SUMMIT BUILDINGS

No hotel or overnight lodging for the public is available on the summit of Mt. Washington. From Columbus Day to Memorial Day no buildings are open to hikers for shelter or refuge. The principal summit building serving tourists and hikers was named to honor Sherman Adams, a former New Hampshire governor and special assistant to President Eisenhower who was also a legendary White Mountain woodsman and, in his youth, trailmaster of the AMC Trail Crew. Operated by the NH Division of Parks and Recreation during the summer season (mid-May to mid-October), it has food service, a pack room, a souvenir shop, public restrooms, telephones, and a post office. It houses the Mt. Washington Observatory, the Mt. Washington Museum, and facilities for park personnel.

The first Summit House on Mt. Washington was built in 1852. The oldest building still standing on the summit is the Tip Top House, a hotel first built in 1853 and rebuilt after it suffered a fire in 1915. This stone building, now owned by the state of New Hampshire and part of Mt. Washington State Park, has been restored and is open to the public as a historical site when the public summit facilities are in operation, but is not available for lodging or emergency shelter. The second Summit House, 1873–1908, was destroyed by fire.

There are several other buildings on the summit of Mt. Washington, none of them open to the general public. The Yankee Building, built in 1941 to house transmitter facilities for the first FM station in northern New England, is now leased by WMTW-TV and houses two-way radio equipment for various state, federal, and local organizations. The transmitter building and powerhouse for WMTW-TV and WHOM-FM, built in 1954 and designed to withstand winds of 300 mph, provides living quarters for station personnel and houses television and microwave equipment. The Stage Office, built in 1975 to replace a similar building constructed in 1908, is owned by the Mt. Washington Auto Road Company.

MOUNT WASHINGTON OBSERVATORY

There has been a year-round weather observatory on Mt. Washington from 1870 to 1886, and from 1932 onward. The observatory maintains museum exhibits in the Sherman Adams summit building on Mt. Washington and in a new location on NH 16 just south of North Conway village. The Mt. Washington Observatory is operated by a nonprofit corporation, and individuals from the general public are invited to become members and contribute to the support of its important work. For details contact the Mt. Washington Observatory, Development Dept., PO Box 2448, North Conway, NH 03581 (800-706-0432).

MOUNT WASHINGTON AUTO ROAD

This road from the Glen House site on NH 16 to the summit, often called the Carriage Road, was constructed in 1855–61. Vehicles are charged a toll at the foot of the mountain. With long zigzags and an easy grade, the road climbs the prominent northeast ridge named for Benjamin Chandler, who died of exposure (as hypothermia was then called) on the upper part in 1856. Hiking on the road is not forbidden, but despite easier grades and smoother footing than hiking trails, the distance is long and the competition with automobile traffic is annoying and potentially dangerous. After dark, however, its advantages increase markedly while its disadvantages decrease greatly, so this road may well be the best escape route for hikers faced with the likelihood of becoming benighted on the trails of Mt. Washington. In winter, severe icing and drifting, along with ruts from official snow-vehicle traffic, make the section above treeline a less pleasant and more difficult route than might be anticipated, particularly for skiers. The emergency shelters that were formerly located along the upper part of the road have been removed. The first 4 mi. of the road (below treeline), although still used by snow vehicles, is now officially maintained as a part of the Great Glen cross-country ski trail network and receives considerable use by skiers.

Because of the continual theft and destruction of trail signs, they are often placed on the trails at some distance from the Auto Rd. The names of some trails are painted on rocks at the point where they leave the road.

The Auto Rd. leaves NH 16 opposite the Glen House site (elevation about 1600 ft.), crosses the Peabody River, and starts the long climb. Just above the 2-mi. mark, after sharp curves right and then left, the Appalachian Trail (AT) crosses. To the south, the AT follows the Old Jackson Road (now a foot trail) past junctions with the Nelson Crag Trail and the Raymond Path to Pinkham Notch

Visitor Center. To the north the AT follows the Madison Gulf Trail toward the Great Gulf and the Northern Peaks. Lowe's Bald Spot, a fine viewpoint, can be reached by an easy walk of about 0.3 mi. from the road via the Madison Gulf Trail and a short side path.

The Auto Rd. continues to treeline, passing to the left of the site of the Halfway House (3840 ft.), and soon swings around the Horn, skirting a prominent shoulder known as the Ledge, where there is a fine view to the north. A short distance above the Ledge, the Chandler Brook Trail descends into the Great Gulf on the right, and soon the route used by snow vehicles in winter diverges right.

Just above the 5-mi. mark, on the right exactly at the sharp turn, there are some remarkable folded strata in the rocks beside the road. Here, near Cragway Spring, the Nelson Crag Trail comes close to the left side of the road. At about 5.5 mi. the road passes through the patch of high scrub in which Dr. B. L. Ball survived two nights in a winter storm in October 1856. (Dr. Ball's account of his ordeal, *Three Days on the White Mountains: The Perilous Adventure of Dr. B. L. Ball on Mt. Washington,* published in 1856, is now available in a reprint edition from Bondcliff Books, PO Box 385, Littleton NH 03561.) A short distance above the 6-mi. mark, where the winter route rejoins, the Wamsutta Trail descends on the right to the Great Gulf, and the Alpine Garden Trail diverges left. The trenchlike structures near the road are the remains of the old Glen House Bridle Path, built in 1853. The road soon makes a hairpin turn and circles the left edge of a lawn sometimes called the Cow Pasture, where the Huntington Ravine Trail enters on the left and the remains of an old corral are visible on the right a little farther along. Beyond the 7-mi. post, the Cog Railway approaches and runs above the road on the right; near the tracks, just below the summit, the Bourne monument stands at the spot where Lizzie Bourne perished in September 1855 at the age of 23, the second recorded death on the mountain. Soon the road crosses the Nelson Crag Trail, which enters on the left and climbs to the summit from the right side. The Tuckerman Ravine Trail enters on the left just below the parking-lot complex at about 8 mi. (13 km.), from which the summit buildings are reached by a wooden stairway.

MOUNT WASHINGTON COG RAILWAY

The Mt. Washington Cog Railway, an unusual artifact of 19th-century engineering with a fascinating history, was completed in 1869. It roughly follows the route of Ethan Allen Crawford's second trail up the mountain, which he cut to provide a shorter and more direct route to Mt. Washington than the Crawford Path over the Southern Peaks. Its maximum grade, 13.5 in. to the yd., is equaled by only one other railroad in the world (excluding funicular roads), the railroad on Pilatus in the Alps. The location of the Base Station is called Marshfield, in honor of Sylvester Marsh, an inventor of meatpacking machinery who was the chief promoter and builder of the railway, and Darby Field, leader of the first recorded ascent of Mt. Washington. When the Cog Railway is in operation, walking on the track is not permitted; at other times it is a poor pedestrian route at best. A new public parking area is located on the Base Rd. about 0.5 mi. west of Marshfield. Hikers who wish to visit or park at the Base Station itself should expect to pay an admission fee.

The Cog Railway ascends a minor westerly ridge in a nearly straight line to the treeline, which is reached near the trestle called Jacob's Ladder (4800 ft.). This trestle, standing as much as 30 ft. above the mountainside, is the steepest part of the railroad. After crossing the shoulder that extends toward Mt. Clay, the line curves to the right and runs close to the edge of the Great Gulf; there is a fine view across the gulf toward the Northern Peaks from the vicinity of the Gulf Tank (5600 ft.). It is 3 mi. from Marshfield to the summit, and trains ascend in about 1 hr. 10 min.

SKIING IN THE MOUNT WASHINGTON AREA

A number of cross-country ski trails have been constructed in the vicinity of Pinkham Notch Visitor Center, making it a fine destination for those who wish to enjoy this sport. In addition, several of the hiking trails in the area are also suitable for ski touring. Information on these trails can be obtained at the center's Trading Post and on the AMC *Winter Trails* map.

The slopes of Tuckerman Ravine and the snowfields on and near the summit cone are justly famous for the opportunities they offer for alpine skiing. The skiing season on the Tuckerman headwall starts about the middle of March and may last into June in some years. The ravine area and the John Sherburne Ski Trail (see below) are patrolled by Forest Service rangers and the Mt. Washington Volunteer Ski Patrol. Warning notices about sections that are unsafe because of ice or possible avalanche danger are posted at Pinkham Notch Visitor Center and in the Tuckerman shelter area. Several lives have been lost in recent years from failure to read and heed these warnings. Skiing areas in the ravine, and also those in the Gulf of Slides or on any part of the mountain above timberline, are subject to wide temperature variations within short periods of time. The difference between corn snow and ice, or between bathing suits and parkas, may be an hour—or even less—when clouds roll in or the afternoon sun drops behind a shoulder of the mountain, so skiers should prepare accordingly. There is a sundeck at Hermit Lake but no longer a warming room open to the public.

The Tuckerman Ravine Trail affords an easy ascent route on foot since it is normally well packed, but skiing downhill on it is prohibited because people walking on the trail would be put in jeopardy. Skiers should descend from Tuckerman Ravine on the John Sherburne Ski Trail (WMNF). This trail—named for John H. Sherburne Jr., whose efforts contributed greatly to its establishment—leaves the south end of the parking lot at Pinkham Notch Visitor Center at the same point as the Gulf of Slides Ski Trail. It ascends by a zigzag course, always to the left (south) of the Tuckerman Ravine Trail and the Cutler River, to the foot of the Little Headwall of the ravine, above the shelter area, where it ends. It is 10 to 50 ft. wide, and although the slope is suitable for expert and intermediate skiers at some points, many less expert skiers can also negotiate this trail because of its width.

The Gulf of Slides, which is situated somewhat similarly to Tuckerman Ravine, receives a large volume of snow that remains in the ravine, so open-slope skiing is possible well into spring (April and May). Its slopes, though less severe than those in Tuckerman Ravine, are more uniform and avalanche frequently. The Gulf of Slides Ski Trail leaves the south end of the parking lot at Pinkham Notch Visitor Center at the same point as the John Sherburne Ski Trail, and ascends west about 2200 ft. in 2.5 mi. to the bowl of the Gulf of Slides.

The Old Jackson Road is a good run for intermediate skiers. It drops 650 ft. and can be run in 30 min. The ascent takes 1 hr. Skiers should use the old trail route instead of the relocation; enter the old route below the 2-mi. mark, about 0.2 mi. below where the relocated section and the Madison Gulf Trail meet at the Auto Rd.

The upper half of the Mt. Washington Auto Rd. is not usually suitable for skiing due to windblown bare and icy spots and ruts from snow-vehicle traffic. The snowfields between the top of the Tuckerman headwall and the summit cone, and also those on Chandler Ridge near the 6-mi. mark on the Auto Rd., afford good spring skiing at all levels of skill, but are far more exposed to bad weather and require much more effort to reach because of their elevation. The lower half of the Auto Rd. is maintained as a cross-country ski trail by Great Glen Trails. In particular, it affords a link between the Old Jackson Road at the 2-mi. mark and Connie's Way, a ski trail that runs from Pinkham Notch Visitor Center to the 1-mi. mark on the road.

GEOGRAPHY

Mt. Washington (6288 ft.), the highest peak east of the Mississippi River and north of the Carolinas, was seen from the ocean as early as 1605. Its first recorded ascent was in June 1642 by Darby Field of Exeter NH and one or two Algonkian natives, who may have reached the summit by way of the Southern Peaks—though no conclusive case can be made for any of the several reasonably practical routes, since only two rather meager secondhand accounts of this expedition have survived. Field made a second ascent a month later, and several other ascents were made that year, including one by Thomas Gorges and Richard Vines of Maine. However, the discovery that the mountain's slopes were not strewn with precious stones led to a sharp decline in interest after this flurry of visits, and it was almost two centuries before visits to Mt. Washington returned to this level. The mountain has a long and varied history of human activity, having been the site of several hotels, a road and a railway, a weather observatory, a daily newspaper, a radio station and a television station, and an assortment of auto, foot, and ski races. *The Story of Mt. Washington* by F. Allen Burt treats the entertaining (and frequently unusual) human history of the mountain in great detail, while Peter Randall's *Mount Washington* is a much shorter and less detailed handbook of human and natural history. *Not Without Peril,* by Nicholas Howe, available from AMC Books, provides a fascinating account of many of the accidents and other misadventures that have taken place on the Presidential Range.

Mt. Washington is a broad, massive mountain with great ravines cut deeply into its steep sides, leaving buttress ridges that reach up through the timberline and support the great upper plateau. The timberline occurs at an elevation of 4500 to 5000 ft., depending on the degree of exposure to the mountain's fierce weather. The upper plateau, varying in elevation from 5000 to 5500 ft., bears comparatively gentle slopes interspersed with wide grassy areas strewn with rocks, which are called lawns. The summit cone, covered with fragments of rock and almost devoid of vegetation, rises steeply above this plateau. The upper part of the mountain has a climate similar to that of northern Labrador, and its areas of alpine tundra support a fascinating variety of plant and animal life adapted to the extreme conditions of the alpine environment. Many of these species are found only on other high mountaintops or in the tundra many hundreds of miles farther north, and a few plants are found only or primarily on the Presidential Range. The alpine plants in particular have attracted many professional and amateur scientists (including, among the well-known amateurs, Henry David Thoreau), and many of the features of the mountain are named for early botanists such as Manasseh Cutler, Jacob Bigelow, Francis Boott, William Oakes, and

Edward Tuckerman. Great care should be exercised not to damage the plant life in these areas, as their struggle for survival is already sufficiently severe. Hikers should avoid unnecessary excursions away from the trails, and should step on rocks rather than vegetation wherever possible. The AMC publishes the *AMC Field Guide to the New England Alpine Summits,* a handbook covering the ecological relations of the plants and animals found above treeline, and *At Timberline,* which includes mountain geology and animal life as well as plants. The New Hampshire Department of Resources and Economic Development (PO Box 856, Concord, NH 03301) publishes booklets on geology intended for the general public. The Presidential Range area is covered by *The Geology of the Mt. Washington Quadrangle* (currently out of print) and *The Geology of the Crawford Notch Quadrangle.*

The slopes of Mt. Washington are drained by tributaries of three major rivers: the Androscoggin, the Connecticut, and the Saco. The high, massive **Northern Presidentials** or **Northern Peaks** (see Section 2) continue the rocky alpine terrain of Mt. Washington to the north and northeast in an arc that encloses the **Great Gulf,** the largest glacial cirque in the White Mtns. (A glacial cirque is a landform that results when a glacier excavates a typical V-shaped brook valley with a narrow floor and fairly uniform slopes, turning it into the classic U-shaped cirque with a broad, fairly flat floor and almost vertical walls.)

Moving clockwise from the Great Gulf around the east side of the mountain, **Chandler Ridge** (by which the Mt. Washington Auto Rd. ascends the upper part of the mountain) passes over the small peak of **Nelson Crag** before merging into the summit cone; this ridge divides the Great Gulf from the great ravines of the east face: **Huntington Ravine,** the **Ravine of Raymond Cataract, Tuckerman Ravine** (which is one of the finest examples of the glacial cirque), and the **Gulf of Slides.** Chandler Ridge also forms the north boundary of the lawn that is called the **Alpine Garden** for its colorful displays of alpine flowers in late June, which lies at the foot of the summit cone just above the three eastern ravines. **Lion Head,** a pinnacled buttress named for its appearance when seen from points on NH 16 just north of Pinkham Notch Visitor Center, caps the north wall of Tuckerman Ravine.

The steep eastern slopes of the mountain bear several notable waterfalls. **Raymond Cataract** falls through a series of wild and beautiful cascades in the Ravine of Raymond Cataract, but brush has covered a former footway, so this series of falls can be reached only by those intrepid explorers who are highly skilled in off-trail travel. **Crystal Cascade** is easily reached from Pinkham Notch Visitor Center by a walk of about 0.4 mi. on the Tuckerman Ravine Trail. **Glen**

Ellis Falls, located deep in the Ellis River valley, can be easily reached from the parking area located on NH 16, 0.8 mi. south of Pinkham Notch Visitor Center, by a gravel path 0.3 mi. long, with rock steps and handrails, that passes under the highway through a tunnel. The main fall is 70 ft. high, and below it are several pools and smaller falls.

Boott Spur (5500 ft.), the great southeast shoulder of Mt. Washington, forms the south wall of Tuckerman Ravine and the north wall of the Gulf of Slides. The flat ridge connecting Boott Spur with the cone of Mt. Washington bears **Bigelow Lawn,** the largest of the Presidential Range lawns. Both the **Montalban Ridge** and the **Rocky Branch Ridge** descend from Boott Spur and quickly drop below treeline, continuing south in thick woods with occasional open summits. **Oakes Gulf,** at the headwaters of the Dry River, lies west of Boott Spur and east of Mt. Monroe. The **Southern Presidentials** or **Southern Peaks,** running southwest from Mt. Washington, form the second most prominent ridge in the range (after the Northern Peaks), dropping to the treeline slowly and rising above it again several times before the final descent into the woods below Mt. Pierce. The Mt. Washington Cog Railway ascends the minor unnamed ridge that separates the much less spectacular (but still quite impressive) principal ravines of Mt. Washington's western face, **Ammonoosuc Ravine** and **Burt Ravine,** which lie between the Southern Peaks and the Northern Peaks.

Three major ridges run southwest or south from Mt. Washington, separated by deep river valleys from each other and from the ranges to the west and east. The most impressive of these ridges, formed by the **Southern Peaks,** runs southwest from Mt. Washington and ends abruptly at the cliffs of Mt. Webster, which make up the most impressive section of the eastern wall of Crawford Notch. The peaks that rise along this ridge are (from northeast to southwest) Mts. Monroe, Franklin, Eisenhower (formerly called Pleasant), Pierce (also commonly known as Clinton), Jackson, and Webster. To the northwest, the headwaters of the Ammonoosuc River (a Connecticut River tributary) flow across the Fabyan Plain—a broad, relatively flat expanse that separates the Southern Peaks from the much lower Cherry-Dartmouth Range; on the other side of the Southern Peaks ridge, the Dry River begins high on Mt. Washington in Oakes Gulf and runs to the Saco River below Crawford Notch through a deep, steep-sided valley between the Southern Peaks and the Montalban Ridge. Beyond the Dry River valley rises the Montalban Ridge, the longest of all Mt. Washington's subsidiary ridges, extending about 20 mi. from the summit. This ridge first runs generally south over Boott Spur, Mt. Isolation, Mt. Davis, Stairs Mtn., Mt. Resolution, and Mt. Parker, then swings east to Mts. Langdon, Pickering, and Stanton, the low peaks above the intervales of Bartlett and Glen near the confluence of the Rocky Branch and Saco River. The Bemis Ridge is a significant spur running from Mt. Resolution southwest over Mt. Crawford, then south to Hart Ledge, which overlooks the great bend in the Saco. East of the Montalbans lies the Rocky Branch of the Saco River, and to the east of that stream rises the Rocky Branch Ridge, a long, wide-spreading assortment of humps and flat ridges running south from Boott Spur via Slide Peak, with no noteworthy summit except Iron Mtn. at the far south end. Still farther east the Ellis River flows down from Pinkham Notch, with NH 16 running through the valley and the ridges of Wildcat Mtn. rising on the opposite side.

The **Southern Presidentials** or **Southern Peaks**—the names are used interchangeably—form a great ridge that extends about 8 mi. southwest from the summit of Mt. Washington to the Webster Cliffs above Crawford Notch. The Ammonoosuc River lies to the northwest and the Dry River to the southeast. The summits on this ridge decrease steadily in elevation from northeast to southwest.

Mt. Monroe (5372 ft.), the highest of the Southern Peaks, is a sharply pointed pyramid that rises abruptly from the flat area around the Lakes of the Clouds, with a secondary summit, a small crag sometimes called **Little Monroe** (5225 ft.), on its west ridge. The summit, crossed by the Mount Monroe Loop, is completely above treeline and affords fine views of the deep chasm of Oakes Gulf on the east, the **Lakes of the Clouds,** and the nearby summit of Mt. Washington. The Lakes of the Clouds are two small alpine tarns that lie in a small bowl on the northwest side of the ridge near the low point between Mt. Washington and Mt. Monroe. The larger lake, often called the Lower Lake, is at an elevation of 5025 ft., while the much smaller Upper Lake lies to the north of the Lower Lake at an elevation of 5050 ft. The flat region between Mt. Monroe and the Lakes of the Clouds supports a bountiful number of alpine plants, including the extremely rare Robbins' cinquefoil *(Potentilla robbinsiana),* making it the most significant and thus the most vulnerable habitat in the White Mtns. Part of this area is closed to all public entry due to damage caused in the past by hikers coming to admire these plants, which can withstand the full violence of above-treeline weather but not the tread of hikers' boots. Sadly, we can now pay homage to some of these rare survivors only from a distance. Due in large part to the sensitivity of hikers for the protection of the plant, in August 2002, the *Potentilla robbinsiana* was removed from the federal endangered species list, thanks to the efforts of the AMC, New England Wildflower Society, and the USFS.

Mt. Franklin (5001 ft.) is a flat shoulder of Monroe that appears impressive only when seen from below, in the Franklin-Eisenhower col. The summit's exact location (and even existence) among a group of low, rolling ridges is not entirely obvious; it lies a short distance to the east of the Crawford Path and commands an excellent view straight down into Oakes Gulf.

Mt. Eisenhower (4760 ft.), previously called Mt. Pleasant, was renamed after the former president's death. While there is a good deal of scrub on the lower slopes of this dome-shaped mountain, the top is completely bald. Its summit is crossed by the Mount Eisenhower Loop.

Mt. Pierce (4312 ft.) was named for Franklin Pierce, the only US president born in New Hampshire, by act of the New Hampshire legislature in 1913. Although this name is officially recognized by the Board of Geographic Names and appears on all USGS maps, it was not universally accepted, and the mountain's former name, Mt. Clinton, persists in the Mt. Clinton Rd. and the Mount Clinton Trail, which ascends the southeast slope of the mountain. Mt. Pierce is wooded almost to the top of its flat summit on the west, but a broad open area on the east side affords fine views. Its summit lies on the Webster Cliff Trail just above its junction with the Crawford Path.

Mt. Jackson (4052 ft.)—named for Charles Jackson, a 19th-century New Hampshire state geologist, and not (as many would suppose) for President Andrew Jackson—has a square, ledgy summit with steep sides and a flat top, affording possibly the finest views overall among the Southern Peaks. Its summit is crossed by the Webster Cliff Trail and is also reached by the Jackson branch of the Webster-Jackson Trail.

Mt. Webster (3910 ft.), once called Notch Mtn., was renamed for Daniel Webster, the great 19th-century orator, US senator, secretary of state, and unsuccessful aspirant to the presidency, probably the best-known and most eminent native the state of New Hampshire can claim. Webster visited the summit of Mt. Washington once with Ethan Allen Crawford as his guide, but unfortunately found the summit swathed in its customary blanket of clouds. Undaunted, the great orator delivered a short address to his large audience, the mountain itself: "Mount Washington, I have come a long distance, have toiled hard to arrive at your summit, and now you seem to give me a cold reception, for which I am extremely sorry, as I shall not have time enough to view this grand prospect which now lies before me, and nothing prevents but the uncomfortable atmosphere in which you reside!" Thousands of visitors have shared his experience of Mt. Washington and his regrets for the lack of a view, though few presumably have remonstrated so directly and eloquently with the mountain itself. The summit of Mt. Webster is crossed by the Webster Cliff Trail, which is intersected by the Webster branch of the Webster-Jackson Trail not far from the top.

To the southeast of the Southern Peaks lies the **Dry River,** running down the central valley of the Presidential–Dry River Wilderness. This river has also been called the Mt. Washington River, but Dry River has won the battle, possibly because of the ironic quality of the name. The Dry River runs from Oakes Gulf to the Saco through a deep, narrow, steep-walled ravine. Though in a dry season the flow is a bit meager, with lots of rocks lying uncovered in the streambed, its watershed has extremely rapid runoff and its sudden floods are legendary—it has drowned unwary hikers. No other logging railroad ever constructed in the White Mtns. had as many river crossings in so short a distance as the railroad that was built up this valley, and no other logging railroad ever had all its trestles swept away by floods so quickly after ceasing operations.

Access to the Dry River area has always been somewhat difficult, and ascents of the Southern Peaks from this side have always been relatively arduous. But since the Presidential Range–Dry River Wilderness was established and the number of wilderness-seeking visitors increased sharply, the WMNF has made access somewhat easier by eliminating many river crossings through trail relocations and the construction of a major suspension bridge at the first (and usually most difficult) remaining crossing. However, it is still an area where visitors need to keep a careful watch on the weather and take account of any substantial rainfall in the previous few days.

The **Montalban Ridge** extends southward from Boott Spur, forming the longest subsidiary ridge in the Presidential Range, running for about 20 mi. between the Rocky Branch on the east and the Dry River and Saco River on the west. At Mt. Resolution the main ridge curves to the east along the Saco valley, while the short **Bemis Ridge** carries the line of the upper ridge south to the great bend in the Saco. The peaks of the Montalban Ridge, in order from the north, include **Mt. Isolation** (4003 ft.), **Mt. Davis** (3819 ft.), **Stairs Mtn.** (3463 ft.), **Mt. Resolution** (3415 ft.), **Mt. Parker** (3004 ft.), **Mt. Langdon** (2390 ft.), **Mt. Pickering** (1930 ft.), and **Mt. Stanton** (1716 ft.). The peaks of the Bemis Ridge include **Mt. Crawford** (3119 ft.), **Mt. Hope** (2505 ft.), and **Hart Ledge** (2020 ft.). **Cave Mtn.** (1439 ft.), a low spur of the range near Bartlett village, is much better known for the cave on its south face than for its summit.

The views from the summits of Mts. Isolation, Davis, and Crawford are among the finest in the White Mtns., and Mts. Resolution and Parker also offer excellent outlooks. The **Giant Stairs** are a wild and picturesque feature of the region, offering a spectacular view from the top of the cliff that forms the upper stair. These two great steplike ledges at the south end of the ridge of Stairs Mtn. are quite regular in form, and are visible from many points. A third and somewhat similar cliff, sometimes called the Back Stair, lies east of the main summit but has no trail. Mt. Stanton and Mt. Pickering are wooded, but several open ledges near their summits afford interesting views in various directions.

All of the peaks named above are reached by well-maintained trails, except Mt. Hope and Hart Ledge. Mt. Hope is heavily wooded and very seldom climbed. The fine cliff of Hart Ledge rises more than 1000 ft. above the meadows at the great bend in the Saco River just above Bartlett and affords commanding views to the east, west, and south. There is no regular trail, but intrepid bushwhackers may follow the roads that run west along the north side of the river, passing under the cliffs, then climb up the slope well to the west of the cliffs.

East of the Montalban Ridge, beyond the Rocky Branch but west of the Ellis River valley, lies the **Rocky Branch Ridge.** This heavily wooded ridge runs south from Slide Peak, and is sharply defined for only about 3 mi., then spreads out and flattens. It has no important peaks. **Iron Mtn.** (2726 ft.), a small mountain near Jackson with a fine north outlook and a magnificent bare ledge at the top of its south cliff, is the most significant summit on this long stretch of uplands between the Rocky Branch and the Ellis River—though the Rocky Branch Ridge ceases to be an outstanding ridge long before it reaches Iron Mtn. **Green Hill** (2181 ft.) is a shoulder of Iron Mtn. with an interesting view reached by an unofficial path.

HUTS

For current information on AMC huts, Pinkham Notch Visitor Center, or the Highland Center at Crawford Notch, contact the Reservation Office, Pinkham Notch Visitor Center, PO Box 298, Gorham, NH 03581 (603-466-2727) or www.outdoors.org.

Pinkham Notch Visitor Center (AMC)

Pinkham Notch Visitor Center is a unique mountain sports facility in the heart of the WMNF. This facility, originally built in 1920 and greatly enlarged since then, is located on NH 16 practically at the height-of-land in Pinkham Notch, about 20 mi. north of Conway and 11 mi. south of Gorham. It is also 0.8 mi. north of Glen Ellis Falls and 0.5 mi. south of the base of the Wildcat Mountain Ski Area. Pinkham Notch Visitor Center offers food and lodging to the public throughout the year and is managed similarly to the AMC huts. Pets are not allowed inside any building of the visitor center. The telephone number for the reservation office is 603-466-2727; the number for general information is 603-466-2721.

Concord Trailways offers daily bus service to and from Logan Airport and South Station in Boston, and the AMC operates a hiker shuttle bus from the visitor center to most of the principal trailheads in the White Mtns. during the summer.

The Joe Dodge Lodge accommodates more than 100 guests in a variety of bunk and family rooms. It also offers overnight guests a library that commands a spectacular view of the nearby Wildcat Ridge, and a living room where accounts of the day's activities can be shared around an open fireplace. The center features a 65-seat conference room equipped with audiovisual facilities.

The Trading Post, a popular meeting place for hikers, has been a center of AMC educational and recreational activities since 1920. Weekend workshops, seminars, and lectures are conducted throughout the year. The building houses a dining room, and an information desk where basic equipment, guidebooks, maps, and other AMC publications are available. The pack room downstairs is open 24 hours a day for hikers to stop in, relax, use the coin-operated showers, and repack their gear.

Pinkham Notch Visitor Center is the most important trailhead on the east side of Mt. Washington. Free public parking is available, although sleeping in cars is not permitted. Additional parking is available in designated areas along NH 16 in both directions, but a USFS recreational permit is required. The Tuckerman Ravine Trail, the Lost Pond Trail, and the Old Jackson Road all start at the center, giving access to many more trails, and a number of walking trails have been constructed for shorter, easier trips in the Pinkham vicinity. Among these are the Crew-Cut Trail, George's Gorge Trail, Liebeskind's Loop, and the Square Ledge Trail. There are also several ski-touring trails; for information consult personnel at the Trading Post main desk.

The Highland Center at Crawford Notch (AMC)

Located at the head of Crawford Notch in the heart of the WMNF, the new Highland Center, scheduled for opening in fall 2003, is a lodging and outdoor program center open to the public year-round. It is located at the site of the Crawford House grand hotel on US 302, about 20 mi. west of North Conway and 8.5 mi. east of the traffic lights in Twin Mountain village.

Plans call for 35 lodging rooms accommodating a total of 120 beds, including shared rooms with shared baths and private rooms with private baths. Reservations are encouraged and may be made through the Pinkham Notch Visitor Center reservation office (603-466-2727). The center's construction utilizes energy-efficient materials and is designed to complement the landscape while paying tribute to the intriguing human history in Crawford Notch. Meals consisting of hearty mountain fare will be served in a family-style setting.

A wide variety of educational programs and skills training for children, teens, and adults will be offered at the Highland Center, aiming to help participants increase their understanding of the natural environment and gain proficiency in outdoor skills such as map and compass use or wilderness medicine. Day-hikers, backpackers, and other visitors will be able to access trail and weather information at the center.

The Macomber Family Information Center is located in the historic Crawford's Depot, a former train station renovated by the AMC, and houses interpretive displays, an information desk, and a small store that stocks last-minute hiker supplies, guidebooks, AMC publications, and souvenir items. It is also a major stop and transfer point for the AMC hiker shuttle bus, which operates during the summer and early fall, and serves as a depot for the excursion trains that run on the Crawford Notch line during the tourist season.

From the AMC's Crawford Notch property, many trails can be accessed, including the Mount Willard Trail and the Avalon Trail. Parking next to the Macomber Family Information Center is limited to 30 minutes. Parking for overnight guests is located on the Highland Center property near the main building. Parking for the Crawford Path is available in the USFS lot (recreational permit required) located just off Mt. Clinton Rd. near its junction with US 302. Other trails easily accessed from the Highland Center include the Around-the-Lake Trail, Red Bench Trail, Saco Lake Trail, and Webster-Jackson Trail.

Lakes of the Clouds Hut (AMC)

The original stone hut was built in 1915 and has been greatly enlarged since then. It is located on a shelf near the foot of Mt. Monroe about 50 yd. west of the larger lake at an elevation of 5012 ft. It is reached by the Crawford Path or the Ammonoosuc Ravine Trail, and has accommodations for 90 guests. Pets are not permitted in the hut. The hut is open to the public from June to mid-September, and closed at all other times. Space for backpackers is available at a lesser cost. A refuge room in the cellar is left open in the winter for emergency use only.

Mizpah Spring Hut (AMC)

The newest of the AMC huts was completed in 1965 and is located at about 3800 ft. elevation on the site formerly occupied by the Mizpah Spring Shelter, at the junction of the Webster Cliff Trail and the Mount Clinton Trail, near the Mizpah

Cutoff. The hut accommodates 60 guests, with sleeping quarters in eight rooms containing from 4 to 10 bunks. This hut is open to the public from mid-May to mid-October (caretaker basis in May). Pets are not permitted in the hut. There are tentsites nearby (caretaker, fee charged).

CAMPING
Presidential Range–Dry River Wilderness
Wilderness regulations, intended to protect Wilderness resources and promote opportunities for challenge and solitude, prohibit use of motorized equipment or mechanical means of transportation of any sort. Camping and wood or charcoal fires are not allowed within 200 ft. of any trail except at designated campsites. Hiking and camping group size must be no larger than 10 people. Camping and fires are also prohibited above the treeline (where trees are less than 8 ft. tall) except in winter, when camping is permitted above the treeline in places where snow cover is at least 2 ft. deep, but not on any frozen body of water. Many shelters have been removed, and the remaining ones will be dismantled when major maintenance is required; one should not count on using any of these shelters.

Forest Protection Areas
The WMNF has established a number of Forest Protection Areas (FPAs)—formerly known as Restricted Use Areas—where camping and wood or charcoal fires are prohibited throughout the year. The specific areas are under continual review, and areas are added to or subtracted from the list in order to provide the greatest amount of protection to areas subject to damage by excessive camping, while imposing the lowest level of restrictions possible. A general list of FPAs in this section follows, but since there are often major changes from year to year, one should obtain current information on FPAs from the WMNF.

(1) No camping is permitted above treeline (where trees are less than 8 ft. tall), except in winter, and then only in places where there is at least 2 ft. of snow cover on the ground—but not on any frozen body of water, and not on the east face of Mt. Washington's summit cone from Boott Spur to Nelson Crag (the area above Tuckerman and Huntington Ravines, including the Alpine Garden area). The point where the above-treeline restricted area begins is marked on most trails with small signs, but the absence of such signs should not be construed as proof of the legality of a site.

(2) No camping is permitted within a quarter mile of any trailhead, picnic area, or any facility for overnight accommodation such as a hut, cabin, shelter, tentsite, or campground, except as designated at the facility itself. In the area covered by Section 1, camping is also forbidden within a quarter mile of Glen Ellis Falls.

(3) No camping is permitted within 200 ft. of certain trails. In 2002 designated trails included the Ammonoosuc Ravine Trail.

(4) No camping is permitted on WMNF land within a quarter mile of certain roads (camping on private roadside land is illegal except by permission of the landowner). In 2002 these roads included US 302 west of Bartlett NH, NH 16 north of Glen Ellis Falls, the Base Road (FR 173), the Jefferson Notch Rd. from the Base Rd. to the Caps Ridge Trail trailhead, and the Rocky Branch Rd. (FR 27, a.k.a. Jericho Rd.).

(5) In Tuckerman and Huntington Ravines (Cutler River drainage, including the Alpine Garden and the east face of the Mt. Washington summit cone), camping is prohibited throughout the year; the only year-round exception is the Hermit Lake Shelters and adjoining tent platforms (management policies described below under campsites). Visitors in the ravine areas may not kindle charcoal or wood fires; people intending to cook must bring their own small stoves. Day visitors and shelter users alike are required to carry out all their own trash and garbage—no receptacles are provided. This operating policy is under continual review, so it can change from time to time; current information is available at Pinkham Notch Visitor Center or the Tuckerman Ravine caretaker's residence, or from WMNF offices. There is no warming room open to the public, and refreshments are not available.

Crawford Notch State Park

No camping is permitted in Crawford Notch State Park, except at the public Dry River Campground (fee charged).

Established Trailside Campsites

Hermit Lake Campsite (AMC/WMNF), located in Tuckerman Ravine, consists of 10 open-front shelters with a capacity of 86 and three tent platforms open to the public. Tickets for shelter and tentsite space (nontransferable and nonrefundable) must be purchased for a nominal fee at Pinkham Notch Visitor Center in person (first come, first served). Campers are limited to a maximum of seven consecutive nights, and pets are not allowed to stay overnight.

Nauman Tentsite (AMC) consists of seven tent platforms near Mizpah Spring Hut. In summer there is a caretaker and a fee is charged.

Lakes of the Clouds Hut (AMC) has limited space available for backpackers at a substantially lower cost than the normal hut services.

Rocky Branch Shelter #1 and Tentsite (WMNF) is located near the junction of the Rocky Branch and Stairs Col Trails, just outside the Presidential Range–Dry River Wilderness.

Rocky Branch Shelter #2 (WMNF) is located at the junction of the Rocky Branch and Isolation Trails, within the Presidential Range–Dry River Wilderness. Following the established policy for management of Wilderness, this shelter will be removed when major maintenance is required.

Dry River Shelter #3 (WMNF) is located on the Dry River Trail, 6.3 mi. from US 302, within the Presidential Range–Dry River Wilderness. This shelter will be removed when major maintenance is required.

Resolution Shelter (AMC) is located on a spur path that leaves the Davis Path at its junction with the Mount Parker Trail, within the Presidential Range–Dry River Wilderness. The water source is scanty in dry seasons. This shelter will be removed when major maintenance is required.

Mt. Langdon Shelter (WMNF) is located at the junction of the Mount Langdon and Mount Stanton Trails, at the edge of the Presidential Range–Dry River Wilderness.

THE TRAILS

Tuckerman Ravine Trail (WMNF)

This trail to the summit of Mt. Washington from NH 16 at Pinkham Notch Visitor Center is probably the most popular route of ascent on the mountain. From Pinkham Notch Visitor Center, it uses a rocky tractor road to the floor of Tuckerman Ravine. From there to the top of the headwall it is a well-graded path, steady but not excessively steep. Its final section ascends the cone of Mt. Washington steeply over fragments of rock. In spring and early summer the WMNF often closes the section of trail on the ravine headwall because of snow and ice hazards, and notice is posted at Pinkham Notch Visitor Center. In these circumstances the Lion Head Trail is usually the most convenient alternative route. In winter conditions the headwall is often impassable except by experienced and well-equipped technical snow and ice climbers, and it is frequently closed by the WMNF even to such climbers due to avalanche and icefall hazards. The winter route of the Lion Head Trail, which now begins on the Huntington Ravine Fire Road 0.1 mi. from the Tuckerman Ravine Trail, bypasses the headwall and usually provides the easiest and safest route for ascending Mt. Washington from the east in winter.

The Tuckerman Ravine Trail starts behind the Trading Post at Pinkham Notch Visitor Center; the Old Jackson Road diverges right 50 yd. from here. Be careful to avoid numerous side paths, including the Blanchard Ski Trail, in this area. In 0.3 mi. it crosses a bridge to the south bank of the Cutler River, begins its moderate but relentless climb, and soon passes a side path leading 20 yd. right to the best viewpoint for Crystal Cascade. The Boott Spur Trail diverges on the left at a sharp curve to the right, 0.4 mi. from Pinkham Notch Visitor Center, and at 1.3 mi. the Huntington Ravine Trail diverges on the right. At 1.5 mi. the Tuckerman Ravine Trail crosses a tributary, then at 1.6 mi. the main branch of the Cutler River. At 1.7 mi. the Huntington Ravine Fire Road, which is the easiest route to Huntington Ravine in winter but offers very rough footing on some parts in summer, leaves on the right. The Lion Head winter route now begins about 0.1 mi. up this road. At 2.1 mi. the Raymond Path enters on the right at a point where the Tuckerman trail turns sharp left, and at 2.3 mi. the Lion Head Trail leaves on the right. In another 0.1 mi. the Boott Spur Link leaves on the left, opposite the buildings located at the floor of Tuckerman Ravine near Hermit Lake. Views from the floor of the ravine are impressive: the cliff on the right is Lion Head, while the more distant crags on the left are the Hanging Cliffs of Boott Spur.

The main trail keeps to the right (north) of the main stream and ascends a well-constructed footway into the upper floor of the ravine. At the foot of the headwall it bears right and ascends a steep slope, where the Snow Arch can be seen on the left in spring and early summer of most years. In the early part of the hiking season, the snowfield above the Snow Arch usually extends across the trail, and the trail is often closed to hiking until this potentially hazardous snow slope has melted away. Some snow may persist in the ravine until late summer. The arch (which does not always form) is carved by a stream of snowmelt water that flows under the snowfield. *Caution:* Do not approach too near the arch and under no circumstances cross over it or venture beneath it, since sections weighing many tons may break off at any moment. One death and several narrow escapes have occurred. When ascending the headwall, be careful not to dislodge rocks and start them rolling—this may put hikers below you in serious danger. There have been several serious accidents in recent years involving hikers who slipped off the side of the trail on the upper part of the headwall, often in adverse weather conditions, especially when the trail was slippery. Though the trail itself is relatively easy and quite safe, it passes within a very short distance of some extremely dangerous terrain, so a minor misstep off the side of the trail can have grave consequences.

Turning sharp left at the top of the debris slope and traversing under a cliff, the trail emerges from the ravine and climbs almost straight west up a grassy, ledgy slope. At 3.4 mi., a short distance above the top of the headwall, the Alpine Garden Trail diverges right. At Tuckerman Junction, located on the lower edge of Bigelow Lawn at 3.6 mi., the Tuckerman Crossover leads almost straight ahead (southwest) to the Crawford Path near the Lakes of the Clouds Hut; the Southside Trail diverges from the Tuckerman Crossover in 30 yd. and leads west, skirting the cone to the Davis Path; and the Lawn Cutoff leads left (south) toward Boott Spur. The Tuckerman Ravine Trail turns sharp right at this junction and ascends the steep rocks, marked by cairns and paint on ledges. At 3.8 mi., at Cloudwater Spring about a third of the way up the cone, the Lion Head Trail re-enters on the right. The Tuckerman trail continues to ascend to the Auto Rd. a few yards below the lower parking area, from which wooden stairways lead to the summit area.

Tuckerman Ravine Trail (map 1:F9)

Distances from Pinkham Notch Visitor Center (2032′)

to Boott Spur Trail (2275′): 0.4 mi., 250 ft., 20 min.

to Huntington Ravine Trail (3031′): 1.3 mi., 1000 ft., 1 hr. 10 min.

to Huntington Ravine Fire Road (3425′): 1.7 mi., 1400 ft., 1 hr. 35 min.

to Raymond Path (3675′): 2.1 mi., 1650 ft., 1 hr. 55 min.

to Lion Head Trail (3825′): 2.3 mi., 1800 ft., 2 hr. 5 min.

to Boott Spur Link and Hermit Lake shelters (3875′): 2.4 mi., 1850 ft., 2 hr. 10 min.

to Snow Arch (4525′): 3.1 mi., 2500 ft., 2 hr. 50 min.

to Alpine Garden Trail (5125′): 3.4 mi., 3100 ft., 3 hr. 15 min.

to Tuckerman Junction (5383′): 3.6 mi., 3350 ft., 3 hr. 30 min.

to Lion Head Trail, upper junction (5675′): 3.8 mi., 3650 ft., 3 hr. 45 min.

to Mt. Washington summit (6288′): 4.2 mi. (6.8 km.), 4250 ft., 4 hr. 15 min.

Lion Head Trail (AMC)

The Lion Head Trail follows the steep-ended ridge—aptly named for the appearance of its upper portion when viewed from points on NH 16 north of Pinkham Notch Visitor Center—that forms the north wall of Tuckerman Ravine. The trail begins and ends on the Tuckerman Ravine Trail and thus provides an alternative route to that heavily used trail, although it is much steeper in parts. It is especially important as an alternative when the Tuckerman Ravine Trail over the headwall is closed on account of snow or ice hazard. The winter route of the Lion Head Trail is considered the least dangerous route for ascending Mt. Washington in winter conditions, and is the most frequently used winter ascent route. An avalanche late in 1995 destroyed the former winter route, and a new winter route has been constructed; this route leaves the Huntington Ravine Fire Road just past the crossing of the Raymond Path, about 0.1 mi. from the Tuckerman Ravine Trail, and rejoins the summer Lion Head Trail at treeline. The signs and markings are changed at the beginning and end of the winter season to ensure that climbers take the proper route for prevailing conditions; the winter route is not open for summer use.

The Lion Head Trail diverges right from the Tuckerman Ravine Trail 2.3 mi. from Pinkham Notch Visitor Center and 0.1 mi. below Hermit Lake. Running north, it passes a side path on the left to one of the Hermit Lake shelters and crosses the outlet of Hermit Lake. It soon begins to climb the steep slope by switchbacks, scrambling up several small ledges with very rough footing. It reaches treeline at 0.4 mi., where the winter route enters on the right as the main trail bears left. (Descending, the summer trail turns right and the winter route descends almost straight ahead.) The trail then ascends an open slope to the lower Lion Head and continues to the upper Lion Head at 0.9 mi., where it runs mostly level, with impressive views from the open spur, until it crosses the Alpine Garden Trail at 1.1 mi. After passing through a belt of scrub, it ascends to the Tuckerman Ravine Trail, which it enters at Cloudwater Spring about a third of the way up the cone of Mt. Washington, about 0.4 mi. and 600 ft. below the summit.

Lion Head Trail (map 1:F9)

Distances from lower junction with Tuckerman Ravine Trail (3825')

    to Alpine Garden Trail (5175'): 1.1 mi., 1350 ft., 1 hr. 15 min.

    to upper junction with Tuckerman Ravine Trail (5675'): 1.6 mi. (2.5 km.), 1850 ft., 1 hr. 45 min.

Distance from Pinkham Notch Visitor Center (2032′)

to Mt. Washington summit (6288′) via Lion Head Trail and Tuckerman Ravine Trail: 4.1 mi. (7.0 km.), 4250 ft., 4 hr. 10 min.

Huntington Ravine Trail (AMC)

Caution: This is the most difficult regular hiking trail in the White Mtns. Many of the ledges demand proper use of handholds for safe passage, and extreme caution must be exercised at all times. Although experienced hikers who are reasonably comfortable on steep rock will probably encounter little difficulty when conditions are good, the exposure on several of the steepest ledges is likely to prove extremely unnerving to novices and to those who are uncomfortable in steep places. Do not attempt this trail if you tend to feel queasy or have difficulty on ledges on ordinary trails. Hikers encumbered with large or heavy packs may experience great difficulty in some places. This trail is very dangerous when wet or icy, and its use for descent at any time is strongly discouraged. Since retreat under unfavorable conditions can be extremely difficult and hazardous, one should never venture beyond the Fan in deteriorating conditions or when weather on the Alpine Garden is likely to be severe. During late fall, winter, and early spring, this trail (and any part of the ravine headwall) should be attempted only by those with full technical ice-climbing training and equipment. In particular, the ravine must not be regarded as a feasible escape route from the Alpine Garden in severe winter conditions.

This trail diverges right from the Tuckerman Ravine Trail 1.3 mi. from Pinkham Notch Visitor Center. In 0.2 mi. it crosses the Cutler River and, at 0.3 mi., the brook that drains Huntington Ravine. At 0.5 mi. it goes straight across the Raymond Path. It crosses the Huntington Ravine Fire Road and then climbs to meet it again, turning left on the road; at this junction a fine view of the ravine can be obtained by following the road to a small rise about 100 yd. in the opposite direction. Above this point the trail and road separate, rejoin, or cross several times; the junctions are not always well marked, but both routes lead to the same objective, and the major advantage of the trail is somewhat better footing. At 1.3 mi. the first-aid cache in the floor of the ravine is reached. Just beyond here there are some interesting boulders near the path whose tops afford good views of the ravine. Beyond the scrubby trees is a steep slope covered with broken rock, known as the Fan, whose tip lies at the foot of the deepest gully. To the left of this gully are precipices; the lower one is called the Pinnacle.

After passing through the boulders, the path ascends to the left side of the Fan and, marked by yellow blazes on the rocks, crosses the talus diagonally. It then turns left and ascends in scrub along the north (right) side of the Fan to its tip at 1.8 mi., crossing a small brook about two-thirds of the way up. The trail then recrosses the brooklet and immediately attacks the rocks to the right of the main gully, climbing about 650 ft. in 0.3 mi. The route up the headwall follows the line of least difficulty and should be followed carefully over the ledges, which are dangerous, especially when wet. The first pitch above the Fan—a large, fairly smooth, steeply sloping ledge—is probably the most difficult scramble on the trail. Above the first ledges the trail climbs steeply through scrub and over short sections of rock, including some fairly difficult scrambles. About two-thirds of the way up it turns sharp left at a promontory with a good view, then continues to the top of the headwall, where it crosses the Alpine Garden Trail at 2.1 mi. From this point it ascends moderately, and at 2.3 mi. it crosses the Nelson Crag Trail, by which the summit can be reached in 0.8 mi. by turning left at this junction. Soon the Huntington Ravine Trail reaches the Mt. Washington Auto Rd. just below the 7-mi. mark, 1.1 mi. below the summit.

Huntington Ravine Trail (map 1:F9)

Distances from Tuckerman Ravine Trail (3031')

   to Raymond Path (3425'): 0.5 mi., 400 ft., 25 min.

   to first-aid cache in ravine floor (4075'): 1.3 mi., 1050 ft., 1 hr. 10 min.

   to Alpine Garden Trail crossing (5475'): 2.1 mi., 2450 ft., 2 hr. 15 min.

   to Auto Rd. (5725'): 2.4 mi. (3.8 km.), 2700 ft., 2 hr. 35 min.

Distance from Pinkham Notch Visitor Center (2032')

   to Mt. Washington summit (6288') via Tuckerman Ravine, Huntington Ravine, and Nelson Crag Trails: 4.3 mi. (6.9 km.), 4250 ft., 4 hr. 15 min.

Nelson Crag Trail (AMC)

This trail, which now runs to the summit of Mt. Washington, begins on the Old Jackson Road at a point 1.7 mi. from Pinkham Notch Visitor Center and 0.2 mi. from the Auto Rd. It is an attractive trail, relatively lightly used, fairly steep in the lower part and greatly exposed to weather in the upper part.

Leaving the Old Jackson Road, this trail follows and soon crosses a small brook, then climbs steadily, soon becoming quite steep. At about 1.1 mi. it rises out of the scrub, emerging on the crest of Chandler Ridge, from which there is an unusual view of Pinkham Notch in both directions. From this point the trail is above treeline and very exposed to the northwest winds. It then bears northwest, climbs moderately over open ledges, and passes close by the Auto Rd. near Cragway Spring (unreliable), at the sharp turn about 0.3 mi. above the 5-mi. mark. The trail then climbs steeply to the crest of the ridge. It passes over Nelson Crag and crosses the Alpine Garden Trail, swings left and travels across the Huntington Ravine Trail and up the rocks to Ball Crag (6112 ft.), then finally runs across the Auto Rd. and the Cog Railway to the summit. To descend on this trail, follow the walkway down along the lower side of the Sherman Adams summit building.

Nelson Crag Trail (map 1:F9)

Distances from Old Jackson Road (2625′)

to closest approach to the Auto Rd. near Cragway Spring (4825′): 1.7 mi., 2200 ft., 1 hr. 55 min.

to Huntington Ravine Trail (5725′): 2.8 mi., 3100 ft., 2 hr. 55 min.

to Mt. Washington summit (6288′): 3.6 mi. (5.8 km.), 3700 ft., 3 hr. 30 min.

Boott Spur Trail (AMC)

This trail runs from the Tuckerman Ravine Trail near Pinkham Notch Visitor Center to the Davis Path near the summit of Boott Spur. It follows the long ridge that forms the south wall of Tuckerman Ravine and affords fine views. Grades are mostly moderate, but the trail is above treeline and thus greatly exposed to any bad weather for a considerable distance.

This trail diverges left from the Tuckerman Ravine Trail at a sharp right turn 0.4 mi. from Pinkham Notch Visitor Center, about 150 yd. above the side path to Crystal Cascade. It immediately crosses the John Sherburne Ski Trail, then climbs through a ledgy area, crosses a tiny brook, and climbs steeply up a crevice in a ledge to the ridgecrest. At 0.5 mi., after a slight descent, there is a sharp right turn where a side trail (left) leads in 50 yd. down to a restricted view east. The trail next passes through some interesting woods, crosses a moist region, and then ascends northwest up a steeper slope toward a craggy shoulder. Halfway up this section, a side trail leads left 100 yd. to a small brook (last water). At the ridgecrest, 1.0 mi. from the Tuckerman Ravine Trail, the main trail turns left and a side trail leads right (east) 25 yd. to an interesting though restricted outlook to Huntington Ravine. The main trail continues upward at moderate grades, reaching a ledgy ridgecrest that affords some views, and at 1.7 mi. a side trail on the right leads in 30 yd. to Harvard Rock, which provides an excellent view of Tuckerman Ravine and of Lion Head directly in front of the summit of Mt. Washington.

The trail emerges from the scrub at 1.9 mi., then soon bears left and angles up the slope to Split Rock, which one can pass through or go around, at 2.0 mi. The trail then turns right, passes through a final patch of fairly high scrub, and rises steeply over two minor humps to a broad, flat ridge, where, at 2.2 mi., the Boott Spur Link descends on the right to the Tuckerman Ravine Trail near Hermit Lake. Above this point the trail follows the ridge, which consists of a series of alternating steplike levels and steep slopes. The views of the ravine are excellent, particularly where the path skirts around the potentially dangerous Hanging Cliff, 1500 ft. above Hermit Lake. After passing just to the right (north) of the summit of Boott Spur, the trail ends at the Davis Path.

Boott Spur Trail (map 1:F9)

Distances from Tuckerman Ravine Trail (2275')

to Harvard Rock (4046'): 1.7 mi., 1750 ft., 1 hr. 45 min.

to Split Rock (4337'): 2.0 mi., 2050 ft., 2 hr.

to Boott Spur Link (4650'): 2.2 mi., 2400 ft., 2 hr. 20 min.

to Davis Path junction (5450'): 2.9 mi. (4.7 km.), 3200 ft., 3 hr. 5 min.

Distances from Pinkham Notch Visitor Center (2032')

to Davis Path junction (5450'): 3.4 mi., 3400 ft., 3 hr. 25 min.

to Mt. Washington summit (6288') via Davis and Crawford Paths: 5.4 mi. (8.7 km.), 4300 ft., 4 hr. 50 min.

Boott Spur Link (AMC)

This steep but interesting trail climbs the south wall of Tuckerman Ravine, connecting the main floor of the ravine with the upper part of Boott Spur. The lower trailhead has been recently relocated to a point about 0.1 mi. farther up the Tuckerman Ravine Trail, so the Boott Spur Link now leaves the south side of the Tuckerman trail at the southeast corner of the clearing opposite the buildings at Hermit Lake, 2.4 mi. from Pinkham Notch Visitor Center. From this clearing it descends south-southeast and soon crosses the Cutler River on a bridge, then crosses the John Sherburne Ski Trail and swings to the left, reaching a junction with the old route of the trail at 0.2 mi. Here it turns right and climbs straight up the slope very steeply through woods and scrub, with rapidly improving views back into the ravine. It then continues to climb steeply over open rocks to the crest of Boott Spur, where it meets the Boott Spur Trail.

Boott Spur Link (map 1:F9)
Distance from Tuckerman Ravine Trail (3875′)
   to Boott Spur Trail (4650′): 0.6 mi. (1.0 km.), 850 ft., 45 min.

Gulf of Slides Ski Trail (WMNF)

This trail leads from Pinkham Notch Visitor Center on NH 16 into the Gulf of Slides, a ravine somewhat similar to Tuckerman Ravine but far less well known and crowded than its illustrious neighbor on the other side of Boott Spur. While this trail is not specifically maintained as a summer hiking trail and may be wet in spots, it still provides a good route to a relatively secluded valley. This is a dead-end trail, so hikers must return by the same route unless they choose to make the challenging trailless ascent of the ravine headwall.

The trail leaves the south end of the parking lot at Pinkham Notch Visitor Center in common with the John Sherburne Ski Trail. In a short distance it turns left where the Blanchard Ski Trail continues straight, crosses the Cutler River and a smaller side channel on bridges, and immediately turns left where the Sherburne Trail turns right. After crossing a branch of the New River on a bridge, it bears right along this stream, passes a junction where the Avalanche Brook Ski Trail diverges left, recrosses the stream, and climbs moderately up into the Gulf of Slides, staying mostly well to the north of the New River. At 1.9 mi. it swings left where the Graham Ski Trail (marked by can tops) goes right toward Tuckerman Ravine. At 2.2 mi. it passes a first-aid cache, ascends roughly for a short distance, then descends for a short distance to the headwaters of the New River near the base of the steep slopes of the ravine's headwall. Soon the trail reaches the base of ski trails leading into the major gullies and ends.

Gulf of Slides Ski Trail (map 1:F9–G9)
Distance from Pinkham Notch Visitor Center (2032′)
   to Gulf of Slides (3900′): 2.6 mi. (4.2 km.), 1900 ft., 2 hr. 15 min.

Glen Boulder Trail (AMC)

This trail ascends past the famous Glen Boulder to the Davis Path 0.4 mi. below Boott Spur. It begins on the west side of NH 16 at the Glen Ellis Falls parking area south of Pinkham Notch Visitor Center. Parts of it are rather rough, but it reaches the treeline and views relatively quickly.

The trail leaves the parking area and ascends gradually for about 0.4 mi. to the base of a small cliff, then climbs around to the right of the cliff and meets the

Direttissima, which enters from the right (north) coming from Pinkham Notch Visitor Center. At this junction the trail turns sharp left (south) and soon passes a short branch trail that leads left to an outlook on the brink of a cliff, which commands a fine view of Wildcat Mtn. and Pinkham Notch. The main trail turns west, rises gradually, then steepens. At 0.8 mi. it crosses the Avalanche Brook Ski Trail, which is marked with blue plastic markers (but not maintained for hiking). The Glen Boulder Trail soon reaches the north bank of a brook draining the minor ravine south of the Gulf of Slides. After following the brook, which soon divides, the trail then turns southwest and crosses both branches. It is level for 200 yd., then rapidly climbs the northeast side of the spur through conifers, giving views of the minor ravine and spur south of the Gulf of Slides. Leaving the trees, it climbs over open rocks and at 1.6 mi. reaches the Glen Boulder, an immense rock perched on the end of the spur that is a familiar landmark for travelers through Pinkham Notch. The view is wide, from Chocorua around to Mt. Washington, and is particularly fine of Wildcat Mtn.

From the boulder the trail climbs steeply up the open ridgecrest to its top at 2.0 mi., then re-enters high scrub and ascends moderately. At 2.3 mi. a side trail descends right about 60 yd. to a fine spring. The main trail continues to Slide Peak (also called Gulf Peak), the rather insignificant peak heading the Gulf of Slides, at 2.6 mi. It then turns north and descends slightly, leaving the scrub, and runs entirely above treeline—greatly exposed to the weather—to the Davis Path just below a minor crag.

Glen Boulder Trail (map 1:G9)

Distances from Glen Ellis Falls parking area on NH 16 (1975')

to the Direttissima (2300'): 0.4 mi., 350 ft., 25 min.

to Avalanche Brook Ski Trail (2600'): 0.8 mi., 650 ft., 45 min.

to Glen Boulder (3729'): 1.6 mi., 1750 ft., 1 hr. 40 min.

to Slide Peak (4806'): 2.6 mi., 2850 ft., 2 hr. 45 min.

to Davis Path junction (5175'): 3.2 mi. (5.2 km.), 3200 ft., 3 hr. 10 min.

to Boott Spur Trail (5450') via Davis Path: 3.7 mi., 3500 ft., 3 hr. 35 min.

to Mt. Washington summit (6288') via Davis and Crawford Paths: 5.7 mi. (9.2 km.), 4400 ft., 5 hr. 5 min.

The Direttissima (AMC)

For hikers desiring access to the Glen Boulder Trail from Pinkham Notch Visitor Center, this trail eliminates a road walk on NH 16. Although in general it is almost level, there are several significant ups and downs. The trail begins about 0.2 mi. south of Pinkham Notch Visitor Center, just south of the highway bridge over the Cutler River, indicated by a sign at the edge of the woods. Marked by paint blazes, the trail turns sharp left about 30 yd. into the woods and follows a cleared area south. It turns slightly west at the end of this clearing and winds generally south, crossing a small brook. It skirts through the upper (west) end of a gorge and then crosses the gorge on a bridge at 0.5 mi. The trail continues past an excellent viewpoint looking down Pinkham Notch, passes along the top of a cliff and then the bottom of another cliff, and ends at the Glen Boulder Trail.

The Direttissima (map 1:F9–G9)

Distance from NH 16 near Cutler River bridge (2025′)

  to Glen Boulder Trail (2300′): 1.0 mi. (1.6 km.), 400 ft. (rev. 100 ft.), 40 min.

Alpine Garden Trail (AMC)

This trail leads from the Tuckerman Ravine Trail to the Mt. Washington Auto Rd. through the grassy lawn called the Alpine Garden. Although its chief value is the beauty of the flowers (in season) and the views, it is also a convenient connecting link between the trails on the east side of the mountain, making up a part of various routes for those who do not wish to visit the summit. It is completely above treeline and exposed to bad weather, although it is on the mountain's east side, which usually bears somewhat less of the brunt of the mountain's worst weather.

The tiny alpine flowers that grow here are best seen in the middle to late part of June. Especially prominent in this area are the five-petaled white diapensia, the bell-shaped pink-magenta Lapland rosebay, and the very small pink flowers of the alpine azalea. (See the AMC's *Field Guide to the New England Alpine Summits* and *Wildflowers of the White Mountains,* published by Huntington Graphics.) No plants should ever be picked or otherwise damaged. Hikers are urged to stay on trails or walk very carefully on rocks so as not to kill the fragile alpine vegetation.

The trail diverges right from the Tuckerman Ravine Trail a short distance above the ravine headwall, about 0.2 mi. below Tuckerman Junction. It leads northeast, bearing toward Lion Head, and crosses the Lion Head Trail at 0.3 mi. Beyond this junction the trail ascends gradually northward, its general direction from here to the Auto Rd. It traverses the Alpine Garden and crosses a tiny stream that is the headwater of Raymond Cataract. (This water may be contaminated by drainage from the summit buildings.) The trail soon approaches the top of Huntington Ravine and crosses the Huntington Ravine Trail at 1.2 mi. Here, a little off the trail, there is a fine view down into this impressive ravine. In winter and spring, take care not to approach too close to the icy gullies that drop precipitously from the edge of the Alpine Garden. Rising to the top of the ridge leading from Nelson Crag, the trail crosses the Nelson Crag Trail at 1.4 mi., then descends and soon enters the old Glen House Bridle Path, constructed in 1853, whose course is still plain although it was abandoned more than a century ago. In a short distance the Alpine Garden Trail turns left and in a few yards enters the Auto Rd. a short distance above the 6-mi. mark, opposite the upper terminus of the Wamsutta Trail.

Alpine Garden Trail (map 1:F9)

Distances from Tuckerman Ravine Trail (5125')

to Lion Head Trail (5175'): 0.3 mi., 50 ft., 10 min.

to Huntington Ravine Trail (5475'): 1.2 mi., 350 ft., 45 min.

to Nelson Crag Trail (5575'): 1.4 mi., 450 ft., 55 min.

to Auto Rd. junction (5305'): 1.8 mi. (2.9 km.), 450 ft. (rev. 250 ft.), 1 hr. 10 min.

Southside Trail (AMC)

This trail forms a direct link between Tuckerman Ravine and the Crawford Path and Westside Trail. It diverges right (west) from the Tuckerman Crossover about 30 yd. southwest of the Tuckerman Ravine Trail at Tuckerman Junction and, skirting the southwest side of Mt. Washington's summit cone, enters the Davis Path near its junction with the Crawford Path.

Southside Trail (map 1:F9)

Distance from Tuckerman Junction (5383')

to Davis Path (5575'): 0.3 mi. (0.5 km.), 200 ft., 15 min.

Tuckerman Crossover (AMC)

This trail connects Tuckerman Ravine with Lakes of the Clouds Hut. It is totally above treeline and crosses a high ridge where there is much exposure to westerly winds. It leaves the Tuckerman Ravine Trail left (southwest) at Tuckerman

Junction, where the latter trail turns sharp right to ascend the cone. In 30 yd. the Southside Trail diverges to the right. The Tuckerman Crossover then rises gradually across Bigelow Lawn, crosses the Davis Path, and descends moderately to the Crawford Path, which it meets along with the Camel Trail a short distance above the upper Lake of the Clouds. After a left turn on the Crawford Path, the Lakes of the Clouds Hut is reached in 0.2 mi.

Tuckerman Crossover (map 1:F9)

Distances from Tuckerman Junction (5383′)

    to Davis Path (5475′): 0.5 mi., 100 ft., 20 min.

    to Crawford Path (5125′): 0.8 mi. (1.3 km.), 100 ft. (rev. 350 ft.), 25 min.

    to Lakes of the Clouds Hut (5012′) via Crawford Path: 1.0 mi. (1.6 km.), 100 ft. (rev. 100 ft.), 30 min.

Lawn Cutoff (AMC)

This trail provides a direct route between Tuckerman Junction and Boott Spur, entirely above treeline. It leaves the Tuckerman Ravine Trail at Tuckerman Junction and ascends gradually southward across Bigelow Lawn to the Davis Path about 0.5 mi. north of Boott Spur.

Lawn Cutoff (map 1:F9)

Distance from Tuckerman Junction (5383′)

    to Davis Path (5475′): 0.4 mi. (0.6 km.), 100 ft., 15 min.

Camel Trail (AMC)

This trail, connecting Boott Spur with the Lakes of the Clouds Hut, is named for ledges on Boott Spur that resemble a kneeling camel when seen against the skyline.

    This is the right-hand trail of the two that diverge right (east) from the Crawford Path 0.2 mi. northeast of Lakes of the Clouds Hut (the Tuckerman Crossover, the other trail that also diverges here, is the left-hand trail of the two). The Camel Trail ascends easy grassy slopes, crosses the old location of the Crawford Path, and continues in a practically straight line across the level stretch of Bigelow Lawn. It aims directly toward the ledges that form the camel, passes under the camel's nose, and joins the Davis Path about 200 yd. northwest of the Lawn Cutoff.

Camel Trail (map 1:F9)

Distance from Crawford Path (5125')
   to Davis Path (5475'): 0.7 mi. (1.1 km.), 350 ft., 30 min.

Westside Trail (WMNF)

This trail was partly constructed by pioneer trail maker J. Rayner Edmands; as was Edmands's practice, many segments are paved with carefully placed stones. It is wholly above timberline, very much exposed to the prevailing west and northwest winds. However, as a shortcut between the Gulfside Trail and Crawford Path that avoids the summit of Mt. Washington, it saves about 0.7 mi. in distance and 600 ft. in elevation between objectives in the Northern Peaks and Southern Peaks regions.

The trail diverges left from the Crawford Path at the point where the latter path begins to climb the steep part of the cone of Mt. Washington. It skirts the cone, climbing for 0.6 mi. at an easy grade, then descends moderately, passes under the tracks of the Mt. Washington Cog Railway, and soon ends at the Gulfside Trail.

Westside Trail (map 1:F9)

Distance from Crawford Path (5625')
   to Gulfside Trail (5500'): 0.9 mi. (1.4 km.), 50 ft. (rev. 150 ft.), 30 min.

Trinity Heights Connector (NHDP)

This trail was created to allow the Appalachian Trail to make a loop over the summit of Mt. Washington; formerly the true summit was a side trip, albeit a very short one, from the AT, so technically the AT did not pass over it. Trinity Heights is a name formerly used for the summit region of Mt. Washington. From the true summit (marked by a large sign), the path runs approximately northwest over the rocks to the Gulfside Trail less than 0.1 mi. to the north of its junction with the Crawford Path.

Trinity Heights Connector (map 1:F9)

Distance from true summit of Mt. Washington (6288')
   to Gulfside Trail (6100'): 0.2 mi. (0.3 km.), 0 ft. (rev. 200 ft.), 5 min.

Raymond Path (AMC)

This trail, one of the older paths in the region, begins on the Old Jackson Road 1.7 mi. from Pinkham Notch Visitor Center and 0.3 mi. from the Auto Rd., at a point about 100 yd. south of the beginning of the Nelson Crag Trail. It ends at the Tuckerman Ravine Trail about 0.3 mi. below Hermit Lake. Its grades are mostly easy to moderate.

After diverging from the Old Jackson Road the trail crosses several small branches of the Peabody River, climbing moderately to the crest of a small ridge at 0.8 mi. where there is an excellent view to Lion Head and Boott Spur. It then descends moderately for a short distance to a small mossy brook, then begins to ascend easily, crossing Nelson Brook at 1.2 mi. and the Huntington Ravine Trail at 1.8 mi. From here it drops down a steep bank to cross the brook that drains Huntington Ravine on a ledge at the brink of Vesper Falls—one should use great care here in high water or icy conditions, and perhaps consider a detour upstream. (This crossing can be avoided entirely by following the Huntington Ravine Trail north 0.1 mi. to the Huntington Ravine Fire Road, then following the Fire Road south until it crosses the Raymond Path.) Soon the path crosses the brook coming from the Ravine of Raymond Cataract (sign) and then the Huntington Ravine Fire Road, then climbs 0.3 mi. at a moderate grade to the Tuckerman Ravine Trail.

Raymond Path (map 1:F9)

Distances from Old Jackson Road (2625')

  to Huntington Ravine Trail (3425'): 1.8 mi., 800 ft., 1 hr. 20 min.

  to Tuckerman Ravine Trail (3675'): 2.4 mi. (3.9 km.), 1050 ft., 1 hr. 45 min.

  to Hermit Lake (3850') via Tuckerman Ravine Trail: 2.7 mi., 1250 ft., 2 hr.

Old Jackson Road (AMC)

This trail runs north from Pinkham Notch Visitor Center to the Mt. Washington Auto Rd., providing access to a number of other trails along with the most direct route from the visitor center to the Great Gulf. It is part of the Appalachian Trail and is blazed in white. Since it is used as a cross-country ski trail in winter, it is usually also marked with blue diamonds year-round.

It diverges right from the Tuckerman Ravine Trail about 50 yd. from the trailhead at the rear of the Trading Post. After about 0.3 mi. the Blanchard and Connie's Way Ski Trails cross, and at 0.4 mi. the Link Ski Trail enters right just before a bridge and the Crew-Cut Trail leaves right (east) just after the bridge.

Soon the Old Jackson Road begins to ascend moderately—more steeply in fact than one would expect of an old road—and crosses a small brook that runs in an interesting gorge with a small waterfall just above the trail. At 0.9 mi., George's Gorge Trail enters on the right (east), and the Old Jackson Road rises easily across the flat divide between the Saco and Androscoggin drainages and then descends slightly, crossing several small brooks. Just before reaching a larger brook it makes a sharp left turn uphill, then after a short, steep climb it turns right and runs nearly level. At 1.7 mi. the Raymond Path leaves on the left, and in another 100 yd., just after a small brook is crossed, the Nelson Crag Trail leaves on the left. Continuing north, the trail climbs slightly up an interesting little rocky hogback, passes through an old gravel pit, and meets the Auto Rd. just above the 2-mi. mark, at a small parking area opposite the Madison Gulf Trail trailhead.

Old Jackson Road (map 1:F9)

Distance from Pinkham Notch Visitor Center (2032′)

  to Mt. Washington Auto Rd. (2675′): 1.9 mi. (3.1 km.), 700 ft., 1 hr. 20 min.

Crew-Cut Trail (AMC)

The Crew-Cut Trail, George's Gorge Trail, and Liebeskind's Loop, a small network of paths in the region north of Pinkham Notch Visitor Center, were originally located and cut by Bradford Swan. These trails provide pleasant walking at a modest expenditure of effort, passing through fine woods with small ravines and ledges.

The Crew-Cut Trail leaves the Old Jackson Road on the right about 0.4 mi. from the visitor center, just after a stream crossing and just before the point where the Old Jackson Road starts to climb more steeply. After crossing a stony, dry brook bed it runs generally east-northeast, crossing two small brooks. On the east bank of the second brook, at 0.2 mi., the George's Gorge Trail leaves left. The Crew-Cut Trail continues generally northeast, rising gradually up the slope through open woods and crossing several gullies. It skirts southeast of the steeper rocky outcroppings until, at 0.5 mi. from the Old Jackson Road, Liebeskind's Loop enters left, coming down from George's Gorge Trail. The spur path to Lila's Ledge, which affords fine views, leaves Liebeskind's Loop less than 0.1 mi. from this junction. The Crew-Cut Trail passes under the base of a cliff and turns right, then descends steeply over a few small ledges and through open woods until it passes east of a small high-level bog formed by an old beaver dam. Shortly thereafter, it crosses a small stream and the Connie's Way Ski Trail, and goes through open woods again, emerging at the top of the grassy embankment on NH 16 almost exactly opposite the south end of the Wildcat Ski Area parking lot.

Crew-Cut Trail (map 1:F9–F10)

Distances from Old Jackson Road (2075′)

to Liebeskind's Loop (2350′): 0.5 mi., 300 ft., 25 min.

to NH 16 (1950′): 1.0 mi. (1.6 km.), 300 ft. (rev. 400 ft.), 35 min.

George's Gorge Trail (AMC)

This trail leaves the Crew-Cut Trail on the left 0.2 mi. from the Old Jackson Road, on the east bank of a small brook (the infant Peabody River). It leads up the brook, steeply in places, passing Chudacoff Falls and crossing the brook twice, then swings rather sharply away from the brook. Liebeskind's Loop leaves on the right at 0.5 mi., and George's Gorge Trail then climbs nearly to the top of a knob and descends west to the Old Jackson Road in the flat section near its halfway point, 0.9 mi. from Pinkham Notch Visitor Center.

George's Gorge Trail (map 1:F9)

Distance from Crew-Cut Trail (2100′)

to Old Jackson Road (2525′): 0.8 mi. (1.3 km.), 600 ft. (rev. 150 ft.), 40 min.

Liebeskind's Loop (AMC)

Liebeskind's Loop makes possible a loop hike starting on the Old Jackson Road 0.4 mi. from the Pinkham Notch Visitor Center (using the Crew-Cut, George's Gorge, Loop, and Crew-Cut Trails) without resorting to returning either by NH 16 or by the section of the Old Jackson Road that is markedly steeper than the rest of the trail. This loop hike is best made in the sequence referred to above, since George's Gorge is more interesting on the ascent and Liebeskind's Loop is more interesting on the descent.

Liebeskind's Loop leaves right (east) near the high point of the George's Gorge Trail, 0.3 mi. from Old Jackson Road, and descends to a swampy flat, then rises through a spruce thicket to the top of a cliff, where there is a fine lookout called Brad's Bluff with a good view to the south down Pinkham Notch. Here the trail turns left and runs along the edge of the cliff, finally descending by an easy zigzag in a gully to a beautiful open grove of birches. The trail continues east, descending through a small gorge and skirting the east end of several small swells until it finally descends to a small notch in the ridgecrest. Here a spur trail leads left 0.1 mi. to Lila's Ledge (named by Brad Swan in memory of his wife), which affords excellent views of Pinkham Notch and the eastern slope of Mt. Washington; the lower ledge is accessed by a short, steep descent that may be dangerous in wet or icy conditions. Liebeskind's Loop then descends on the other side of the ridge to join the Crew-Cut Trail, which can then be followed back to the starting point.

Liebeskind's Loop (map 1:F9–F10)

Distances from George's Gorge Trail (2575′)

to Crew-Cut Trail (2350′): 0.6 mi. (1.0 km.), 0 ft. (rev. 250 ft.), 20 min.

for complete loop from Pinkham Notch Visitor Center (2032′) via Old Jackson Road, Crew-Cut Trail, George's Gorge Trail, Liebeskind's Loop, Crew-Cut Trail, and Old Jackson Road: 2.6 mi. (4.2km.), 600 ft., 1 hr. 35 min.

Crawford Path (WMNF)

This trail is considered to be the oldest continuously maintained footpath in America. The first section, leading up Mt. Pierce (Mt. Clinton), was cut in 1819 by Abel Crawford and his son Ethan Allen Crawford. In 1840 Thomas J. Crawford, a younger son of Abel, converted the footpath into a bridle path, but more than a century has passed since its regular use for ascents on horseback ended. The trail still follows the original path, except for the section between Mt. Monroe and the Westside Trail, which was relocated to take it off the windswept ridge and down past the shelter at Lakes of the Clouds. From the junction just north of Mt. Pierce to the summit of Mt. Washington, the Crawford Path is part of the Appalachian Trail and is blazed in white.

Caution: Parts of this trail are dangerous in bad weather. Several lives have been lost on the Crawford Path due to failure to observe proper precautions. Below Mt. Eisenhower there are a number of ledges exposed to the weather, but they are scattered, and shelter is usually available in nearby scrub. From the Eisenhower-Franklin col the trail runs completely above treeline, exposed to the full force of all storms. The most dangerous part of the path is the section on the cone of Mt. Washington, beyond Lakes of the Clouds Hut. Always carry a compass and study the map before starting. If trouble arises on or above Mt. Monroe, take refuge at Lakes of the Clouds Hut or go down the Ammonoosuc Ravine Trail. The Crawford Path is well marked above treeline with large cairns topped by yellow-painted rocks, and in poor visibility great care should be exercised to stay on it, since many of the other paths in the vicinity are much less clearly marked. If the path is lost in bad weather and cannot be found again after diligent effort, one should travel west, descending into the woods and following streams downhill to the roads. On the southeast, toward the Dry River valley, nearly all the slopes are more precipitous, the river crossings are potentially dangerous, and the distance to a highway is much greater.

The main parking area at the south end of this trail is now located on the Mt. Clinton Rd. a short distance from its junction with US 302. The former parking lot on US 302 has been closed, and Crawford Path hikers are requested to use the Mt. Clinton Rd. lot, since the parking spaces at other lots in the area are needed for the trails that originate from them. For historical reasons the name Crawford Path continues to be attached to the old route of the trail that leads directly from US 302, and the short path that connects the Crawford Path to the Mt. Clinton Rd. parking lot is called the Crawford Connector. However, in the descriptions that follow, the main route will be described and distances given starting from Mt. Clinton Rd. via the Crawford Connector, which will now be the usual route for most hikers using this trail.

The following description of the path is in the northbound direction (toward Mt. Washington). See below for a description of the path in the reverse direction.

Leaving the parking lot and soon crossing Mt. Clinton Rd., the Crawford Connector climbs gradually for 0.4 mi. until it reaches the bridge over Gibbs Brook. Here the Crawford Cliff Spur diverges left.

Crawford Cliff Spur. This short side path leaves the Crawford Connector at the west end of the bridge over Gibbs Brook and follows the brook to a small flume and pool. It then climbs steeply above the brook, turns left at an old illegible sign, becomes very rough, and reaches a ledge with an outlook over Crawford Notch and the Willey Range, 0.4 mi. (20 min.) from the Crawford Path.

The Crawford Connector continues across the bridge and ends at the Crawford Path 0.2 mi. from its trailhead on US 302 opposite the AMC Highland Center at Crawford Notch. To continue ascending on the Crawford Path, turn left here. The Crawford Path follows the south bank of Gibbs Brook, and at 0.6 mi. a side path leads 40 yd. left to Gibbs Falls. Soon the trail passes an information sign for the Gibbs Brook Scenic Area, then climbs moderately but steadily. At about 1.2 mi. from Mt. Clinton Rd. the trail begins to climb away from the brook, angling up the side of the valley. At 1.9 mi. the Mizpah Cutoff diverges east for Mizpah Spring Hut. The Crawford Path continues to ascend at easy to moderate grades, crossing several small brooks, then reaches its high point on the shoulder of Mt. Pierce and runs almost level, breaking into the open with fine views. At 3.1 mi. it reaches the junction with the Webster Cliff Trail, which leads right (south) to the summit of Mt. Pierce in about 0.1 mi.

From Mt. Pierce to Mt. Eisenhower the path runs through patches of scrub and woods with many open ledges that give magnificent views in all directions. Cairns and the marks left by many feet on the rocks indicate the way. The path winds about heading generally in a northeasterly direction, staying fairly near the poorly defined crest of the broad ridge, which is composed of several rounded humps. At 3.8 mi. the trail crosses a small stream in the col, then ascends mostly on ledges to the junction with the Mount Eisenhower Loop, which diverges left at 4.3 mi. The trip over this summit adds only 0.2 mi. and 300 ft. of climbing and provides excellent views in good weather. The Crawford Path bears somewhat to the right at this junction and runs nearly level—though with somewhat rough footing—through scrub on the southeast side of the mountain; this is the better route in bad weather. The Mount Eisenhower Loop rejoins the Crawford Path on the left at 4.8 mi., just above the sag between Mt. Eisenhower and Mt. Franklin, on a ledge that overlooks Red Pond, a small alpine tarn of stagnant water. The Edmands Path can be reached from this junction by following the Mount Eisenhower Loop for a short distance.

At 5.0 mi. the Mount Eisenhower Trail from the Dry River valley enters right. The Crawford Path then begins the ascent of the shoulder called Mt. Franklin, first moderately, then steeply for a short distance near the top. At 5.5 mi. the trail reaches the relatively level shoulder and continues past an unmarked path on the right at 6.0 mi. that leads in 130 yd. to the barely noticeable summit of Mt. Franklin, from which there are excellent views, particularly into Oakes Gulf. At 6.2 mi. the Mount Monroe Loop diverges left to cross both summits of Monroe, affording excellent views. It is about the same length as the parallel section of the Crawford Path but requires about 350 ft. more climbing. The Crawford Path is safer in inclement conditions, since it is much less exposed to the weather. The Crawford Path continues along the edge of the precipice that forms the northwest wall of Oakes Gulf, then follows a relocated section, passing an area that has been closed to public entry to preserve the habitat of the dwarf cinquefoil, an endangered species of plant. The area between the two ends of the Mount Monroe Loop is one of great fragility and botanical importance. To protect this area—probably the most significant tract of rare vegetation in the entire White Mtn. region—the most scrupulous care is required on the part of visitors. At 6.9 mi. the Mount Monroe Loop rejoins on the left, and the Crawford Path descends easily to Lakes of the Clouds Hut at 7.0 mi.

The Ammonoosuc Ravine Trail enters on the left at the corner of the hut, and in another 30 yd. the Dry River Trail enters on the right. The Crawford Path crosses the outlet of the larger lake and passes between it and the second lake, and in a short distance the Camel Trail to Boott Spur and the Tuckerman Crossover to Tuckerman Ravine diverge right at the same point. The Crawford Path then ascends moderately on the northwest side of the ridge, always some distance below the crest. The Davis Path, which has been following the original, less sheltered location of the Crawford Path, enters on the right at 7.9 mi., at the foot of the cone of Mt. Washington. In another 50 yd. the Westside Trail, a shortcut to the Northern Peaks, diverges left. The Crawford Path runs generally north, switching back and forth as it climbs the steep cone through a trench in the rocks. At the plateau west of the summit, it meets the Gulfside Trail at 8.3 mi., then turns right, passes through the old corral in which saddle horses from the Glen House used to be kept, and from there ascends past buildings to the summit.

Crawford Path (map 1:G8–F9)

Distances from Mt. Clinton Rd. parking area (1920') via Crawford Connector

  to Mizpah Cutoff (3380'): 1.9 mi., 1450 ft., 1 hr. 40 min.

  to Webster Cliff Trail (4250'): 3.1 mi., 2350 ft., 2 hr. 45 min.

  to south end of Mount Eisenhower Loop (4425'): 4.3 mi., 2650 ft., 3 hr. 30 min.

  to Mount Eisenhower Trail (4475'): 5.0 mi., 2750 ft., 3 hr. 55 min.

  to Lakes of the Clouds Hut (5012'): 7.0 mi., 3450 ft., 5 hr. 15 min.

  to Westside Trail (5625'): 7.9 mi., 4050 ft., 6 hr.

  to Gulfside Trail (6150'): 8.3 mi., 4600 ft., 6 hr. 30 min.

  to Mt. Washington summit (6288'): 8.5 mi. (13.7 km.), 4750 ft., 6 hr. 40 min.

Crawford Path (WMNF) [in reverse]

Descending from the summit of Mt. Washington, the path is on the right (west) side of the railroad track. After passing between the buildings it leads generally south, then west. After passing the old corral it reaches a junction where the Gulfside Trail turns sharp right. Here the Crawford Path turns sharp left and zigzags downward through a trench in the rocks. At 0.6 mi. the Westside Trail enters on the right and in another 50 yd. the Davis Path diverges left, following the original, less sheltered route of the Crawford Path. The Crawford Path now descends moderately on the northwest side of the ridge well below the crest, and the Tuckerman Crossover and the Camel Trail enter on the left at the same point just before the trail reaches the Lakes of the Clouds. It then passes between the lakes and reaches Lakes of the Clouds Hut at 1.5 mi., where the Dry River Trail enters on the left and the Ammonoosuc Ravine Trail enters on the right.

The Crawford Path now climbs up to the base of Mt. Monroe, where the north end of the Mount Monroe Loop diverges right to cross both summits of Monroe, affording excellent views. The loop over the summits is about the same length as the parallel section of the Crawford Path but requires about 350 ft. more climbing. The Crawford Path is safer in inclement conditions, as it is much less exposed to the weather. It circles around the foot of this sharp peak, following a relocated section past an area that has been closed to public entry to preserve the habitat of the dwarf cinquefoil, an endangered species of plant. The area between the two ends of the Mount Monroe Loop is one of great fragility and botanical importance. To protect this area—probably the most significant tract of rare vegetation in the entire White Mtn. region—the most scrupulous care is required on the part of visitors. The Crawford Path continues along the edge of the precipice that forms the northwest wall of Oakes Gulf, the Mount Monroe Loop rejoins on the right, and the main path continues along the flat ridge, passing an unmarked path on the left at 2.6 mi. that leads in 130 yd. to the barely noticeable summit of Mt. Franklin, from which there are excellent views, particularly into Oakes Gulf. At 3.0 mi. the trail drops rather steeply off the end of the shoulder, then descends moderately to the sag, passing the Mount Eisenhower Trail on the left at 3.5 mi. The Mount Eisenhower Loop leaves on the right at 3.7 mi. on a small ledge overlooking Red Pond, a small alpine tarn of stagnant water. The Edmands Path can be reached from this junction by following the Mount Eisenhower Loop for a short distance. The trip over Mt. Eisenhower adds only 0.2 mi. and 300 ft. of climbing and provides excellent views in good weather. The Crawford Path bears left and runs nearly level—though with somewhat rough footing—through scrub on the southeast side of the mountain; this is the better route in bad weather.

The Mount Eisenhower Loop rejoins on the right at 4.2 mi., and the Crawford Path descends on ledges to cross a small stream in the col, then climbs moderately to the junction with the Webster Cliff Trail at 5.4 mi., on an open ledge just below the summit of Mt. Pierce. From here the trail soon enters the scrub and then full woods, descends moderately past the Mizpah Cutoff at 6.6 mi., and continues through the Gibbs Brook Scenic Area. At 8.1 mi., where the Crawford Path continues straight another 0.2 mi. to US 302 opposite the AMC Highland Center at Crawford Notch, the main route turns right on the Crawford

Connector, immediately crosses a bridge over Gibbs Brook and passes the side path on the right to Crawford Cliff (see above), and continues 0.4 mi. to the Mt. Clinton Rd. parking area.

Crawford Path (map 1:G8–F9)

Distances from the summit of Mt. Washington (6288′)

to Gulfside Trail (6150′): 0.2 mi., 0 ft., 5 min.

to Westside Trail (5625′): 0.6 mi., 0 ft., 20 min.

to Lakes of the Clouds Hut (5012′): 1.5 mi., 0 ft., 45 min.

to Mount Eisenhower Trail (4475′): 3.5 mi., 150 ft., 1 hr. 50 min.

to south end of Mount Eisenhower Loop (4425′): 4.2 mi., 200 ft., 2 hr. 10 min.

to Webster Cliff Trail (4250′): 5.4 mi., 350 ft., 2 hr. 55 min.

to Mizpah Cutoff (3380′): 6.6 mi., 350 ft., 3 hr. 30 min.

to Mt. Clinton Rd. parking area (1920′) via Crawford Connector: 8.5 mi. (13.7 km.), 350 ft., 4 hr. 25 min.

Mount Eisenhower Loop (AMC)

This short trail parallels the Crawford Path, climbing over the bare, flat summit of Mt. Eisenhower, which provides magnificent views. It diverges from the Crawford Path 4.3 mi. from Mt. Clinton Rd. at the south edge of the summit dome, climbs easily for 0.1 mi., then turns sharp left in a flat area and ascends steadily to the summit at 0.4 mi. From there it descends moderately to a ledge overlooking Red Pond, then drops steeply over ledges, passes through a grassy sag just to the left of Red Pond, and finally climbs briefly past a junction on the left with the Edmands Path to rejoin the Crawford Path on a small, rocky knob.

Mount Eisenhower Loop (map 1:G8)

Distances from south junction with Crawford Path (4425′)

to Mt. Eisenhower summit (4760′): 0.4 mi., 350 ft., 25 min.

to north junction with Crawford Path (4475′): 0.8 mi. (1.2 km.), 350 ft. (rev. 300 ft.), 35 min.

Mount Monroe Loop (AMC)

This short trail runs parallel to the Crawford Path and passes over the summits of Mt. Monroe and Little Monroe. The views are fine, but the summits are very exposed to the weather. The trail diverges from the Crawford Path 6.2 mi. from Mt. Clinton Rd. and quickly ascends the minor crag called Little Monroe, then descends into the shallow, grassy sag beyond. It then climbs steeply to the summit of Mt. Monroe at 0.4 mi., follows the northeast ridge to the end of the shoulder, and drops sharply to the Crawford Path 0.1 mi. south of Lakes of the Clouds Hut.

Mount Monroe Loop (map 1:F9)

Distances from south junction with Crawford Path (5075′)

to summit of Mt. Monroe (5372′): 0.4 mi., 350 ft., 20 min.

to north junction with Crawford Path (5075′): 0.7 mi. (1.1 km.), 350 ft. (rev. 350 ft.), 30 min.

Ammonoosuc Ravine Trail (WMNF)

The Ammonoosuc Ravine Trail ascends to Lakes of the Clouds Hut from a parking lot on the Base Rd., 1.1 mi. east of its junction with the Mt. Clinton Rd. and the Jefferson Notch Rd. It can also be reached on foot from the Jefferson Notch Rd. via the Boundary Line Trail (see Section 2). Together with the upper section of the Crawford Path, this trail provides the shortest route to Mt. Washington from the west. The trail follows the headwaters of the Ammonoosuc River with many fine falls, cascades, and pools, and affords excellent views from its upper section. It is the most direct route to Lakes of the Clouds Hut, and the best route to or from the hut in bad weather, since it lies in woods or scrub except for the last 200 yd. to the hut. The section above Gem Pool is extremely steep and rough, and is likely to prove quite arduous to many hikers, particularly those with limited trail-walking experience. Many hikers also find it somewhat unpleasant to descend this section because of the steep, often slippery rocks and ledges.

Leaving the parking lot, this trail follows a path through the woods, crossing Franklin Brook at 0.3 mi. then passing over a double pipeline as it skirts the Base Station area. It joins the old route of the trail at the edge of the Ammonoosuc River at 1.0 mi., after a slight descent. (The lower section of the old route, marked by a sign, leads left from here 0.3 mi. to the Base Station.) The main trail bears right along the river, following the old route for the rest of the way. It ascends mostly by easy grades, though with some rough footing, crossing Monroe Brook at 1.7 mi. At 2.1 mi. it crosses the outlet of Gem Pool, a beautiful emerald pool at the foot of a cascade.

Now the very steep, rough ascent begins. At 2.3 mi. a side path (sign) leads right about 80 yd. to a spectacular viewpoint at the foot of the gorge. Above this point the main brook falls about 600 ft. down a steep trough in the mountainside at an average angle of 45°, while another brook a short distance to the north does the same, and these two spectacular water slides meet in a pool at the foot of the gorge. The main trail continues its steep ascent, passes an outlook over the cascades to the right of the trail, and at 2.5 mi. crosses the main brook on flat ledges at the head of the highest fall, a striking viewpoint. The grade now begins to ease, and the trail crosses several more brooks. Ledges become more frequent and the scrub becomes smaller and more sparse. At 3.0 mi. the trail emerges from the scrub and follows a line of cairns directly up some rock slabs (which are slippery when wet), passes through one last patch of scrub, and reaches the Crawford Path at the south side of Lakes of the Clouds Hut.

Ammonoosuc Ravine Trail (map 1:F8–F9)

Distances from the Base Rd. parking lot (2500′)

to Gem Pool (3450′): 2.1 mi., 950 ft., 1 hr. 30 min.

to brook crossing on flat ledges (4175′): 2.5 mi., 1700 ft., 2 hr. 5 min.

to Lakes of the Clouds Hut (5012′): 3.1 mi. (5.0 km.), 2500 ft., 2 hr. 50 min.

to Mt. Washington summit (6288′) via Crawford Path: 4.5 mi. (7.2 km.), 3800 ft., 4 hr. 10 min.

Edmands Path (WMNF)

The Edmands Path climbs to the Mount Eisenhower Loop near its junction with the Crawford Path in the Eisenhower-Franklin col, starting from a parking lot on the east side of the Mt. Clinton Rd. 2.3 mi. north of its junction with US 302. This trail provides the shortest route to the summit of Mt. Eisenhower, and a relatively easy access to the middle portion of the Crawford Path and the Southern Presidentials. The last 0.2-mi. segment before it joins the Mount Eisenhower Loop and Crawford Path is very exposed to northwest winds and, although short, can create a serious problem in bad weather. The ledgy brook crossings in the upper part of the trail can be treacherous in icy conditions.

J. Rayner Edmands, the pioneer trail maker, relocated and reconstructed this trail in 1909. The rock cribbing and paving in the middle and upper sections of the trail testify to the diligent labor that Edmands devoted to constructing a trail with constant comfortable grades in rather difficult terrain. Most of his work has survived the weather and foot traffic of many decades well, and though erosion has made the footing noticeably rougher in recent years, the trail retains what is probably the easiest grade and footing of any comparable trail in the White Mtns. It is nearly always comfortable, and almost never challenging.

From its trailhead the path runs nearly level across two small brooks, then at 0.4 mi. it crosses Abenaki Brook and turns sharp right onto an old logging road on the far bank. At 0.7 mi. the trail diverges left off the old road and crosses a wet area. Soon it begins to climb steadily, undulating up the west ridge of Mt. Eisenhower, carefully searching out the most comfortable grades. At 2.2 mi. the trail swings left and angles up the mountainside on a footway supported by extensive rock cribbing, then passes through a tiny stone gateway. At 2.5 mi. it crosses a small brook running over a ledge, and soon the grade becomes almost level as the trail contours around the north slope of Mt. Eisenhower, affording excellent views out through a fringe of trees. At 2.8 mi. it breaks into the open, crosses the nose of a ridge on a footway paved with carefully placed stones, and reaches the Mount Eisenhower Loop a few yards from the Crawford Path.

Edmands Path (map 1:G8)

Distances from Mt. Clinton Rd. (2000')

to stone gateway (4000'): 2.2 mi., 2000 ft., 2 hr. 5 min.

to Mount Eisenhower Loop junction (4450'): 2.9 mi. (4.7 km.), 2450 ft., 2 hr. 40 min.

to Mt. Eisenhower summit (4760') via Mount Eisenhower Loop: 3.3 mi. (5.3 km.), 2750 ft., 3 hr.

Webster-Jackson Trail (AMC)

This trail connects US 302 at a small parking area just south of the Macomber Family Information Center (Crawford Depot) with the summits of both Mt. Webster and Mt. Jackson, and provides the opportunity for an interesting loop trip, since the two summits are linked by the Webster Cliff Trail.

The trail, blazed in blue, leaves the east side of US 302 0.1 mi. south of the Crawford Depot and 0.1 mi. north of the Gate of the Notch. It runs through a clearing, enters the woods, and at 0.1 mi. from US 302 passes the side path leading right to Elephant Head.

Elephant Head Spur. Elephant Head is an interesting ledge that forms the east side of the Gate of the Notch, a mass of gray rock striped with veins of white quartz providing a remarkable likeness to an elephant's head and trunk. The path runs through the woods parallel to the highway at an easy grade, then ascends across the summit of the knob and descends 40 yd. to the top of the ledge, which overlooks Crawford Notch and affords fine views; it is 0.2 mi. (10 min.) from the Webster-Jackson Trail.

The main trail climbs along the south bank of Elephant Head Brook, well above the stream, then turns right, away from the brook, at 0.2 mi. Angling up the mountainside roughly parallel to the highway, nearly level stretches alternating with sharp uphill pitches, it crosses Little Mossy Brook at 0.3 mi., and at 0.6 mi. from US 302 a side path leads right 60 yd. to Bugle Cliff. This is a massive ledge overlooking Crawford Notch, where the view is well worth the slight extra effort required; if ice is present, exercise extreme caution. The main trail rises fairly steeply and crosses Flume Cascade Brook at 0.9 mi. At 1.4 mi., within sound of Silver Cascade Brook, the trail divides, the left branch for Mt. Jackson and the right for Mt. Webster.

Mount Webster Branch

The Webster (right) branch immediately descends steeply to Silver Cascade Brook, crosses it just below a beautiful cascade and pool, then bears left and climbs steeply up the bank. The trail then climbs steadily south 1.0 mi., meeting the Webster Cliff Trail on the high plateau northwest of the summit of Mt. Webster, 2.4 mi. from US 302. The ledgy summit of Mt. Webster, with an excellent view of Crawford Notch and the mountains to the west and south, is 0.1 mi. right (south) via the Webster Cliff Trail. For Mt. Jackson and Mizpah Spring Hut, turn left.

Mount Jackson Branch

The Jackson (left) branch ascends gradually until it comes within sight of Silver Cascade Brook, then begins to climb moderately. About 0.5 mi. above the junction, it crosses three branches of the brook in quick succession. At 1.0 mi. from the junction, a short distance below the base of the rocky summit cone, it passes Tisdale Spring (unreliable, often scanty and muddy). The trail soon swings right and ascends steep ledges to the open summit, 2.6 mi. from US 302.

Webster-Jackson Trail (map 1:G8)

Distances from US 302 (1900')

to Bugle Cliff (2450'): 0.6 mi., 550 ft., 35 min.

to Flume Cascade Brook (2500'): 0.9 mi., 600 ft., 45 min.

to Mt. Webster–Mt. Jackson fork (2800'): 1.4 mi., 900 ft., 1 hr. 10 min.

to Webster Cliff Trail (3840') via Webster branch: 2.4 mi., 2050 ft., 2 hr. 15 min.

to summit of Mt. Webster (3910') via Webster Cliff Trail: 2.5 mi. (4.1 km.), 2100 ft., 2 hr. 20 min.

to summit of Mt. Jackson (4052') via Jackson branch: 2.6 mi. (4.2 km.), 2150 ft., 2 hr. 25 min.

for loop trip over summits of Webster and Jackson (via Webster Cliff Trail): 6.5 mi. (10.5 km.), 2500 ft., 4 hr. 30 min.

Webster Cliff Trail (AMC)

This trail, a part of the Appalachian Trail, leaves the east side of US 302 opposite the road to Willey House Station, about 1 mi. south of the Willey House Recreation Area at the Willey House site. It ascends along the edge of the spectacular cliffs that form the east wall of Crawford Notch, then leads over Mts. Webster, Jackson, and Pierce to the Crawford Path 0.1 mi. north of Mt. Pierce.

From US 302, it runs nearly east 0.1 mi. to a bridge on which it crosses the Saco River. The Saco River Trail joins from the left at 0.2 mi. and departs on the right at 0.3 mi. Then the Webster Cliff Trail climbs steadily up the south end of the ridge, winding up the steep slope, swinging more to the north and growing steeper as it approaches the cliffs. At 1.8 mi. from US 302 it reaches the first open ledge, and from here on, as the trail ascends the ridge with easier grades, there are frequent outlook ledges giving ever-changing perspectives of the notch and the mountains to the south and west. At 2.4 mi. a ledge affords a view straight down to the state park buildings, and a short distance farther there is a ledge with an outlook to Mt. Washington. After climbing steadily and scrambling up a few fairly steep pitches, the trail reaches the jumbled, ledgy summit at 3.3 mi.

The trail then descends north, and in 0.1 mi. the Webster branch of the Webster-Jackson Trail from the Macomber Family Information Center (Crawford Depot) on US 302 enters left. The Webster Cliff Trail swings east and crosses numerous wet gullies, finally ascending the steep, ledgy cone of Mt.

Jackson to reach the summit at 4.7 mi., where the Jackson branch of the Webster-Jackson Trail enters left.

The trail leaves the summit of Mt. Jackson toward Mt. Pierce, following a line of cairns running north, and descends the ledges at the north end of the cone quite rapidly into the scrub, then enters and winds through open alpine meadows. At 5.2 mi., where an overgrown side path leads right 40 yd. to an outlook, the trail turns sharp left and drops into the woods. It continues up and down along the ridge toward Mt. Pierce, then descends gradually to the junction at 6.3 mi. with the Mizpah Cutoff, which leads left (west) to the Crawford Path. At 6.4 mi. Mizpah Spring Hut (where there are also tentsites for backpackers) is reached, and the Mount Clinton Trail to the Dry River valley diverges right (southeast), starting off diagonally down the hut clearing. Continuing past the hut, the trail soon ascends very rapidly, passes an outlook toward Mt. Jackson, and reaches an open ledge with good views at 6.6 mi. The grade lessens, and after a sharp right turn in a ledgy area the trail reaches the summit of the southwest knob of Mt. Pierce, which affords a view of the summit of Mt. Washington rising over Mt. Pierce. The trail descends into a sag and ascends easily through scrub to the summit of Mt. Pierce at 7.2 mi., where it comes into the open. It then descends moderately in the open in the same direction (northeast) about 150 yd. to its junction with the Crawford Path.

Webster Cliff Trail (map 1:G8)

Distances from US 302 (1275′)

to first open ledge (3100′): 1.8 mi., 1850 ft., 1 hr. 50 min.

to summit of Mt. Webster (3910′): 3.3 mi., 2700 ft., 3 hr.

to summit of Mt. Jackson (4052′): 4.7 mi., 3050 ft. (rev. 250 ft.), 3 hr. 50 min.

to Mizpah Spring Hut (3800′): 6.4 mi., 3250 ft. (rev. 250 ft.), 4 hr. 50 min.

to Crawford Path (4250′): 7.3 mi. (11.7 km.), 3800 ft. (rev. 100 ft.), 5 hr. 35 min.

Mizpah Cutoff (AMC)

This short trail provides a direct route from the Macomber Family Information Center (Crawford Depot) area to Mizpah Spring Hut. It diverges right (east) from the Crawford Path 1.9 mi. from the Mt. Clinton Rd. parking area, climbs the ridge at a moderate grade, passes through a fairly level area, and descends slightly to join the Webster Cliff Trail 0.1 mi. south of Mizpah Spring Hut.

50 Section 1

Mizpah Cutoff (map 1:G8)

Distance from Crawford Path (3380′)

   to Mizpah Spring Hut (3800′): 0.7 mi. (1.1 km.), 400 ft., 35 min.

Distance from Mt. Clinton Rd. parking area (1920′)

   to Mizpah Spring Hut (3800′) via Crawford Connector, Crawford Path, and Mizpah Cutoff: 2.6 mi. (4.2 km.), 1900 ft., 2 hr. 15 min.

Sam Willey Trail (NHDP)

This trail provides a short, easy walk at the base of the Webster Cliffs from the Willey House site on US 302, starting from the parking area on the east side of the road.

   Leaving the road, the trail crosses the wooden dam over the Saco River. Beyond a sign, the Sam Willey Trail bears right, and the Pond Loop Trail (providing a 0.2-mi. loop walk beside Willey Pond, with views up to the surrounding mountains, returning to a point near the dam) bears left. The Sam Willey Trail follows a graded path south and comes to its loop junction at 0.4 mi. Going left (clockwise), the loop reaches the junction at 0.5 mi. where the Saco River Trail continues ahead (south). The Sam Willey Trail swings around back to the north, passes a scenic spot by the Saco River and a view up to the Webster Cliffs, and returns to the loop junction in another 0.1 mi. To return to the Willey House site, turn left.

Sam Willey Trail (map 1:G8)

Distance from Willey House site (1300′)

   to Saco River Trail (1300′): 0.5 mi. (0.8 km), 0 ft., 15 min.

   for complete loop: 1.0 mi. (1.6 km.), 0 ft., 30 min.

Saco River Trail (NHDP)

This trail, blazed in blue, provides easy walking through attractive forests along the floor of Crawford Notch, linking the Willey House site (via the Sam Willey Trail) with the Webster Cliff Trail and Dry River Trail.

   Leaving the most southerly point of the southern loop section of the Sam Willey Trail, 0.5 mi. from the Willey House site, the trail runs briefly alongside the Saco River, then bears left away from the river and traverses several minor ups and downs. At 0.5 mi. it dips to the edge of an open swamp, where there is a view of Mt. Willey. At 0.7 mi. the Saco River Trail meets the Webster Cliff Trail (0.2 mi. from its trailhead on US 302) and turns left on it. The two trails coincide, climbing steadily eastward. At 0.8 mi. the Saco River Trail turns right off the Webster Cliff Trail and descends easily, working down to the floor of the valley. At 1.2 mi. it crosses several channels of Webster Brook and continues south through open hardwoods; in places the footway must be followed with care. At 1.6 mi. the trail passes a rustic bench and skirts a beaver swamp, crossing a small brook. After traversing a rocky section it ends at the Dry River Trail, 0.5 mi. from that trail's trailhead on US 302 and directly across from the junction with the Dry River Connection 0.4 mi. from Dry River Campground.

Saco River Trail (map 1:G8–H8)

Distances from Sam Willey Trail (1300')

to lower (west) junction with Webster Cliff Trail (1350'): 0.7 mi., 50 ft., 25 min.

to Dry River Trail (1300'): 2.4 mi. (3.9 km), 150 ft. (rev. 150 ft.), 1 hr. 15 min.

Saco Lake Trail (AMC)

This very short trail makes a loop around the east shore of Saco Lake, beginning and ending on US 302. It starts opposite the AMC Highland Center at Crawford Notch and ends after crossing the dam at the south end of Saco Lake. In addition to being an attractive short walk, it provides an alternative to part of the road walk between the beginning points of the Crawford Path and Webster-Jackson Trail.

Saco Lake Trail (map 1:G8)

Distance from north junction with US 302 (1890')

to south junction with US 302 (1890'): 0.3 mi. (0.5 km.), 0 ft., 10 min.

Dry River Trail (WMNF)

The Dry River Trail is the main trail from US 302 up the valley of the Dry River and through Oakes Gulf to Lakes of the Clouds Hut, giving access to Mt. Washington, the Southern Peaks, and the upper portion of the Montalban Ridge. It leaves the east side of US 302, 0.3 mi. north of the entrance to Dry River

Campground and 2.6 mi. south of the Willey House site. This trail in general is somewhat rougher than most similar valley trails elsewhere in the White Mtns. The first 5 mi. follows fairly close to the route of an old logging railroad, although the river and its tributaries have eradicated much of the old roadbed, and the relocations cut to eliminate the numerous potentially hazardous river crossings have bypassed much of the remaining grade. When water levels are high, the few Dry River crossings that remain on this trail—and on the trails that diverge from it—are at best difficult and can be very dangerous. At such times it is prudent not to descend into this valley if major stream crossings lie between you and your destination. This trail is almost entirely within the Presidential Range–Dry River Wilderness. Dry River Shelters #1 and #2 have been removed; Dry River Shelter #3 will be removed whenever major maintenance is required (contact Saco Ranger District office for information).

From the highway the trail follows a wide woods road generally northeast for 0.5 mi. to its junction with the bed of the old logging railroad (signed as the Dry River Connection), which reaches this point from Dry River Campground in 0.4 mi. At this junction the Saco River Trail, connecting to the Webster Cliff Trail and (via the Sam Willey Trail) the Willey House site, enters on the left. From here the Dry River Trail follows the railroad bed, enters the Presidential Range–Dry River Wilderness at 0.7 mi., and leaves the railroad grade sharp left at 0.9 mi., staying on the west side of the river where the railroad formerly crossed it. Just downstream from this point there is a pleasant pool. The trail climbs over a low bluff, rejoins the roadbed, then leaves it again and climbs over a higher bluff, where there is a restricted but beautiful outlook up the Dry River to Mt. Washington, Mt. Monroe, and the headwall of Oakes Gulf. At 1.7 mi., after a short, fairly steep descent, the trail crosses the Dry River on a suspension bridge and continues up the east bank, occasionally using portions of the old railroad grade. At 2.9 mi. it turns sharp right off the railroad grade where the Mount Clinton Trail diverges left to cross the river and ascend to Mizpah Spring Hut. At 4.2 mi. the Dry River Trail makes a sharp turn away from the river, then turns left and continues along the bank at a higher level. At 4.9 mi. it crosses Isolation Brook, turns right along the brook bank, and in 60 yd. the Isolation Trail diverges right, heading up along the brook.

The Dry River Trail continues straight along the high east bank of the Dry River and passes a cleared outlook over the river; at 5.2 mi. the Mount Eisenhower Trail diverges sharp left and descends the steep bank to cross the river and climb to the Crawford Path. The Dry River Trail continues along the east bank, passing at 5.4 mi. a side path (sign) on the left that leads down 40 yd. to the pool at the foot of Dry River Falls, a very attractive spot. The top of the falls, with an interesting pothole, can also be reached from here. At 5.6 mi. the trail crosses the river to the west side; the crossing is normally fairly easy but could be a serious problem at high water. At 6.3 mi. Dry River Shelter #3 is passed; it will be removed when major maintenance is required. In another 60 yd. the trail crosses a major tributary of the Dry River at the confluence and continues along the bank of the main stream, gradually rising higher above the river.

At 7.4 mi. the trail begins to swing away from the river, which has been at least audible to this point, and gradually climbs into Oakes Gulf. After it crosses a small ridge and descends sharply on the other side, views begin to appear, although the trail remains well sheltered in the scrub. At 8.7 mi. there is a good outlook perch just to the right of the trail. The trail soon climbs out of the scrub, turns left, and crosses a small brook at a right angle. At 9.1 mi. the trail turns sharp right from the gully it once ascended, where signs forbid public entry into the area formerly crossed by the trail. (The closed area is the habitat of the dwarf cinquefoil, an endangered plant species.) The trail continues to climb, passing the Presidential Range–Dry River Wilderness boundary sign in a patch of scrub, and reaches the height-of-land on the southwest ridge of Mt. Washington at 9.4 mi. It then descends to the larger of the two Lakes of the Clouds, follows its south edge, and ends at Lakes of the Clouds Hut.

Dry River Trail (map 1:H8–F9)

Distances from US 302 (1205')

to Dry River Connection and Saco River Trail (1250'): 0.5 mi., 50 ft., 15 min.

to suspension bridge (1600'): 1.7 mi., 500 ft. (rev. 100 ft.), 1 hr. 5 min.

to Mount Clinton Trail (1900'): 2.9 mi., 800 ft., 1 hr. 50 min.

to Isolation Trail (2600'): 4.9 mi., 1500 ft., 3 hr. 10 min.

to Mount Eisenhower Trail (2650'): 5.2 mi., 1550 ft., 3 hr. 25 min.

to Dry River Shelter #3 (3125'): 6.3 mi., 2000 ft., 4 hr. 10 min.

to Lakes of the Clouds Hut (5012'): 9.6 mi. (15.5 km.), 4000 ft., 6 hr. 50 min.

Mount Clinton Trail (WMNF)

This trail connects the lower part of the Dry River to Mizpah Spring Hut and the southern part of the Southern Peaks, and lies almost entirely within the Presidential Range–Dry River Wilderness. *Caution:* The crossing of the Dry River on this trail near its junction with the Dry River Trail can vary from an easy skip over the stones to a waist-high ford in a torrent, and there may be no safe way across. In high-water conditions it would be prudent not to descend from Mizpah Spring Hut by this trail, since the only safe course on reaching the Dry River (other than returning to the hut) might be a rough bushwhack south along the riverbank for about 1.2 mi.

The trail diverges left from the Dry River Trail 2.9 mi. from US 302, and immediately makes the potentially hazardous crossing of the Dry River. On the west side of the river it follows a short stretch of old railroad grade, then swings left up the bank of a major tributary, following an old logging road at a moderate grade much of the way. At 0.5 mi. the trail crosses this brook for the first of seven times, then scrambles up a washed-out area on the other bank. At 1.2 mi. the trail turns sharp left off the road and descends to the brook, crosses at a ledgy spot, and soon regains the road on the other side. It follows close to the brook, crossing many tributaries as well as the main brook, to the seventh crossing of the main brook at 1.8 mi. Above an eroded section where a small brook has taken over the road, the walking on the old road becomes very pleasant, and the Dry River Cutoff enters on the right at 2.5 mi. From here the trail ascends past a large boulder to the Presidential Range–Dry River Wilderness boundary at 2.9 mi., and soon enters the clearing of Mizpah Spring Hut, where it joins the Webster Cliff Trail.

Mount Clinton Trail (map 1:G8)

Distances from Dry River Trail (1900')

to Dry River Cutoff (3425'): 2.5 mi., 1550 ft., 2 hr.

to Mizpah Spring Hut (3800'): 3.0 mi. (4.8 km.), 1900 ft., 2 hr. 25 min.

Mount Eisenhower Trail (WMNF)

This trail connects the middle part of the Dry River valley to the Crawford Path at the Eisenhower-Franklin col and lies almost entirely within the Presidential Range–Dry River Wilderness. Its grades are mostly easy to moderate and it runs above the treeline for only a short distance at the ridgecrest.

The trail diverges left from the Dry River Trail about 5.2 mi. from US 302, and descends rather steeply on a former route of the Dry River Trail through an area with many side paths; care must be taken to stay on the proper trail. The trail crosses the Dry River (may be difficult or impassable at high water) and follows the bank downstream. At 0.2 mi. it joins its former route and bears right up a rather steep logging road, and the Dry River Cutoff diverges left at 0.3 mi.

Soon the grade on the Mount Eisenhower Trail eases as it leads generally north, keeping a bit to the west of the crest of the long ridge that runs south from a point midway between Mts. Franklin and Eisenhower. At 1.3 mi. it passes through a blowdown patch with views of Mt. Pierce, and from here on there are occasional views to the west from the edge of the ravine. At 1.8 mi. it turns sharp right, then left, and soon ascends more steeply for a while. At 2.4 mi. the trail finally gains the crest of the ridge and winds among rocks and scrub, passing the Presidential Range–Dry River Wilderness boundary 50 yd. before reaching the Crawford Path in the Eisenhower-Franklin col, at a point 0.2 mi. north of the Crawford Path's northern junction with the Mount Eisenhower Loop.

Mount Eisenhower Trail (map 1:G8)

Distances from Dry River Trail (2650′)

to Dry River Cutoff (2650′): 0.3 mi., 100 ft. (rev. 100 ft.), 10 min.

to Crawford Path (4475′): 2.7 mi. (4.3 km.), 1950 ft., 2 hr. 20 min.

Dry River Cutoff (AMC)

This trail connects the middle part of the Dry River valley to Mizpah Spring Hut and the southern section of the Southern Peaks. Grades are mostly easy with some moderate sections. This trail is entirely within the Presidential Range–Dry River Wilderness.

The trail diverges left from the Mount Eisenhower Trail 0.3 mi. from the latter trail's junction with the Dry River Trail. In 0.1 mi. it crosses a substantial brook after a slight descent, turns sharp left and climbs the bank, crosses a tributary, then swings back and climbs above the bank of the tributary. It crosses several branches of the tributary and gains the height-of-land on the southeast ridge of Mt. Pierce at 1.3 mi., then runs almost on the level to its junction with the Mount Clinton Trail at 1.7 mi. Mizpah Spring Hut is 0.5 mi. to the right from this junction via the Mount Clinton Trail.

Dry River Cutoff (map 1:G8)

Distance from Mount Eisenhower Trail (2650′)

to Mount Clinton Trail (3425′): 1.7 mi. (2.8 km.), 800 ft., 1 hr. 15 min.

Davis Path (AMC)

The Davis Path, completed by Nathaniel T. P. Davis in 1845, was the third (and longest) bridle path constructed to the summit of Mt. Washington. It was in use until 1853 or 1854 but became impassable soon afterward; eventually it went out of existence entirely until it was reopened as a foot trail by the AMC in 1910. At that time it was so overgrown that some sections could be located only by one of the original laborers, then a very old man, who relied on his memory of where the path had been built. The sections leading up the dauntingly steep southern slopes of Mt. Crawford and Stairs Mtn. give some idea of the magnitude of the task Davis performed in building a trail passable to horses along this ridge. The resolution that enabled Davis to push forward with this apparently hopeless task was the inspiration for the naming of Mt. Resolution. This trail is almost entirely within the Presidential Range–Dry River Wilderness.

The path leaves US 302 on the west side of the Saco River at a paved parking lot near the Notchland Inn, 5.6 mi. south of the Willey House site in Crawford Notch State Park.

It follows the bank of the river about 200 yd. upstream to the new suspension footbridge (Bemis Bridge). Beyond the east end of the bridge, the trail passes through private land, continuing straight east across an overgrown field near a camp, then turns left into a path along a power line and crosses a small brook. It then enters the woods and the WMNF, and soon joins and follows a logging road along the bed of a small brook (normally dry in summer). It crosses the brook bed at a point where there may be running water upstream, soon recrosses it, and begins to climb away from it, shortly passing into the Presidential Range–Dry River Wilderness. At 0.9 mi. it turns sharp right and soon enters the old, carefully graded bridle path and begins to ascend the steep ridge between Mt. Crawford and Mt. Hope by zigzags. Attaining the crest at 1.9 mi., the Davis Path follows this ridge north, rising over bare ledges with good outlooks, particularly to Carrigain and Tripyramid.

At 2.2 mi. from US 302, at the foot of a large, sloping ledge, a side trail diverges left and climbs 0.3 mi. (15 min.) to the bare, peaked summit of Mt. Crawford, from which there is a magnificent view of Crawford Notch, the Dry River valley, and the surrounding ridges and peaks.

From this junction the Davis Path turns northeast, descends slightly to the col between the peak of Mt. Crawford and its ledgy, domelike east knob (sometimes called Crawford Dome), and resumes the ascent. It soon passes over a ledgy shoulder of Crawford Dome, with good views back to the impressively precipitous face of the small peak of Mt. Crawford, and dips to the Crawford-

Resolution col. Leaving this col, the path runs north, rises slightly, and keeps close to the same level along the steep west side of Mt. Resolution.

At 3.7 mi. the Mount Parker Trail diverges right (east) and leads in about 0.6 mi. to open ledges near the summit of Mt. Resolution, then continues to the Mount Langdon Trail and Bartlett village. Fine views can be obtained from open ledges by ascending this trail for only a little more than 0.1 mi. from the Davis Path junction.

At this junction also, a spur trail leaves opposite the Mount Parker Trail and descends steeply for about 120 yd. to the AMC Resolution Shelter, an open camp with room for eight, situated on a small branch of Sleeper Brook. (WMNF Wilderness policies call for removal of this shelter when major maintenance is required.) Ordinarily there is water just behind the shelter, but in dry seasons it may be necessary to go down the brook a short distance. In most seasons, this is the first water after the brook at the base of the climb up from the Saco valley; in dry seasons it may be the last water available on the entire remainder of the trail unless one descends well down one of the branches of the Isolation Trail, since all of the water sources near this ridgecrest trail are unreliable.

At 4.0 mi. the path passes just west of Stairs Col, the small, wild pass between Mt. Resolution and Stairs Mtn. Here the Stairs Col Trail to the Rocky Branch diverges right. The Davis Path now veers northwest, passing west of the precipitous Giant Stairs, ascending gradually along a steep mountainside, then zigzagging boldly northeast—with occasional steep scrambles on ledges—toward the flat top of Stairs Mtn. As the path turns sharp left shortly before reaching the top of the slope, a branch trail leads right a few steps to the Down-look, a good viewpoint at the brink of a cliff. (On the descent, where the main trail turns sharp right, take care not to follow this side path inadvertently since it ends at the drop-off very abruptly.) At the top of the climb, 4.4 mi. from US 302, a branch trail leads right (southeast) 0.2 mi., passing just south of the summit of Stairs Mtn., to the top of the Giant Stairs, where there is an inspiring view to the east and south.

The Davis Path continues down the north ridge of Stairs Mtn. for 1.0 mi., then runs east in a sag for about 0.1 mi. Turning north again and crossing a small brook (watch for this turn), it passes over a small rise and descends into another sag. The path next begins to ascend the long north and south ridge of Mt. Davis, keeping mostly to the west slopes. At 6.1 mi. there is a small spring on the right, and at 6.5 mi. a small brook is crossed. At 8.5 mi. a side path diverges right (east) and climbs steeply 0.2 mi. to the summit of Mt. Davis, which commands perhaps the finest view on the Montalban Ridge and one of the best in the mountains. The main path now descends to the col between Mt. Davis and Mt. Isolation, where it crosses a small brook and then ascends Mt. Isolation. At 9.7 mi. a spur path (which is signed, but easily missed) diverges left at a ledgy spot, leading in 125 yd. to the open summit of Mt. Isolation, which provides magnificent views in all directions.

The path descends moderately for 0.2 mi. and then runs north along the ridge at easy grades. At 10.5 mi. the path leads past the site of the former Isolation Shelter, and at 10.6 mi. the east branch of the Isolation Trail enters on the right from the Rocky Branch valley. Water can be obtained by going down the Isolation Trail to the right (east); decent-appearing water (which is nevertheless unsafe to drink without treatment) may be a considerable distance down. The Davis Path continues to climb steadily, and at 10.9 mi., as it reaches the top of the ridge and the grade decreases, the west branch of the Isolation Trail diverges and descends to the left into the Dry River valley. The Davis Path passes over a hump and runs through a sag at 11.5 mi., then ascends steadily to the treeline at 12.1 mi. From here the trail is above the treeline and completely exposed to the weather. At 12.5 mi. the Glen Boulder Trail joins on the right just below a small crag; at 13.0 mi. the path passes just west of the summit of Boott Spur, and the Boott Spur Trail from AMC Pinkham Notch Visitor Center enters on the right (east).

Turning northwest, the path leads along the almost level ridges of Boott Spur and crosses Bigelow Lawn. At 13.6 mi. the Lawn Cutoff diverges right to Tuckerman Junction, and, 200 yd. farther on, the Camel Trail diverges left (west) to the Lakes of the Clouds Hut. At 14.0 mi. the Davis Path begins to follow the original location of the Crawford Path and crosses the Tuckerman Crossover, and in another 0.3 mi. the Davis Path is joined on the right by the Southside Trail. At 14.4 mi. the Davis Path ends at the present Crawford Path, which climbs to the summit of Mt. Washington in another 0.6 mi.

Davis Path (maps 1/3:H8–F9)

Distances from parking area near US 302 (1000')

to Mt. Crawford spur path (2900'): 2.2 mi., 1900 ft., 2 hr. 5 min.

to Mount Parker Trail (3040'): 3.7 mi., 2250 ft. (rev. 200 ft.), 3 hr.

to Stairs Col Trail (3040'): 4.0 mi., 2250 ft., 3 hr. 10 min.

to Giant Stairs spur path (3450'): 4.4 mi., 2650 ft., 3 hr. 30 min.

to Mt. Davis spur path (3720'): 8.5 mi., 3750 ft. (rev. 800 ft.), 6 hr. 10 min.

to Mt. Isolation spur path (3950'): 9.7 mi., 4150 ft. (rev. 150 ft.), 7 hr.

to Isolation Trail, east branch (3850'): 10.6 mi., 4300 ft. (rev. 250 ft.), 7 hr. 30 min.

to Isolation Trail, west branch (4150'): 10.9 mi., 4600 ft., 7 hr. 45 min.

to Glen Boulder Trail (5175'): 12.5 mi., 5650 ft. (rev. 100 ft.), 9 hr. 5 min.

to Boott Spur Trail (5425'): 13.0 mi., 5900 ft., 9 hr. 30 min.

to Lawn Cutoff (5475'): 13.6 mi., 5950 ft. (rev. 100 ft.), 9 hr. 50 min.

to Crawford Path (5625'): 14.4 mi. (23.2 km.), 6150 ft. (rev. 50 ft.), 10 hr. 15 min.

to Lakes of the Clouds Hut (5012') via Camel Trail: 14.4 mi., 5950 ft. (rev. 450 ft.), 10 hr. 10 min.

to Mt. Washington summit (6288') via Crawford Path: 15.0 mi. (24.1 km.), 6750 ft., 10 hr. 55 min.

Stairs Col Trail (AMC)

This trail connects the Rocky Branch valley with Stairs Col on the Davis Path, providing, in particular, the easiest route to the Giant Stairs. Note that there is usually water in small streams in the upper part of this trail, but very little on the Davis Path. This trail is almost entirely within the Presidential Range–Dry River Wilderness.

It leaves the Rocky Branch Trail opposite the side path to the Rocky Branch Shelter #1 area and follows an old railroad siding for 50 yd. It then turns sharp left, crosses a swampy area, and climbs briefly to a logging road, where it enters the Presidential Range–Dry River Wilderness. From here nearly to Stairs Col, the trail follows logging roads along the ravine of Lower Stairs Brook, becoming quite steep at 1.3 mi. and crossing the headwaters of the brook at about 1.5 mi., where it enters a birch glade. The trail becomes gradual as it approaches Stairs Col, then it crosses this small, ferny pass below the cliffs of Stairs Mtn. and continues down the west slope a short distance to meet the Davis Path. For the Giant Stairs, turn right.

Stairs Col Trail (map 1:H9)

Distance from Rocky Branch Trail (1420')

to Davis Path junction (3040'): 1.8 mi. (2.9 km.), 1600 ft., 1 hr. 40 min.

Rocky Branch Trail (WMNF)

This trail provides access to the valley of the Rocky Branch of the Saco River, which lies between the two longest subsidiary ridges of Mt. Washington: the

Montalban Ridge to the west and the Rocky Branch Ridge to the east. In the upper part of the valley, the forest is still recovering from fires that swept the slopes in 1912 to 1914. The lack of mature trees, particularly conifers, is evident in many areas. *Caution:* There are four river crossings between the junctions with the Stairs Col Trail and the Isolation Trail, and one just beyond the Isolation Trail junction; these crossings are wide, difficult, and possibly dangerous at high water. The northeast terminus of this trail is located at a paved parking lot on NH 16 about 5 mi. north of Jackson, just north of the highway bridge over the Ellis River. The Jericho (south) trailhead is reached by following Jericho Rd.—called Rocky Branch Rd. (FR 27) by the USFS—which leaves US 302 just east of the bridge over the Rocky Branch, 1 mi. west of the junction of US 302 and NH 16 in Glen; it is paved for about 1 mi., then a good gravel road up to the beginning of the trail about 4.4 mi. from US 302.

At the northeast terminus, on NH 16 below Pinkham Notch, the trail leaves the north end of the parking lot (avoid a gravel road that branches left just below the parking lot) and climbs moderately on an old logging road. At about 0.5 mi. the Avalanche Brook Ski Trail enters from the left and leaves on the right at 0.7 mi. At 1.3 mi. the trail swings left, away from the bank of a small brook, and continues to ascend, then turns sharp left at 1.8 mi. and follows an old, very straight road on a slight downhill grade. After about 0.5 mi. on this road, it swings gradually right and climbs moderately, following a brook part of the way, and reaches the Presidential Range–Dry River Wilderness boundary just east of the ridge top. Passing the almost imperceptible height-of-land at 2.8 mi., the trail follows a short bypass to the left of a very wet area and runs almost level, then descends easily, with small brooks running in and out of the trail.

At 3.5 mi. the trail begins to swing left, descends gradually to the Rocky Branch and follows it downstream for a short distance, then crosses it at 3.7 mi. This crossing may be very difficult, and the trail can be difficult to follow from this crossing for travelers going toward NH 16, since it is poorly marked and there are well-beaten side paths to campsites—heading for NH 16, the main trail first parallels the river going upstream and then swings gradually away from the river on a well-defined old road. (*Note:* If you are climbing to Mt. Isolation from NH 16, and the river is high, you can avoid two possibly difficult crossings by bushwhacking upstream along the east side of the river for 0.4 mi., since the Isolation Trail, which begins on the opposite bank, soon crosses back to the east bank.)

On the west bank of the river at this crossing is the junction with the Isolation Trail, which turns right (north), following the riverbank upstream on the old railroad grade. The Rocky Branch Trail turns left downstream, also following the old railroad grade from this junction, and passes Rocky Branch Shelter #2 in 60 yd. (USFS Wilderness policies call for removal of this shelter when major maintenance is required.) The trail then runs generally south along the west bank for about 2.4 mi., at times on the old railroad grade, then follows the grade more closely, crossing the river four times. These crossings are difficult at high water; it may be practical to avoid some or all—particularly the upstream pair, which are a bit more than 0.1 mi. apart, while the downstream pair are 0.4 mi. apart—by bushwhacking along the west bank. After the fourth crossing at 6.8 mi., the trail leaves the Presidential Range–Dry River Wilderness, crosses Upper Stairs Brook, and begins a bypass on the uphill side of the old railroad grade that is almost 0.5 mi. long. Returning to the grade, the trail reaches a junction at 7.8 mi. with the Stairs Col Trail on the right, and, 20 yd. farther along the trail, a spur path on the left leads 60 yd. to WMNF Rocky Branch Shelter #1 and tentsite. Continuing south along the river on the railroad grade, the trail crosses Lower Stairs Brook, makes a shorter bypass on the uphill side of a boggy section of the grade, and at 9.4 mi. enters a new gravel logging road and follows it for another 0.4 mi. to Jericho Rd., crossing the river and Otis Brook on logging-road bridges just before reaching its south terminus. In the reverse direction, where the new road swings to the left about 0.4 mi. from Jericho Rd., the trail continues straight ahead on the old railroad grade, which looks like an old grassy road.

Rocky Branch Trail (map 3:G10–H9)

Distances from parking lot off NH 16 (1200′)

to height-of-land (3100′): 2.8 mi., 1900 ft, 2 hr. 20 min.

to Isolation Trail (2800′): 3.7 mi., 1900 ft. (rev. 300 ft.), 2 hr. 50 min.

to Stairs Col Trail (1420′): 7.8 mi., 1900 ft. (rev. 1400 ft.), 4 hr. 50 min.

to Jericho Rd. (1100′): 9.8 mi. (15.8 km.), 1900 ft. (rev. 300 ft.), 5 hr. 50 min.

Isolation Trail (WMNF)

This trail links the Dry River valley (Dry River Trail), the Montalban Ridge (Davis Path), and the Rocky Branch valley (Rocky Branch Trail), crossing the ridgecrest north of Mt. Isolation. It is entirely within the Presidential Range–Dry River Wilderness.

This trail diverges from the Rocky Branch Trail just north of Rocky Branch Shelter #2 (which will be removed when major maintenance is required), on the west bank of the river at the point where the Rocky Branch Trail crosses it. The Isolation Trail follows the river north along the west bank on what is left of the old railroad grade, crossing the river at 0.4 mi. At 0.7 mi. the trail turns sharp right off the railroad grade, climbs briefly, then follows a logging road that at first runs high above the river. The trail crosses the river three more times; the next two crossings are only 70 yd. apart and so can be fairly easily avoided by a short bushwhack along the riverbank. The last crossing comes at 1.7 mi., after which the trail swings away from the main stream and climbs easily along a tributary, reaching the Davis Path at 2.6 mi. after passing through an area of confusing side paths among bootleg campsites where the main trail must be followed with care.

Now coinciding with the Davis Path, the Isolation Trail climbs steadily north for about 0.3 mi. until it approaches the ridgecrest and the grade decreases, where it turns left off the Davis Path. It runs level for 0.2 mi., then descends moderately southwest into the Dry River valley. At 4.3 mi. the trail reaches Isolation Brook, a branch of the Dry River, and follows its northwest bank on an old logging road disrupted by numerous small slides until it ends at the Dry River Trail, 4.9 mi. from US 302.

Isolation Trail (map 1:G9–G8)

Distances from Rocky Branch Trail (2800')

- *to* fourth crossing of the Rocky Branch (3423'): 1.7 mi., 600 ft., 1 hr. 10 min.
- *to* Davis Path, south junction (3850'): 2.6 mi., 1050 ft., 1 hr. 50 min.
- *to* Davis Path, north junction (4150'): 2.9 mi., 1350 ft., 2 hr. 10 min.
- *to* Isolation Brook (3300'): 4.3 mi., 1400 ft. (rev. 900 ft.), 2 hr. 50 min.
- *to* Dry River Trail (2600'): 5.3 mi. (8.6 km.), 1400 ft. (rev. 700 ft.), 3 hr. 20 min.

Distances from Rocky Branch Trail at parking area on NH 16 (1200')

- *to* Isolation Trail (2800') via Rocky Branch Trail: 3.8 mi., 1900 ft. (rev. 300 ft.), 2 hr. 50 min.
- *to* Davis Path, south junction (3850'): 6.4 mi., 2950 ft., 4 hr. 40 min.
- *to* Mt. Isolation summit (4004') via Davis Path: 7.3 mi. (11.8 km.), 3250 ft. (rev. 150 ft.), 5 hr. 15 min.

Mount Langdon Trail (WMNF)

This trail runs to the Mt. Langdon Shelter from the road on the north side of the Saco near Bartlett village, meeting both the Mount Parker Trail and the Mount Stanton Trail, and thus gives access to both the higher and lower sections of the Montalban Ridge. It should be noted that despite its name this trail does not get particularly close to the summit of Mt. Langdon, which is crossed by the Mount Stanton Trail. Most of this trail is either within or close to the boundary of the Presidential Range–Dry River Wilderness; Mt. Langdon Shelter is just outside the Wilderness.

From the four corners at the junction of US 302 and the Bear Notch Rd. in Bartlett village, follow the road that leads north across a bridge over the Saco to an intersection at 0.4 mi. The trail, marked by a sign, begins almost straight ahead; there are two entrances that very soon converge. The trail follows a fairly recent gravel logging road, and at 0.3 mi. the path to Cave Mtn. (unsigned and easily missed) diverges left. The road gradually becomes older and less evident. The trail enters the Presidential Range–Dry River Wilderness and passes a trail register just before it crosses a good-sized brook at 1.0 mi., after which it climbs more steadily, bearing sharp right twice as the road fades away.

The Mount Langdon Trail crosses Oak Ridge at 2.2 mi., passing through an unusual stand of red oak, and descends, sharply at times, to the Oak Ridge–Mt. Parker col, where it bears right at 2.5 mi. at the junction with the Mount Parker Trail. The Mount Langdon Trail then descends gradually to the WMNF Mt. Langdon Shelter, capacity eight, where this trail and the Mount Stanton Trail both end. Some care is required to follow the trail near the shelter. Water may be found in a brook 60 yd. from the shelter on the Mount Stanton Trail, although in dry weather the brook bed may have to be followed downhill for a distance.

Mount Langdon Trail (map 3:I9–H9)

Distances from the road on the north bank of the Saco River (700′)

to Mount Parker Trail (1894′): 2.5 mi., 1450 ft. (rev. 250 ft.), 2 hr.

to Mt. Langdon Shelter (1760′): 2.9 mi. (4.7 km.), 1450 ft. (rev. 100 ft.), 2 hr. 10 min.

to high point on Mt. Langdon (2380′) via Mount Stanton Trail: 3.7 mi., 2050 ft., 2 hr. 55 min.

Mount Parker Trail (SSOC)

This pleasant, rugged, lightly used trail passes several excellent viewpoints and provides access from Bartlett to Mt. Parker, Mt. Resolution, the Stairs Col area, and the upper Montalban Ridge. It runs almost entirely within or close to the boundary of the Presidential Range–Dry River Wilderness. There is no reliable water on this trail.

This trail begins in the Oak Ridge–Mt. Parker col 2.5 mi. from Bartlett, continuing straight ahead to the north where the Mount Langdon Trail turns right (east). It climbs moderately with many switchbacks through beech and oak woods severely damaged by the January 1998 ice storm, descends briefly, and then continues its winding ascent to the open summit of Mt. Parker at 1.4 mi., where there are excellent views.

Continuing north, the trail follows the long ridge between Mt. Parker and Mt. Resolution and passes over three bumps, alternating between spruce woods and semi-open ledges with restricted views. Some blowdown may be encountered in this area. It then runs along the west and south slopes of the remainder of the ridge (swinging inside the Presidential Range–Dry River Wilderness for the rest of its length) until it reaches the southeast corner of Mt. Resolution. Here it turns sharp right and zigzags up to the col between the main summit ridge and a southerly knob at 3.2 mi., where a somewhat overgrown branch trail leads left 0.1 mi. to the top of this knob, which is an open ledge with excellent views. Beyond this junction the trail winds along the flat top of Mt. Resolution until it reaches a large cairn on an open ledge with excellent views at 3.8 mi. The true summit is probably just above this cairn; there is another knob of almost equal elevation about 0.1 mi. east-northeast that affords excellent views north, but there is no path to it. From the cairn the trail descends into a gully where it crosses a small, sluggish brook (unreliable water), then heads down northwest over fine open ledges and finally drops steeply to the Davis Path, opposite the branch trail to Resolution Shelter.

Mount Parker Trail (map 3:H9)

Distances from Mount Langdon Trail (1894')

to summit of Mt. Parker (3004'): 1.4 mi., 1100 ft., 1 hr. 15 min.

to branch trail to open southerly knob (3200'): 3.2 mi., 1500 ft. (rev. 300 ft.), 2 hr. 20 min.

to high point on Mt. Resolution (3400'): 3.8 mi., 1700 ft., 2 hr. 45 min.

to Davis Path junction (3100'): 4.3 mi. (6.8 km.), 1700 ft. (rev. 300 ft.), 3 hr.

Mount Stanton Trail (SSOC)

This trail passes over the low eastern summits of the Montalban Ridge and affords many views from scattered ledges. A new east trailhead is being constructed in the vicinity of the old trailhead, and the beginning of the trail will be relocated; directions given here are for the old trailhead and trail, but the relocation of both should make only a minor difference. To reach the east trailhead (the west trailhead is at Mt. Langdon Shelter), leave the north side of US 302 1.8 mi. west of its junction with NH 16 in Glen and a short distance east of the bridge over the Saco River. Follow a paved road (Covered Bridge Ln.) west about 0.2 mi., then bear right on Oak Ridge Dr., and almost immediately turn sharp right onto Hemlock Dr. (In winter continue on Oak Ridge Dr. and take the next right after Hemlock Dr., which leads to the upper part of Hemlock Dr.) Park at the trail sign near a crossroads 0.6 mi. from US 302; the trail begins just uphill on the left side of the gravel driveway that leads to the right from the crossroads.

In 100 yd. the trail passes to the right of a red-blazed WMNF boundary corner and bears right, then at 0.3 mi. it turns sharp left with yellow blazes where the red-blazed WMNF boundary continues straight ahead. (This section will probably be changed by the relocation.) The trail climbs steeply at times, but there are gentler sections, and the outlooks from White's Ledge begin at about 0.8 mi. The trail climbs steeply again after passing a large boulder on the right of the trail, and at 1.2 mi. it turns sharp right on a ledge, where there is a good viewpoint just to the left of the trail and climbing becomes easier. At 1.4 mi. it passes about 15 yd. to the right of the true summit of Mt. Stanton. The summit area is covered with a fine stand of red (Norway) pines, and there are good views from nearby scattered ledges.

The trail descends to the Stanton-Pickering col, then ascends steadily, crosses a ledgy ridge and descends slightly, then climbs again and at 2.1 mi. passes 30 yd. to the right of the true summit of Mt. Pickering. It then leads to ledges on a slightly lower knob, where there are excellent views. The trail descends to a minor col, then crosses over several interesting small humps sometimes called the Crippies (the origin of this peculiar name is one of the mysteries of White Mtn. nomenclature). These humps have scattered outlook ledges, and the best view is from the fourth and last Crippie, which is crossed at 3.3 mi.

After the last Crippie the trail may be less well cleared and harder to follow. It descends somewhat along the north side of the ridge toward Mt. Langdon, then climbs north moderately with a few steep pitches, passing an outlook to Carter Dome, Carter Notch, and Wildcat Mtn. At 4.5 mi. the trail passes about 35 yd. to the right of the summit of Mt. Langdon, which is wooded and viewless, then descends easily to a gravel slope, turns right, and continues downward to a brook that is crossed 60 yd. east of Mt. Langdon Shelter, where the Mount Stanton Trail ends.

Mount Stanton Trail (map 3:H10–H9)

Distances from the trailhead off Hemlock Drive (700')

to high point on Mt. Stanton (1700'): 1.4 mi., 1000 ft., 1 hr. 10 min.

to high point on Mt. Pickering (1900'): 2.1 mi., 1400 ft. (rev. 200 ft.), 1 hr. 45 min.

to fourth Crippie (1888'): 3.3 mi., 1750 ft. (rev. 300 ft.), 2 hr. 30 min.

to high point on Mt. Langdon (2380'): 4.5 mi., 2450 ft. (rev. 200 ft.), 3 hr. 30 min.

to Mount Langdon Trail at Mt. Langdon Shelter (1760'): 5.3 mi. (8.5 km.), 2450 ft. (rev. 600 ft.), 3 hr. 55 min.

Cave Mountain Path

Cave Mtn. (located on private property) is remarkable for the shallow cave near its wooded summit. It is reached from Bartlett by following the Mount Langdon Trail for 0.3 mi. to an unsigned but well-worn branch path that forks left (watch for it carefully) and skirts the east side of Cave Mtn. After 0.3 mi. this path swings right and leads up a steep gravel slope to the cave. A rough, poorly marked trail to the right of the cave leads, after a short scramble, to the top of the cliff in which the cave is located, where there is a good view of Bartlett and the Saco River.

Cave Mountain Path (map 3:H9)

Distances from Mount Langdon Trail (800')

to cave (1200'): 0.3 mi., 400 ft., 20 min.

to outlook (1350'): 0.4 mi. (0.6 km.), 550 ft., 30 min.

Winniweta Falls Trail (WMNF)

This trail provides easy access to a waterfall. Its trailhead (limited parking) is located on the west side of NH 16, 3 mi. north of the bridge over the Ellis River in Jackson. Hikers using this trail must ford the wide bed of the Ellis River, which is often a rather shallow stream, but the crossing can require wading in even moderate flow and may be dangerous or impassable at high water. During the winter months the crossing is even more treacherous, since there is often considerable running water under a seemingly stable snow- and ice pack. This trail makes use of several cross-country ski trails maintained by the Jackson Ski Touring Foundation. During the winter months hikers should avoid walking on ski tracks and should yield to skiers, who have the right of way.

After reaching the far bank of the Ellis River, this trail bears right and skirts the north side of an open field, crossing the Ellis River Ski Trail at 0.2 mi. It then follows the Winniweta Falls Ski Trail upstream along the north bank of Miles Brook on an old logging road. At an arrow, the path turns left from the road and soon reaches the falls. The ski trail continues uphill along the logging road for over a mile and ends at the Hall Ski Trail, which connects Dana Place with Green Hill Rd.

Winniweta Falls Trail (map 1:G10)

Distance from NH 16 (950′)

  to Winniweta Falls (1350′): 0.9 mi. (1.4 km.), 400 ft., 40 min.

Iron Mountain Trail (JCC)

The summit of this mountain is wooded with somewhat restricted views, but an outlook on the north side and the fine south cliffs provide very attractive views for relatively little effort. Somewhat down the slope to the east of the cliffs are abandoned iron mines. A prominent easterly ridge, on which there was once a trail, descends over the open summit of Green Hill to the cliff called Duck's Head, named for its shape when seen from a point on NH 16 just north of the Jackson covered bridge. The trail is reached by leaving NH 16 in Jackson, next to the golf course and about 0.2 mi. north of the red covered bridge that leads to Jackson village, and following a road prominently signed Green Hill Rd. At 1.2 mi. the pavement ends, and at 1.4 mi. the road (FR 119) bears left at a fork where FR 325 bears right. The road now becomes fairly steep, a bit rough, and very narrow (be prepared to back up if required for other cars to pass); above the fork the road is not passable in mud season and winter. At 2.6 mi. from NH 16, where the road ahead soon becomes very poor, park in a designated area generously provided by the landowner on either side of the road near the house of the former Hayes Farm (now a summer residence).

The trail starts at a sign on the left 10 yd. up the road. It crosses a field, where there are fine views, traverses a smaller field, then passes through a band of trees and emerges at the base of a clearcut slope. Marked with wooden stakes and small cairns, it ascends the open slope, swinging left, then right, and enters the woods at the top edge at 0.2 mi. The path climbs up a badly eroded footway, steeply at times, entering the WMNF at 0.3 mi. At 0.6 mi. there is a side path right 20 yd. to a fine outlook up the Rocky Branch valley to Mt. Washington, with the Southern Presidentials visible over the Montalban Ridge. The main trail continues to the summit at 0.9 mi., where there are remains of the former fire tower. The trail descends steadily along a rocky ridge, dropping about 300 ft., then crosses several small humps in thick woods. At 1.5 mi. a faintly marked side path descends left 0.2 mi. and 250 ft. to the old mines (tailings, water-filled shaft, tunnel), while the main trail ascends in a short distance to ledges and the edge of the cliffs, where wide views to the south and west can be enjoyed.

Iron Mountain Trail (map 3:H10)

Distances from Hayes Farm (1920′)

to summit of Iron Mtn. (2726′): 0.9 mi., 800 ft., 50 min.

to south cliffs (2430′): 1.6 mi. (2.6 km.), 850 ft. (rev. 300 ft.), 1 hr. 15 min.

SUGGESTED HIKES

For more information on suggested hikes, see p. xxx.

Easy Hikes

Crystal Cascade [rt: 0.6 mi., 200 ft., 0:25]. A short jaunt up the Tuckerman Ravine Trail to a fine waterfall.

Elephant Head [rt: 0.6 mi., 150 ft., 0:25]. An easy climb up the Webster-Jackson Trail and a spur trail to a ledge with a view of Crawford Notch.

Liebeskind's Loop [lp: 2.6 mi., 600 ft., 1:35]. An interesting loop with views of Pinkham Notch, using the Old Jackson Road, Crew-Cut Trail, George's Gorge Trail, and Liebeskind's Loop.

Iron Mtn. [rt: 3.2 mi., 1150 ft., 2:10]. This mountain, reached by the Iron Mountain Trail, has a fine north outlook and a broad ledge with an excellent view on its south end.

Moderate Hikes

Glen Boulder [rt: 3.2 mi., 1750 ft., 2:30]. A fairly steep and rough but short route to the treeline via the Glen Boulder Trail, with good views and a huge boulder perched on the mountainside.

Lowe's Bald Spot [rt: 4.4 mi., 900 ft., 2:40]. An attractive walk from Pinkham Notch Camp via the Old Jackson Road and Madison Gulf Trail, with an outlook providing interesting views of the Presidentials.

Hermit Lake [rt: 4.8 mi., 1850 ft., 3:20]. A moderate climb up the Tuckerman Ravine Trail to views into the famed glacial cirque.

Mt. Stanton and Mt. Pickering [rt: 4.2 mi., 1600 ft., 2:55]. These two small mountains offer beautiful red pine woods with scattered ledges, each with a different interesting view. They are on the Mount Stanton Trail, which continues over several small ledgy peaks called the Crippies; the trail is not recommended beyond the last Crippie [rt: 6.6 mi., 2250 ft., 4:25].

Mt. Crawford [rt: 5.0 mi., 2100 ft., 3:40]. This beautiful rock peak, reached by the Davis Path, offers extensive views. It is also part of an excellent longer trip that includes Stairs Mtn. [rt: 9.8 mi., 3000 ft., 6:25], Mt. Resolution [rt: 9.2 mi., 2800 ft., 6:00], or both of these excellent viewpoints [rt: 11.0 mi., 3400 ft., 7:10].

Mts. Jackson and Webster. The open summit of Mt. Jackson is reached by the Jackson branch of the Webster-Jackson Trail [rt: 5.2 mi., 2200 ft., 3:35]. Mt. Webster, another fine viewpoint, is reached by the Webster branch of the Webster-Jackson Trail [rt: 5.0 mi., 2100 ft., 3:35]. A loop can be made over both summits via the Webster Cliff Trail [lp: 6.5 mi., 2500 ft., 4:30]. If a car spot is available, one can ascend Mt. Webster by the Webster-Jackson Trail and then make a leisurely descent of the magnificent Webster Cliff Trail down to the notch [lp: 5.8 mi., 2100 ft., 4:00]. The Webster Cliff Trail can also be enjoyed as an out-and-back route to Mt. Webster [rt: 6.6 mi., 2700 ft., 4:40].

Mt. Pierce and Mizpah Spring Hut [lp: 6.6 mi., 2450 ft., 4:30]. This interesting loop provides good views and a sampling of the alpine zone on Mt. Pierce, with additional views and a visit to a high country hut on the return trip. Use the Crawford Connector, Crawford Path, Webster Cliff Trail, and Mizpah Cutoff.

Mt. Eisenhower [rt: 6.6 mi., 2750 ft., 4:40]. The Edmands Path and Mount Eisenhower Loop provide a moderate, graded route to this bald summit.

Strenuous Hikes

Mt. Monroe [rt: 7.0 mi., 2900 ft., 5:00]. This craggy peak is an excellent alternative to its more notorious neighbor, Mt. Washington, offering superb views. Ascend via the Ammonoosuc Ravine Trail, Crawford Path, and Mount Monroe Loop. With a car spot, a magnificent open ridge walk can be enjoyed along the Crawford Path, with descent via the Edmands Path [lp: 8.2 mi., 2900 ft., 5:35].

Mt. Washington. Few hikers will be able to resist the urge to climb the highest mountain in the Northeast, despite the crowds on the popular trails and the hordes of tourists on the summit. The easiest way to climb it is probably the Jewell Trail–Gulfside Trail combination on the west side [rt: 10.2 mi., 3800 ft., 7:00], which begins at a parking lot on the road to the Cog Railway. Most hikers climbing from this side will be tempted to turn the hike into a loop by combining the Jewell and Gulfside Trails with the Ammonoosuc Ravine Trail, which begins at the same parking lot [lp: 9.6 mi., 3800 ft., 6:40]. The Ammonoosuc Ravine Trail [rt: 9.0 mi., 3800 ft., 6:25] is a much more interesting and beautiful route to Mt. Washington than the Jewell Trail, but the section between Gem Pool and Lakes of the Clouds Hut can be extremely discouraging to a person in poor physical condition. On the descent, this section passes mostly over ledges and rocks, some of which are wet and slippery, and it can be quite tedious and tiring for a person whose agility is limited. On the whole, it is probably better to ascend the Ammonoosuc Ravine Trail and descend the Jewell Trail, but if afternoon thunderstorms are threatening, the descent by the Jewell Trail is probably more hazardous, as it is far less sheltered; on the other hand, in rain without lightning the steep wet rocks on the Ammonoosuc Ravine Trail may be more of a problem, but if it is both cold and rainy the exposure on the Jewell Trail may be more hazardous.

From the east side the Tuckerman Ravine Trail is the easiest and most popular route to the summit [ow: 4.2 mi., 4300 ft., 4:15; rt: 8.4 mi., 4300 ft., 6:20]. There are many other routes available, but though all of them are substantially less crowded they are also either longer or more strenuous. In good weather the Boott Spur Trail offers better views, and though it is longer it is not substantially more difficult; one can ascend by this trail and then descend through Tuckerman Ravine with the crowds, or make the easier, faster ascent through Tuckerman Ravine and then make a leisurely descent via Boott Spur [lp: 9.6 mi., 4300 ft., 6:55]. The Lion Head Trail is about the same length as the Tuckerman Ravine Trail and also offers better views, but it has steeper sections and is generally rougher; for most people, it is probably a better route for the ascent than for descent [ow: 4.1 mi., 4300 ft., 4:10].

Section 2

The Northern Peaks and the Great Gulf

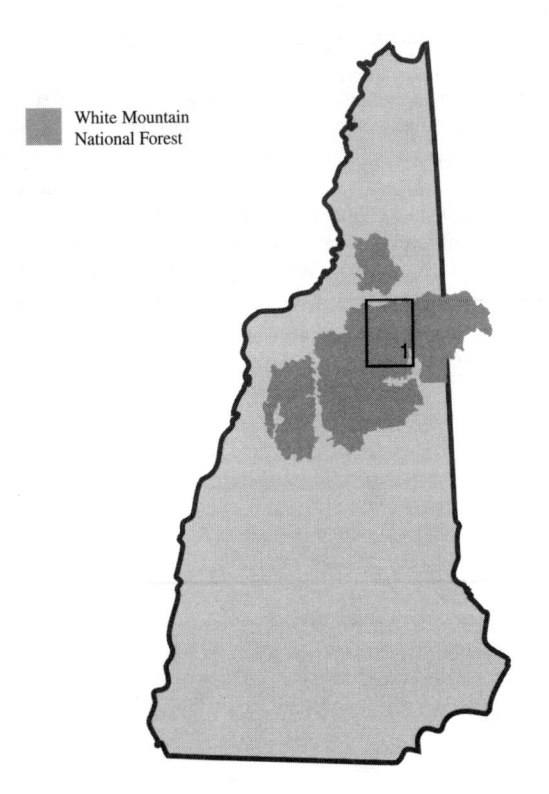

White Mountain
National Forest

Introduction 74
Trail Descriptions 81
Suggested Hikes 142

LIST OF TRAILS

Trails on the Main Ridge
Gulfside Trail 81
Mount Jefferson Loop 90
Mount Clay Loop 90
Edmands Col Cutoff 90
The Cornice 91

Linking Trails on the North and West Slopes of the Range
Randolph Path 92
The Link 94

Trails in the Great Gulf Wilderness
Great Gulf Trail 95
Great Gulf Link Trail 97
Madison Gulf Trail 98
Chandler Brook Trail 100
Wamsutta Trail 101
Sphinx Trail 101
Six Husbands Trail 102
Buttress Trail 103
Osgood Trail 104
Osgood Cutoff 106

Trails on Mount Madison
Daniel Webster–Scout Trail 106
Parapet Trail 107
Pine Link 108
Howker Ridge Trail 109
Kelton Trail 111
Inlook Trail 111
The Brookside 112
Watson Path 113
Valley Way 113
Lower Bruin 115
Upper Bruin 115

Trails on Mount Adams
Air Line 115
Scar Trail 117

Star Lake Trail 118
Short Line 118
King Ravine Trail 119
Chemin des Dames 120
Great Gully Trail 121
The Amphibrach 122
Cliffway 123
Monaway 124
Spur Trail 124
Hincks Trail 125
Gray Knob Trail 125
Perch Path 126
Lowe's Path 126
Cabin-Cascades Trail 128
Israel Ridge Path 128
Emerald Trail 130

Trails on Mount Jefferson
Castle Ravine Trail 130
Castle Trail 132
Caps Ridge Trail 133
Boundary Line Trail 135

Trail on Mt. Clay
Jewell Trail 135

Trails on Pine Mountain
Pine Mountain Trail 136
Pine Mountain Road 137
Ledge Trail 138

Pleasure Paths on the Lower North Slopes of the Range
Town Line Brook Trail 139
Sylvan Way 139
Fallsway 139
Brookbank 140
Maple Walk 140
Beechwood Way 141

This section covers the high peaks of Mt. Washington's massive northern ridge, which curves north and then northeast as a great arm embracing the magnificent glacial cirque called the Great Gulf. This ridge runs for 5 mi. with only slight dips below the 5000-ft. level, and each of the three main peaks rises at least 500 ft. above the cols. The AMC Presidential Range map (map 1) covers the entire area except for the Pine Mountain Trail, which is covered by the AMC Carter Range–Evans Notch map (map 5). The Randolph Mountain Club (RMC) publishes a map of the Randolph Valley and Northern Peaks, printed on plastic-coated paper, and a guidebook, *Randolph Paths,* which can be obtained from many outdoor shops throughout the area or from the RMC, Randolph, NH 03570. The map covers the dense trail network on the northern slope of this region at a larger scale than map 1, and it is useful for people who want to explore some of the attractive, less crowded paths in this section. The RMC maintains a considerable number of paths on the Northern Peaks; many of these paths are very lightly used and are wilder and rougher than most trails in the WMNF. Traditionally they have been less plainly marked, cleared, and trampled out than the heavily used primary trails, but in recent years they have been thoroughly cleared and marked so they are now suitable for almost any hiker. Adventurous hikers will find them a delightful alternative to the heavily used principal throughways on the range. This network of paths also provides opportunities for less strenuous, varied walks to the many waterfalls and other interesting places on the lower slopes of the range. Additional information can be obtained from the RMC website, www.RandolphMountainClub.org.

Caution: The peaks and higher ridges of this range are nearly as exposed to the elements as Mt. Washington, and should be treated with the same degree of respect and caution. Severe winterlike storms can occur at any time of the year, and many lives have been lost in this area from failure to observe the basic principles of safety (see page xii for detailed safety information). In addition, all of the major peaks are strenuous climbs by even the easiest routes. The distances quoted may not seem long to a novice, but there is only one route to a major peak, the Caps Ridge Trail to Mt. Jefferson, that involves less than 3000 ft. of climbing, and that trail is not an easy one. Although the Caps Ridge Trail is relatively short, it is also quite steep with numerous scrambles on ledges that a person unfamiliar with mountain trails might find daunting. Most other routes to the summits involve 4000 to 4500 ft. of climbing, due to the lower elevations of the major trailheads, thus making these ascents roughly equivalent in strenuousness to the ascent of Mt. Washington. The substantial amount of effort required to climb these peaks, together with the threat of sudden and violent storms, should make the need to avoid overextending oneself quite apparent.

The highest points from which to climb the Northern Peaks, not including the summit of Mt. Washington, are Jefferson Notch Rd. at the Caps Ridge Trail (3008 ft.); the parking lot on the Cog Railway Base Rd., 1.1 mi. east of the Jefferson Notch Rd., for the Jewell Trail (2500 ft.); Pinkham Notch Visitor Center (2030 ft.); and the Pinkham B Rd. (Dolly Copp Rd.) at the Pine Link (1650 ft.). Other important parking areas are at a newly constructed area serving the Great Gulf trails located 1.5 mi. south of Dolly Copp Campground on NH 16; at Randolph East, on Pinkham B (Dolly Copp) Rd. near its junction with US 2; at Appalachia, on US 2 about 1 mi. west of Pinkham B Rd.; at Lowe's Store on US 2 (nominal fee charged by owner); and at Bowman, on US 2 about 1 mi. west of Lowe's Store. Several of the trailheads in the region, such as Randolph East, Appalachia, and Bowman, owe their names and locations to their former status as stations on the railroad line, whose tracks were removed in the summer of 1997. The USFS requires a parking permit (fee) for areas located on WMNF land.

The Northern Peaks were observed by Thomas Gorges and Richard Vines from the summit of Mt. Washington in 1642, but the men evidently considered these peaks to be merely a part of Mt. Washington, for on their return the explorers wrote, with considerable geographic confusion, "The mountain runs E. and W. 30 miles, but the peak is above all the rest." In the early summer of 1820, a party consisting of Adino N. Brackett, John W. Weeks, Gen. John Wilson, Charles J. Stuart, Noyes S. Dennison, Samuel A. Pearson, Philip Carrigain, and Ethan Allen Crawford visited Mt. Washington, and from that summit named Mts. Jefferson, Adams, and Madison, but did not explore them. On August 31, 1820, Brackett, Weeks, and Stuart made a second visit to the summit of Mt. Washington in company with Richard Eastman, Amos Legro, Joseph W. Brackett, and Edward B. Moore. Two members of this party spent a part of the day on the Northern Peaks and were probably the first persons of European extraction to visit these summits. In 1828 a more thorough exploration was made by Dr. J. W. Robbins, who spent considerable time there collecting botanical and other specimens.

The first trail on the Northern Peaks was probably the Stillings Path, which was cut about 1852 primarily for transporting building materials from Randolph to the summit of Mt. Washington and did not cross any of the summits. In 1860 or 1861 a partial trail was made over the peaks to Mt. Washington, of which some sections still exist as parts of current trails. Lowe's Path was cut in 1875–76, the branch path through King Ravine was made in 1876, and the Osgood Path was opened in 1878. Many trails were constructed between 1878 and the beginning of lumbering in about 1902, but this network was greatly damaged by the timber cutting, and many trails were obliterated, at least temporarily. The more important ones were restored after the most intensive period of lumbering ceased.

In the Randolph Valley, where the Amphibrach and the Link cross Cold Brook just below scenic Cold Brook Falls, Memorial Bridge stands as a memorial to J. Rayner Edmands, Eugene B. Cook, and other pioneer path makers who helped construct the superb trail network in the Presidential Range, including Thomas Starr King, James Gordon, Charles E. Lowe, Laban M. Watson, William H. Peek, Hubbard Hunt, William G. Nowell, and William Sargent.

In this section the Appalachian Trail follows the Gulfside Trail to Madison Spring Hut from its junction with the Trinity Heights Connector near the summit of Mt. Washington. It then follows the Osgood Trail over Mt. Madison and down into the Great Gulf, proceeding to the Auto Rd. via the Osgood Cutoff, Great Gulf Trail (for a very short distance), and Madison Gulf Trail.

GEOGRAPHY

The upper part of the mass of the **Northern Peaks** is covered with rock fragments; above 5000 ft. there are no trees and little scrub. The southeast side of the range is dominated by the **Great Gulf** and the two smaller cirques that branch off from it, **Jefferson Ravine** and **Madison Gulf.** The two Jefferson "knees," fairly prominent buttresses truncated by the Great Gulf, are the only significant ridges on this side of the range that survived the massive excavations by the glaciers that hollowed out the gulf. Many ridges and valleys radiate from this range on the north and west sides, the most important being, from north to south: on Mt. Madison, the **Osgood Ridge, Howker Ridge, Bumpus Basin, Gordon Ridge,** and the ravine of **Snyder Brook,** which is shared with Mt. Adams; on **Mt. Adams, Durand Ridge, King Ravine, Nowell Ridge, Cascade Ravine,** the **Israel Ridge,** and **Castle Ravine,** which is shared with Mt. Jefferson; on **Mt. Jefferson,** the **Castellated Ridge** and the **Ridge of the Caps;** and on **Mt. Clay,** an **unnamed but conspicuous ridge extending westerly.** The Great Gulf, Bumpus Basin, King Ravine, and Castle Ravine are glacial cirques, a landform that results when a glacier excavates a typical V-shaped brook valley with a narrow floor and fairly uniform slopes, turning it into the classic U-shaped cirque with a broad, fairly flat floor and almost vertical walls.

The Great Gulf is the largest cirque in the White Mtns., lying between Mt. Washington and the Northern Peaks and drained by the West Branch of the Peabody River. The headwall, bounded on the south by the slopes of Mt.

Washington and on the west by the summit ridge of Mt. Clay, rises about 1100 to 1600 ft. above a bowl-shaped valley enclosed by steep walls that extend east for about 3.5 mi. The gulf then continues as a more open valley about 1.5 mi. farther east. The glacial action that formed the Great Gulf and its tributary gulfs is believed to have occurred mainly prior to the most recent ice age. The views from its walls and from points on its floor are among the best in New England, and steep slopes and abundant water result in a great number of cascades. The first recorded observation of the Great Gulf was by Darby Field in 1642, and the name probably had its origin in 1823 from a casual statement made by Ethan Allen Crawford, who, having lost his way in cloudy weather, came to "the edge of a great gulf." For a time it was sometimes called the "Gulf of Mexico," but this name is no longer used. The region was visited in 1829 by J. W. Robbins, a botanist, but was little known until Benjamin F. Osgood blazed the first trail, from the Osgood Trail to the headwall, in 1881.

Mt. Clay (5533 ft.) is the first peak on the ridge north of Mt. Washington. Strictly speaking it is only a shoulder, comparable to Boott Spur on the southeast ridge of its great neighbor, since it rises barely 150 ft. above the connecting ridge. But it offers superb views from the cliffs that drop away practically at the summit to form the west side of the Great Gulf headwall.

Mt. Jefferson (5716 ft.) has three summits a short distance apart, in line northwest and southeast, with the highest in the middle. Perhaps the most striking view is down the Great Gulf with the Carter Range beyond (better views of the gulf itself are obtained from points on the Gulfside Trail to the north of the summit). There are other fine views from the peak, most notably those to Mt. Washington and the other Northern Peaks, to the Fabyan Plain on the southwest, and down the broad valley of the Israel River on the northwest. The **Castellated Ridge,** sharpest and most salient of the White Mtn. ridges, extends northwest, forming the southwest wall of Castle Ravine; the view of the Castles from US 2 near the hamlet of Bowman is unforgettable. The **Ridge of the Caps,** similar in formation but less striking, extends to the west from the base of the summit cone. **Jefferson's Knees,** the two eastern ridges that are cut off abruptly by the Great Gulf, have precipitous wooded slopes and gently sloping tops. South of the peak of Mt. Jefferson is a smooth, grassy plateau called **Monticello Lawn** (about 5400 ft.). In addition to its share of the Great Gulf proper, Jefferson's slopes are cut by two other prominent glacial cirques: **Jefferson Ravine,** a branch of the Great Gulf northeast of the mountain, and **Castle Ravine,** drained by a branch of the **Israel River,** on the north. The boundary between these two cirques is the narrow section of the main Northern Presidential ridge that runs from Mt. Jefferson through **Edmands Col** to Mt. Adams.

Mt. Adams (5799 ft.), second highest of the New England summits, has a greater variety of interesting features than any other New England mountain except Katahdin: its sharp, clean-cut profile; its large area above the treeline; its inspiring views, the finest being across the Great Gulf to Mts. Washington, Jefferson, and Clay; its great northern ridges, sharp, narrow **Durand Ridge** and massive, broad-spreading **Nowell Ridge;** and its four glacial cirques, **King Ravine** and the three that it shares with its neighbors, which are the **Great Gulf, Madison Gulf,** and **Castle Ravine.** Mt. Adams also has several lesser summits and crags, of which the two most prominent are **Mt. Sam Adams** (5585 ft.), a rather flat mass to the west, and **Mt. Quincy Adams** or **J. Q. Adams** (5410 ft.), a sharp, narrow shark-fin ridge to the north.

Mt. Madison (5366 ft.) is the farthest northeast of the high peaks of the Presidential Range, remarkable for the great drop of more than 4000 ft. to the river valleys east and northeast from its summit. The drop to the Androscoggin River at Gorham (4580 ft. in about 6.5 mi.) is probably the closest approach in New England, except at Katahdin, of a major river to a high mountain. The views south and southwest to the neighboring Presidential peaks and into the Great Gulf are very fine; the distant view is excellent in all other directions, and it includes Chocorua, which is visible just to the left of Mt. Washington.

Edmands Col (4938 ft.), named for pioneer trail maker J. Rayner Edmands, lies between Mt. Adams and Mt. Jefferson, and **Sphinx Col** (4959 ft.) lies between Mt. Jefferson and Mt. Clay. The col between Mt. Adams and Mt. Madison has an elevation of about 4890 ft., so there is a range of only about 70 ft. between the lowest and highest of the three major cols on this ridge. In the **unnamed Adams-Madison col** lies **Star Lake,** a small, shallow body of water among jagged rocks, with impressive views, particularly up to Mt. Madison and Mt. Quincy Adams. Nearby is the **Parapet,** a small crag that offers magnificent views into the Great Gulf.

Pine Mtn. (2405 ft.) is a small peak lying to the northeast, between Mt. Madison and the great bend of the Androscoggin River at Gorham. Though low compared to its lofty neighbors, it is a rugged mountain with a fine cliff on the southeast side, and it offers magnificent, easily attained views of its Northern Presidential neighbors and of the mountains and river valleys to the north and east.

HUTS
Madison Hut (AMC)
In 1888 at Madison Spring (4800 ft.), a little north of the Adams-Madison col, the AMC built a stone hut that was later demolished. The present hut, rebuilt and improved after a fire in 1940, accommodates 50 guests in two bunkrooms operated on a coed basis. It is open to the public from early June to mid-September and is closed at all other times. Pets are not permitted in the hut. It is located 6.0 mi. from the summit of Mt. Washington via the Gulfside Trail, and 6.8 mi. from Lakes of the Clouds Hut via the Gulfside Trail, Westside Trail, and Crawford Path. In bad weather the best approach (or exit) is via the Valley Way, which is sheltered to within a short distance of the hut. Nearby points of interest include Star Lake and the Parapet, a crag overlooking Madison Gulf. For current information contact the Reservation Office, Pinkham Notch Visitor Center, PO Box 298, Gorham, NH 03581 (603-466-2727) or www.outdoors.org.

CAMPING
Great Gulf Wilderness
Wilderness regulations, intended to protect Wilderness resources and promote opportunities for challenge and solitude, prohibit use of motorized equipment or mechanical means of transportation of any sort. No camping is allowed within 200 ft. of any trail except at designated campsites (of which there are several between the Bluff and the Sphinx Trail), and wood or charcoal fires are not permitted at any place in the Great Gulf Wilderness. Camping is prohibited on the Great Gulf Trail south of its junction with the Sphinx Trail, including Spaulding Lake and its vicinity. Hiking and camping group size must be no larger than 10 people. Camping and fires are also prohibited above the treeline (where trees are less than 8 ft. tall), except in winter, when camping is permitted above the treeline in places where snow cover is at least 2 ft. deep, but not on any frozen body of water. All former shelters have been removed.

Forest Protection Areas
The WMNF has established a number of Forest Protection Areas (FPAs)—formerly known as Restricted Use Areas—where camping and wood or charcoal fires are prohibited throughout the year. The specific areas are under continual review, and areas are added to or subtracted from the list in order to provide the greatest amount of protection to areas subject to damage by excessive camping, while imposing the lowest level of restrictions possible. A general list of FPAs

in this section follows, but since there are often major changes from year to year, one should obtain current information on FPAs from the WMNF.

(1) No camping is permitted above treeline (where trees are less than 8 ft. tall) except in winter, and then only where there is at least 2 ft. of snow cover on the ground—but not on any frozen body of water. The point where the above-treeline restricted area begins is marked on most trails with small signs, but the absence of such signs should not be construed as proof of the legality of a site.

(2) No camping is permitted within a quarter mile of any trailhead, picnic area, or any facility for overnight accommodation such as a hut, cabin, shelter, tentsite, or campground, except as designated at the facility itself.

(3) No camping is permitted within 200 ft. of certain trails. In 2002 designated trails included the Valley Way south of its junction with the Scar Trail, from that junction up to Madison Hut.

(4) No camping is permitted on WMNF land within a quarter mile of certain roads (camping on private roadside land is illegal except by permission of the landowner). In 2002 these roads included NH 16 north of Glen Ellis Falls, Jefferson Notch Rd. from the Cog Railway Base Rd. to the Caps Ridge Trail trailhead, and the Pinkham B Rd. (also known as Dolly Copp Rd.).

Established Trailside Campsites

The Log Cabin (RMC), first built about 1890 and totally rebuilt in 1985, is located at a spring at 3300 ft. elevation, beside Lowe's Path at the junction with the Cabin-Cascades Trail. The cabin is partly enclosed and has room for about 10 guests. A fee is charged. There is no stove, and no wood fires are permitted in the area. Guests are requested to leave the cabin clean and are required to carry out all trash.

The Perch (RMC) is an open log shelter located at about 4300 ft. on the Perch Path between the Randolph Path and Israel Ridge Path, but much closer to the former. It accommodates eight, and there are also four tent platforms at the site. The caretaker at Gray Knob often visits to collect the overnight fee. Wood fires are not allowed in the area, and all trash must be carried out.

Crag Camp (RMC) is situated at the edge of King Ravine near the Spur Trail at about 4200 ft. It is an enclosed cabin with room for about 20 guests. A fee is charged at all times. During July and August it is maintained by a caretaker. Hikers are required to limit groups to 10. Wood fires are not allowed in the area, and all trash must be carried out.

Gray Knob (RMC) is an enclosed, winterized cabin on Gray Knob Trail at its junction with Hincks Trail, near Lowe's Path, at about 4400 ft. It is staffed by a caretaker year-round, and a fee is charged at all times. Gray Knob has room for about 15 guests and is supplied with cooking utensils. Hikers are required to limit groups to 10. Wood fires are not allowed in the area, and all trash must be carried out.

These RMC shelters are all in Forest Protection Areas, and no camping is allowed within a quarter mile of them, except in the shelters and on the tent platforms themselves. Fees should be mailed to the Randolph Mountain Club, Randolph, NH 03570, if not collected by the caretakers. Any infraction of rules or acts of vandalism should be reported to the above address.

Osgood Campsite (WMNF), consisting of tent platforms, is located near the junction of the Osgood Trail and Osgood Cutoff (which is on the Appalachian Trail).

Valley Way Campsite (WMNF), consisting of two tent platforms, is located on a short spur path off the Valley Way 3.1 mi. from Appalachia.

THE TRAILS
Gulfside Trail (WMNF)

This trail, the main route along the Northern Presidential ridgecrest, leads from Madison Hut to the summit of Mt. Washington. It threads its way through the principal cols, avoiding the summits of the Northern Peaks, and offers extensive, ever-changing views. Its elevations range from about 4800 ft. close to the hut to 6288 ft. on the summit of Mt. Washington. The name Gulfside was given by J. Rayner Edmands who, starting in 1892, located and constructed the greater part of the trail, sometimes following trails that had existed before. All but about 0.8 mi. of the trail was once a graded path, and parts were paved with carefully placed stones—a work cut short by Edmands's death in 1910. The whole trail is part of the Appalachian Trail, except for a very short segment at the south end. For its entire distance it forms the northwestern boundary of the Great Gulf Wilderness, though the path itself is not within the Wilderness.

The trail is well marked with large cairns, each topped with a yellow-painted stone, and, though care must be used, it can often be followed even in dense fog. Always carry a compass and study the map before starting, so you will be aware of your alternatives if a storm strikes suddenly. The trail is continuously exposed to the weather; dangerously high winds and low temperatures may occur with little warning at any season of the year. If such storms threaten serious trouble on the Gulfside Trail, do not attempt to ascend the summit cone of Mt. Washington, where conditions are usually far worse. If you are not close to either of the huts (at Madison Spring or Lakes of the Clouds), descend into one of the ravines on a trail if possible, or without trail if necessary. A night of discomfort in the woods is better than exposure to the weather on the heights, which may prove fatal. Slopes on the Great Gulf (southeast) side are more sheltered but generally steeper and farther from highways. It is particularly important not to head toward Edmands Col in deteriorating conditions; there is no easy trail out of this isolated mountain pass (which often acts like a natural wind tunnel) in bad weather, and hikers have sometimes been trapped in this desolate and isolated place by a storm. The emergency refuge shelter that was once located here was removed in 1982 after years of misuse and abuse (including illegal camping) by thoughtless visitors. In order to enjoy a safe trip through this spectacular but often dangerous area, there is no substitute for studying the map carefully and understanding the hazards and options before setting out on the ridge.

The following description of the path is in the southbound direction (toward Mt. Washington). See below for a description of the path in the reverse direction.

Part I. Madison Hut–Edmands Col

The trail begins about 30 yd. from Madison Hut at a junction with the Valley Way and Star Lake Trail and leads southwest through a patch of scrub. It then aims to the right (north) of Mt. Quincy Adams and ascends its steep, open north slope. At the top of this slope, on the high plateau between King Ravine and Mt. Quincy Adams, it is joined from the right by the Air Line, which has just been joined by the King Ravine Trail. Here there are striking views back to Mt. Madison, and into King Ravine at the Gateway a short distance down on the right. The Gulfside and Air Line coincide for less than 100 yd., then the Air Line branches left toward the summit of Mt. Adams. Much of the Gulfside Trail for about the next 0.5 mi. is paved with carefully placed stones. It rises moderately southwest, then steepens, and at 0.9 mi. from the hut reaches a grassy lawn in the saddle (5490 ft.) between Mt. Adams and Mt. Sam Adams. Here several trails intersect at a spot called Thunderstorm Junction, where there is a massive cairn that once stood about 10 ft. high. Entering the junction on the right is the Great Gully Trail, coming up across the slope from the southwest corner of King Ravine. Here, also, the Gulfside is crossed by Lowe's Path, ascending from Lowe's Store on US 2 to the summit of Mt. Adams. About 100 yd. down Lowe's Path, the Spur Trail branches right for Crag Camp. The summit of Mt. Adams is about 0.3 mi. from the junction (left) via Lowe's Path; a round trip to the summit requires about 25 min.

An unofficial trail, known as the White Trail because its cairns are topped with white rocks, will be seen running from Thunderstorm Junction to the summit of Mt. Sam Adams, and then following its south ridge to the Gulfside at the point where the Israel Ridge Path enters from US 2. Sam Adams is an interesting viewpoint, well worth a visit, but in good weather the cairned path is not necessary, since the route over the rocks between Sam Adams and either starting point is quite plain. However, the cairns are neither prominent enough nor close enough together to be followed reliably when visibility is poor, and the Sam Adams ridge is much more exposed to the wind and weather than the Gulfside.

Continuing southwest from Thunderstorm Junction and beginning to descend, the Gulfside Trail passes a junction on the left with the Israel Ridge Path, which ascends a short distance to Lowe's Path and thence to the summit of Mt. Adams. For about 0.5 mi. the Gulfside Trail and Israel Ridge Path coincide, passing Peabody Spring (unreliable) just to the right in a small, grassy flat; more-reliable water is located a short distance beyond at the base of a conspicuous boulder just to the left of the path. Soon the trail climbs easily across a small ridge, where the Israel Ridge Path diverges right at a point 1.5 mi. from Madison Hut. Near this junction in wet weather there is a small pool called Storm Lake. The Gulfside bears a bit left toward the edge of Jefferson Ravine, and, always leading toward Mt. Jefferson, descends southwest along the narrow ridge that divides Jefferson Ravine from Castle Ravine, near the edge of the southeast cliffs, from which there are fine views into the Great Gulf. This part of the Gulfside was never graded. At the end of this descent the trail reaches Edmands Col at 2.2 mi. from the hut, with 3.8 mi. to go to Mt. Washington.

At Edmands Col (4938 ft.) there is a bronze tablet in memory of J. Rayner Edmands, who made most of the graded paths on the Northern Peaks. Gulfside Spring is 50 yd. south of the col on the Edmands Col Cutoff, and Spaulding Spring (reliable) is about 0.2 mi. north near the Castle Ravine Trail. The emergency shelter once located at this col has been dismantled, and none of the trails leaving this area is an entirely satisfactory escape route in bad weather. From the col, the Edmands Col Cutoff leads south, entering scrub almost immediately, affording the quickest route to this rough form of shelter in dangerous weather; it then continues about 0.5 mi. to the Six Husbands Trail leading down into the Great Gulf, but it is very rough and the Six Husbands Trail is fairly difficult to descend, making it a far less than ideal escape route unless the severity of the weather leaves no choice. The Randolph Path leads north into the Randolph Valley, running above treeline with great exposure to northwest winds for more than 0.5 mi. It is nevertheless probably the fastest, safest route to civilization unless high winds make it too dangerous to cross through Edmands Col. Branching from this path about 0.1 mi. north of the col are the Cornice, a very rough trail leading west entirely above treeline to the Castle Trail, and the Castle Ravine Trail, which descends steeply over very loose talus and may be hard to follow.

Part II. Edmands Col–Sphinx Col

South of Edmands Col the Gulfside Trail ascends steeply over rough rocks, with Jefferson Ravine on the left. It passes flat-topped Dingmaul Rock, from which there is a good view down the ravine, with Mt. Adams on the left. This rock is named for a legendary alpine beast to which it is reputed to bear a remarkable resemblance—the more remarkable since there has never been a verified sighting of the beast. About 100 yd. beyond, the Mount Jefferson Loop branches right and leads 0.4 mi. to the summit of Mt. Jefferson (5716 ft.). The views from the summit are excellent, and the Mount Jefferson Loop is only slightly longer than the parallel section of the Gulfside, though it requires about 300 ft. of extra climbing and about 10 min. more hiking time.

The path now rises less steeply. It crosses the Six Husbands Trail and soon reaches its greatest height on Mt. Jefferson, about 5400 ft. Curving southwest and descending a little, it crosses Monticello Lawn, a comparatively smooth, grassy plateau. Here the Mount Jefferson Loop rejoins the Gulfside about 0.3 mi. from the summit. A short distance beyond the edge of the lawn, the Cornice enters right from the Caps Ridge Trail. The Gulfside descends to the south, and from one point there is a view of the Sphinx down the slope to the left. A few yards north of the low point in Sphinx Col, the Sphinx Trail branches left (east) into the Great Gulf through a grassy passage between ledges. Sphinx Col is 3.7 mi. from Madison Hut, with 2.3 mi. left to the summit of Mt. Washington. In bad weather a fairly quick descent to sheltering scrub can be made via the Sphinx Trail, though once the treeline is reached this trail becomes rather steep and difficult.

Part III. Sphinx Col–Mount Washington

From Sphinx Col the path leads toward Mt. Washington, and soon the Mount Clay Loop diverges left to climb over the summits of Mt. Clay, with impressive views into the Great Gulf. The Mount Clay Loop adds about 300 ft. of climbing and 10 min.; the distance is about the same. The Gulfside Trail is slightly easier and passes close to a spring, but misses the best views. It bears right from the junction with the Mount Clay Loop, runs south, and climbs moderately, angling up the west side of Mt. Clay. About 0.3 mi. above Sphinx Col, a loop leads to water a few steps down to the right. The side path continues about 30 yd. farther to Greenough Spring (more reliable), then rejoins the Gulfside about 100 yd. above its exit point. The Gulfside continues its moderate ascent, and the Jewell

Trail from the Cog Railway Base Rd. enters from the right at 4.6 mi. From this junction the ridgecrest of Mt. Clay can be reached in good weather by a short scramble up the rocks without trail. The Gulfside swings southeast and soon descends slightly to a point near the Clay-Washington col (5391 ft.), where the Mount Clay Loop rejoins it from the left. A little to the east is the edge of the Great Gulf, with fine views, especially of the east cliffs of Mt. Clay.

The path continues southeast, rising gradually on Mt. Washington. About 0.1 mi. above the col, the Westside Trail branches right, crosses under the Cog Railway, and leads to the Crawford Path and Lakes of the Clouds Hut. The Gulfside continues southeast between the Cog Railway on the right and the edge of the gulf on the left. If the path is lost, the railway can be followed to the summit. At the extreme south corner of the gulf, the Great Gulf Trail joins the Gulfside from the left, 5.5 mi. from Madison Hut. Here the Gulfside turns sharp right, crosses the railroad, and continues south to the plateau just west of the summit. Here it passes a junction with the Trinity Heights Connector, a link in the Appalachian Trail, which branches left and climbs for 0.2 mi. to the true summit of Mt. Washington. In another 0.1 mi. the Gulfside joins the Crawford Path just below (north of) the old corral, and the two trails turn left and coincide to the summit.

Gulfside Trail (map 1:F9)

Distances from Madison Hut (4825′)

    to Air Line (5125′): 0.3 mi., 300 ft., 20 min.

    to Thunderstorm Junction (5490′): 0.9 mi., 650 ft., 45 min.

    to Israel Ridge Path, north junction (5475′): 1.0 mi., 650 ft., 50 min.

    to Israel Ridge Path, south junction (5225′): 1.5 mi., 650 ft., 1 hr. 5 min.

    to Edmands Col (4938′): 2.2 mi., 650 ft., 1 hr. 25 min.

    to Mount Jefferson Loop, north end (5125′): 2.4 mi., 850 ft., 1 hr. 40 min.

    to Six Husbands Trail (5325′): 2.7 mi., 1050 ft., 1 hr. 55 min.

    to Mount Jefferson Loop, south end (5375′): 3.1 mi., 1100 ft., 2 hr. 5 min.

    to the Cornice (5325′): 3.2 mi., 1100 ft., 2 hr. 10 min.

    to Sphinx Trail (4975′): 3.7 mi., 1100 ft., 2 hr. 25 min.

    to Mount Clay Loop, north end (5025′): 3.8 mi., 1150 ft., 2 hr. 30 min.

    to Jewell Trail (5400′): 4.6 mi., 1550 ft., 3 hr. 5 min.

    to Mount Clay Loop, south end (5400′): 4.9 mi., 1600 ft., 3 hr. 15 min.

    to Westside Trail (5500′): 5.0 mi., 1700 ft., 3 hr. 20 min.

to Great Gulf Trail (5925′): 5.5 mi., 2150 ft., 3 hr. 50 min.

to Trinity Heights Connector (6100′): 5.7 mi., 2300 ft., 4 hr.

to Crawford Path (6150′): 5.8 mi. (9.3 km.), 2350 ft., 4 hr. 5 min.

to Mt. Washington summit (6288′) via Crawford Path: 6.0 mi. (9.7 km.), 2500 ft., 4 hr. 15 min.

to Lakes of the Clouds Hut (5012′) via Westside Trail and Crawford Path: 6.8 mi. (10.9 km.), 1850 ft., 4 hr. 20 min.

Gulfside Trail (WMNF) [in reverse]
Part I. Mount Washington–Sphinx Col

Descending from the summit of Mt. Washington, coinciding with the Crawford Path, the trail is on the right (west) side of the railroad track. After passing between the buildings it leads generally northwest; avoid random side paths toward the south. Shortly it reaches its point of departure from the Crawford Path, just below the remains of an old corral, and turns sharp right. In 0.1 mi. it passes a junction with the Trinity Heights Connector, a link in the Appalachian Trail, which branches right and climbs for 0.2 mi. to the true summit of Mt. Washington. The Gulfside Trail then descends steadily, crossing the railroad, and at 0.4 mi., as the Gulfside turns sharp left at the extreme south corner of the Great Gulf, the Great Gulf Trail joins on the right. The Gulfside continues northwest between the Cog Railway on the left and the edge of the gulf on the right. At 1.0 mi. the Westside Trail branches left, crosses under the Cog Railway, and leads to the Crawford Path and Lakes of the Clouds Hut. The Gulfside descends gradually to a point near the Clay-Washington col (5391 ft.), where the Mount Clay Loop diverges right to traverse the summits of Mt. Clay, with impressive views into the Great Gulf. The Mount Clay Loop adds about 300 ft. of climbing and 10 min.; the distance is about the same. The Gulfside Trail is slightly easier and passes close to a spring, but misses the best views. A little to the east at this col is the edge of the Great Gulf, with fine views, especially of the east cliffs of Mt. Clay.

After a slight ascent, the Gulfside begins to angle down the west side of Mt. Clay, and the Jewell Trail from the Cog Railway Base Rd. enters from the left at 1.4 mi. From this junction the ridgecrest of Mt. Clay can be reached by a short scramble up the rocks without trail. At about 0.5 mi. beyond this junction, a loop leads left to Greenough Spring (reliable), then rejoins the Gulfside about 100 yd. below its exit point. As the grade levels approaching Sphinx Col, the Mount Clay Loop rejoins on the right. At Sphinx Col, it is 2.3 mi. from Mt. Washington and

3.7 mi. to Madison Hut. In bad weather a fairly quick descent to sheltering scrub can be made via the Sphinx Trail, though once the treeline is reached this trail becomes rather steep and difficult.

Part II. Sphinx Col–Edmands Col

A few yards north of the low point in Sphinx Col, the Sphinx Trail branches right (east) into the Great Gulf through a grassy passage between ledges. The Gulfside ascends to the north, and from one point there is a view of the Sphinx down the slope to the right. The Cornice enters left from the Caps Ridge Trail a short distance before the Gulfside begins to cross Monticello Lawn, a comparatively smooth, grassy plateau. Here the Mount Jefferson Loop branches left and leads 0.3 mi. to the summit of Mt. Jefferson (5716 ft.). The views from the summit are excellent, and the Mount Jefferson Loop is only slightly longer than the parallel section of the Gulfside, though it requires about 300 ft. of extra climbing and about 10 min. more hiking time.

The path now turns northeast and rises less steeply. It crosses the Six Husbands Trail soon after reaching its greatest height on Mt. Jefferson, about 5400 ft., then descends moderately to the point where the Mount Jefferson Loop rejoins on the left about 0.3 mi. from the summit. The trail now descends steeply north over rough rocks, with Jefferson Ravine on the right, and about 100 yd. beyond the junction, it passes flat-topped Dingmaul Rock, from which there is a good view down the ravine, with Mt. Adams on the left. The trail reaches Edmands Col at 3.8 mi. from Mt. Washington, with 2.2 mi. to go to Madison Hut.

At Edmands Col (4938 ft.) there is a bronze tablet in memory of J. Rayner Edmands, who made most of the graded paths on the Northern Peaks. Gulfside Spring (unreliable in dry seasons) is 50 yd. south of the col, and Spaulding Spring (reliable) is about 0.2 mi. north near the Castle Ravine Trail. The emergency shelter once located at this col has been dismantled, and none of the trails leaving this area is a particularly satisfactory escape route in bad weather. From the col, the Edmands Col Cutoff leads south, entering scrub almost immediately, affording the quickest route to this rough form of shelter in dangerous weather; it then continues about 0.5 mi. to the Six Husbands Trail leading down to the Great Gulf, but it is very rough and the Six Husbands Trail is fairly difficult to descend, making it a far less than ideal escape route unless the severity of the weather leaves no choice. The Randolph Path leads north into the Randolph Valley, running above treeline with great exposure to northwest winds for more than 0.5 mi. It is nevertheless probably the fastest, safest route to civilization unless high winds make it too dangerous to cross through Edmands Col. Branching from this path about 0.1 mi. north of the col are the Cornice, a very rough trail leading west entirely above the treeline to the Castle Trail, and the Castle Ravine Trail, which descends steeply over very loose talus and may be hard to follow.

Part III. Edmands Col–Madison Spring Hut

Leaving Edmands Col, the Gulfside climbs moderately along the edge of Jefferson Ravine, ascending northeast along the narrow ridge that divides Jefferson Ravine from Castle Ravine near the edge of the southeast cliffs, from which there are fine views into the Great Gulf. This part of the Gulfside was never graded. About 0.7 mi. above Edmands Col the trail reaches the crest of a small ridge, where the Israel Ridge Path enters left. Near this junction in wet weather there is a small pool called Storm Lake. For about 0.5 mi. the Gulfside Trail and Israel Ridge Path coincide, passing reliable water at the base of a conspicuous boulder just to the right of the path; Peabody Spring (unreliable) is just beyond on the left in a small, grassy flat. The Gulfside Trail continues to ascend and, as it levels out on a grassy lawn in the saddle (5490 ft.) between Mt. Adams and Mt. Sam Adams, the Israel Ridge Path diverges right and ascends a short distance to Lowe's Path and thence to the summit of Mt. Adams.

In another 0.1 mi. several trails intersect at a spot called Thunderstorm Junction, where there is a massive cairn that once stood about 10 ft. high. Entering the junction on the left is the Great Gully Trail, coming up across the slope from the southwest corner of King Ravine. Here, also, the Gulfside is crossed by Lowe's Path, ascending from Lowe's Store on US 2 to the summit of Mt. Adams. About 100 yd. down Lowe's Path, the Spur Trail branches right for Crag Camp. The summit of Mt. Adams is about 0.3 mi. from the junction (right) via Lowe's Path; a round trip to the summit requires about 25 min.

An unofficial trail, known as the White Trail because its cairns are topped with white rocks, runs from Thunderstorm Junction to the summit of Mt. Sam Adams, and then follows its south ridge to the Gulfside at the point where the Israel Ridge Path enters from US 2. Sam Adams is an interesting viewpoint, well worth a visit, but in good weather the cairned path is not necessary, since the route over the rocks between Sam Adams and either starting point is quite plain. However, the cairns are neither prominent enough nor close enough together to be followed reliably when visibility is poor, and the Sam Adams ridge is much more exposed to the wind and weather than the Gulfside.

From Thunderstorm Junction the Gulfside descends northeast, gradually at first, and enters a section about 0.5 mi. long that is paved with carefully placed stones. At the end of this section, on the high plateau between King Ravine and

Mt. Quincy Adams, the Air Line enters on the right, descending from Mt. Adams, and the trails coincide for less than 100 yd. Then the Air Line branches left at the top of the steep, open north slope of Mt. Quincy Adams, and just below this junction the King Ravine Trail branches left from the Air Line. Here there are striking views ahead to Mt. Madison, and into King Ravine at the Gateway a short distance down on the left. The Gulfside then descends the slope and passes through a patch of scrub to a junction with the Valley Way and Star Lake Trail about 30 yd. from Madison Hut.

Gulfside Trail (map 1:F9)

Distances from the summit of Mt. Washington (6288′)

to Crawford Path junction (6150′): 0.2 mi., 0 ft., 5 min.

to Trinity Heights Connector (6100′): 0.3 mi., 0 ft., 10 min.

to Great Gulf Trail (5925′): 0.5 mi., 0 ft., 15 min.

to Westside Trail (5500′): 1.0 mi., 0 ft., 30 min.

to Mount Clay Loop, south end (5400′): 1.1 mi., 0 ft., 35 min.

to Jewell Trail (5400′): 1.4 mi., 50 ft., 45 min.

to Mount Clay Loop, north end (5025′): 2.2 mi., 50 ft., 1 hr. 5 min.

to Sphinx Trail (4975′): 2.3 mi., 50 ft., 1 hr. 10 min.

to the Cornice (5325′): 2.8 mi., 400 ft., 1 hr. 35 min.

to Mount Jefferson Loop, south end (5375′): 2.9 mi., 450 ft., 1 hr. 40 min.

to Six Husbands Trail (5325′): 3.3 mi., 450 ft., 1 hr. 55 min.

to Mount Jefferson Loop, north end (5125′): 3.6 mi., 450 ft., 2 hr.

to Edmands Col (4938′): 3.8 mi., 450 ft., 2 hr. 10 min.

to Israel Ridge Path, south junction (5225′): 4.5 mi., 750 ft., 2 hr. 40 min.

to Israel Ridge Path, north junction (5475′): 5.0 mi., 1000 ft., 3 hr.

to Thunderstorm Junction (5490′): 5.1 mi., 1000 ft., 3 hr. 5 min.

to Air Line (5125′): 5.6 mi., 1000 ft., 3 hr. 20 min.

to Madison Hut (4825′): 6.0 mi. (9.7 km.), 1000 ft., 3 hr. 30 min.

Distance from Lakes of the Clouds Hut (5012′)

to Madison Hut (4825′) via Westside Trail, Crawford Path, and Gulfside Trail: 6.8 mi. (10.9 km.), 1650 ft., 4 hr. 15 min.

Mount Jefferson Loop (AMC)

This trail provides access to the summit of Mt. Jefferson from the Gulfside Trail. It diverges right (west) from the Gulfside, 0.2 mi. south of Edmands Col, and climbs steeply almost straight up the slope. Just below the summit, the Six Husbands Trail enters on the left, then the Castle Trail enters on the right, and soon the junction with Caps Ridge Trail is reached at the base of the summit crag. The true summit is 40 yd. right (west) on the Caps Ridge Trail. The Mount Jefferson Loop then descends to rejoin the Gulfside Trail on Monticello Lawn.

Mount Jefferson Loop (map 1:F9)

Distances from north junction with Gulfside Trail (5125′)

to Mt. Jefferson summit (5716′): 0.4 mi., 600 ft., 30 min.

to south junction with Gulfside Trail (5375′): 0.7 mi. (1.1 km.), 600 ft. (rev. 350 ft.), 40 min.

Mount Clay Loop (AMC)

This trail traverses the summit ridge of Mt. Clay roughly parallel to the Gulfside Trail, providing access to the superb views into the Great Gulf from Clay's east cliffs. The entire trail (except for its end points) is within the Great Gulf Wilderness.

The trail diverges left (east) from the Gulfside Trail about 0.1 mi. south of Sphinx Col, and ascends a somewhat steep, rough slope to the ragged ridgecrest. After crossing the summit and passing over several slightly lower knobs, the trail descends easily to the flat col between Mt. Clay and Mt. Washington, where it rejoins the Gulfside Trail.

Mount Clay Loop (map 1:F9)

Distances from north junction with Gulfside Trail (5025′)

to summit of Mt. Clay (5533′): 0.5 mi., 500 ft., 30 min.

to south junction with Gulfside Trail (5400′): 1.2 mi. (1.9 km.), 650 ft. (rev. 300 ft.), 55 min.

Edmands Col Cutoff (RMC)

This important link, connecting the Gulfside Trail and Randolph Path at Edmands Col with the Six Husbands Trail, makes possible a quick escape from Edmands Col into plentiful sheltering scrub on the lee side of Mt. Jefferson; it also provides a route to civilization through the Great Gulf via the Six Husbands Trail, and although this route is long, with a steep, rough, and rather difficult descent, it may be the safest escape route from the vicinity of Edmands Col in severe weather. Footing on this trail is very rough and rocky. It is almost entirely within the Great Gulf Wilderness.

Leaving Edmands Col, the trail passes Gulfside Spring in 50 yd., then begins a rough scramble over rockslides and through scrub, marked by cairns. The trail is generally almost level but has many small rises and falls over minor ridges and gullies, with good views to the Great Gulf and out to the east. It ends at the Six Husbands Trail 0.3 mi. below that trail's junction with the Gulfside Trail.

Edmands Col Cutoff (map 1:F9)

Distance from Edmands Col (4938′)

   to Six Husbands Trail (4925′): 0.5 mi. (0.8 km.), 100 ft., 20 min.

The Cornice (RMC)

This trail circles the west slope of Mt. Jefferson, running completely above the treeline, with many interesting views. It starts near Edmands Col, crosses the Castle Trail and the Caps Ridge Trail, and returns to the Gulfside at Monticello Lawn, linking the trails on the west and northwest slopes of Jefferson. Its southern segment, which has good footing, provides an excellent shortcut from the Caps Ridge Trail to the Gulfside on Monticello Lawn south of Mt. Jefferson. However, the section leading from Edmands Col to the Caps Ridge Trail is extremely rough, with a large amount of tedious and strenuous rock-hopping, which is very hard on knees and ankles. This section of the trail, therefore, may take considerably more time than the estimates below. As a route between Edmands Col and the Caps Ridge Trail, the Cornice saves a little climbing compared to the route over the summit of Jefferson, but it is much longer, requires more exertion, and is just as exposed to the weather. This makes its value as a route to avoid Jefferson's summit in bad weather very questionable.

The Cornice diverges west from the Randolph Path near Spaulding Spring, 0.1 north of the Gulfside Trail in Edmands Col, where the Castle Ravine Trail also diverges from the Randolph Path. It crosses a small grassy depression where there may be no perceptible footway until it climbs the rocky bank on the other side. It then ascends moderately over large rocks, passing above a rock formation that resembles a petrified cousin of the Loch Ness monster, and circles around the north and west sides of Mt. Jefferson, crossing the Castle Trail above the Upper Castle. It continues across the rocky slope, intersects the Caps Ridge Trail above the Upper Cap, and turns left (east) up the Caps Ridge Trail for about 20 yd., then diverges right (south) and climbs gradually with improved footing to the Gulfside Trail just below Monticello Lawn.

The Cornice (map 1:F9)

Distances from Randolph Path (4900′)

    to Castle Trail (5100′): 0.6 mi., 200 ft., 25 min.

    to Caps Ridge Trail (5025′): 1.3 mi., 200 ft. (rev. 100 ft.), 45 min.

    to Gulfside Trail junction (5325′): 1.8 mi. (2.9 km.), 500 ft., 1 hr. 10 min.

Randolph Path (RMC)

This graded path extends southwest from the Pinkham B (Dolly Copp) Rd. near Randolph village, ascending diagonally up the slopes of Mt. Madison and Mt. Adams to the Gulfside Trail in Edmands Col between Mt. Adams and Mt. Jefferson. In addition to providing a route from Randolph to Edmands Col it crosses numerous other trails along the way and thus constitutes an important linking trail between them. Some sections are heavily used and well beaten, while others bear very little traffic and, though well cleared and marked, have a less obvious footway. The Randolph Path was made by J. Rayner Edmands from 1893 to 1899. Parts of it were reconstructed in 1978 as a memorial to Christopher Goetze, an active RMC member and former editor of *Appalachia,* the AMC's journal.

The path begins at the parking space known as Randolph East, located on the Pinkham B Rd. 0.2 mi. south of US 2 and 0.3 mi. west of the crossing of the former Boston & Maine Railroad grade (tracks removed in the summer of 1997). Coinciding with the Howker Ridge Trail, it quickly crosses the former railroad grade, and 30 yd. beyond turns right (west) where the Howker Ridge Trail diverges left (southeast). The Randolph Path runs along the south edge of the power-line clearing for about 0.3 mi., then swings southwest. (Logging activity in this area has disrupted this trail somewhat in recent years, and trail markings must be observed and followed with great care.) Soon the trail enters a logging road, turns right and follows it for about 150 yd., then leaves it on the right, though continuing to parallel it for a while longer. It crosses the Sylvan Way at 0.7 mi., and at 1.4 mi. it reaches Snyder Brook, where the Inlook Trail and Brookside join on the left. The Brookside and the Randolph Path cross the brook together on the Carolyn Cutter Stevens Memorial Bridge, then the Brookside diverges right and leads down to the Valley Way. After a short climb the Randolph Path crosses the Valley Way, and soon after that joins the Air Line, coincides with it for 20 yd., then leaves it on the right.

At 1.9 mi. the Short Line enters right; by this shortcut route it is 1.3 mi. to US 2 at Appalachia. The Short Line coincides with the Randolph Path for 0.4 mi., then branches left for King Ravine. The Randolph Path descends slightly and crosses Cold Brook on Sanders Bridge, and the Cliffway diverges right just beyond. At 3.1 mi. the King Ravine Trail is crossed at its junction with the Amphibrach, an intersection called the Pentadoi. The Randolph Path continues across Spur Brook on ledges just below some interesting pools and cascades, and just beyond the brook the Spur Trail diverges left. The Randolph Path climbs around the nose of a minor ridge and becomes steeper. Soon the Log Cabin Cutoff diverges right and runs 0.2 mi. to the Log Cabin.

At 3.9 mi. from Randolph East, Lowe's Path is crossed and the grade moderates as the trail angles up the steep west side of Nowell Ridge. At 4.7 mi. good outlooks begin to appear, providing particularly notable views of the Castles nearby and Mt. Lafayette in the distance to the southwest. At 4.9 mi. the Perch Path crosses, leading left (north) to the Gray Knob Trail and right (south) to the Perch and Israel Ridge Path; a small brook runs across the Perch Path about 60 yd. south of the Randolph Path. Above this junction the Randolph Path rises due south through high scrub. At 5.4 mi. the Gray Knob Trail from Crag Camp and Gray Knob enters left at about the point where the Randolph Path rises out of the high scrub. In another 70 yd. the Israel Ridge Path enters right (west), ascending from US 2, and the trails coincide for about 150 yd.; then the Israel Ridge Path branches left for Mt. Adams in an area where views to Jefferson and the Castles are particularly fine. From this point the Randolph Path is nearly level to its end at Edmands Col, curving around the head of Castle Ravine, offering continuous excellent views. It is above treeline, much exposed to the weather, and its footway is visible for a long distance ahead. Near Edmands Col is Spaulding Spring (reliable water), in a small grassy depression on the right. The Castle Ravine Trail from US 2 comes up through the length of this little valley, and the Cornice leading to the Caps and Castles crosses it. In 0.1 mi. more the Randolph Path joins the Gulfside Trail in Edmands Col.

Randolph Path (map 1:E9–F9)

Distances from Randolph East parking area (1225')

to Valley Way (1953'): 1.5 mi., 750 ft., 1 hr. 5 min.

to Air Line (2000'): 1.6 mi., 800 ft., 1 hr. 10 min.

to Short Line, north junction (2275'): 1.9 mi., 1050 ft., 1 hr. 30 min.

to King Ravine Trail and Amphibrach (2925'): 3.1 mi., 1700 ft., 2 hr. 25 min.

to Lowe's Path (3600'): 3.9 mi., 2400 ft., 3 hr. 10 min.

to Perch Path (4325'): 4.9 mi., 3100 ft., 4 hr.

to Israel Ridge Path, north junction (4825'): 5.4 mi., 3600 ft., 4 hr. 30 min.

to Edmands Col and Gulfside Trail (4938'): 6.1 mi. (9.8 km.), 3700 ft., 4 hr. 55 min.

to Mt. Washington summit (6288') via Gulfside Trail and Crawford Path: 9.9 mi. (15.9 km.), 5550 ft. (rev. 450 ft.), 7 hr. 45 min.

The Link (RMC)

This path links the Appalachia parking area and the trails to Mt. Madison with the trails ascending Mt. Adams and Mt. Jefferson, connecting with the Amphibrach, Cliffway, Lowe's Path, and Israel Ridge Path, and the Castle Ravine, Emerald, Castle, and Caps Ridge Trails. It is graded as far as Cascade Brook. The section between the Caps Ridge and Castle Trails, although very rough, makes possible a circuit of the Caps and the Castles from Jefferson Notch Rd. Though some sections are heavily used, much of the trail is very lightly used and, though well cleared and marked, may have little evident footway.

The Link, coinciding with the Amphibrach, diverges right from the Air Line 100 yd. south of Appalachia, just after entering the woods beyond the power-line clearing, and runs west, fairly close to the edge of this clearing. At 0.6 mi. it enters a logging road and bears left; then Beechwood Way diverges left, and, just east of Cold Brook, Sylvan Way enters left. Cold Brook is crossed at 0.7 mi. on the Memorial Bridge, where there is a fine view upstream to Cold Brook Fall, which can be reached in less than 100 yd. by Sylvan Way or by a spur from the Amphibrach. Memorial Bridge is a memorial to J. Rayner Edmands, Eugene B. Cook, and other pioneer path makers: Thomas Starr King, James Gordon, Charles E. Lowe, Laban M. Watson, William H. Peek, Hubbard Hunt, William G. Nowell, and William Sargent.

Just west of the brook the Amphibrach diverges left and the Link continues straight ahead. The Link then follows old logging roads southwest with gradually increasing grades and occasional wet footing. At 2.0 mi. the Cliffway leads left (east) to White Cliff, a fine viewpoint on Nowell Ridge, and the Link swings to the south and climbs at easy grades, crossing Lowe's Path at 2.7 mi. It crosses the north branch of the Mystic Stream at 3.1 mi. and the main Mystic Stream, in a region of small cascades, at 3.3 mi. It soon curves left, rounds the western buttress of Nowell Ridge, and, running southeast nearly level, enters Cascade Ravine on the mountainside high above the stream. At 4.0 mi. it joins the Israel Ridge Path coming up on the right from US 2; the two trails coincide for 50 yd., then the Israel Ridge Path diverges sharp left for Mt. Adams, passing the Cabin-Cascades Trail in about 60 yd. The Link continues straight from this junction, descending sharply to Cascade Brook, which it crosses on a large flat ledge at the top of the largest cascade, where there are fine views down the valley. This crossing may be difficult at high water. The trail makes a steep and very rough climb up the bank of the brook, then swings right, and the grade eases and the footing gradually improves as it rounds the tip of Israel Ridge and runs generally south into Castle Ravine.

At 5.1 mi. the Link joins the Castle Ravine Trail, with which it coincides while the two trails pass the Emerald Trail and cross Castle Brook, then at 5.4 mi. the Link diverges sharp right and ascends steeply west, angling up the southwest wall of Castle Ravine. At 6.0 mi. it crosses the Castle Trail below the first Castle at about 4050 ft., then runs south, generally descending gradually, over a very rough pathway with countless treacherous roots, rocks, and hollows that are very tricky and tedious to negotiate. At 6.5 mi. the trail crosses a gravelly slide with good views, and at 7.0 mi. it crosses a fair-sized brook flowing over mossy ledges. At 7.6 mi. it turns sharp left uphill and in 50 yd. reaches the Caps Ridge Trail 1.1 mi. above the Jefferson Notch Rd., about 100 yd. above the famous ledge with the potholes and the fine view up to Jefferson.

The Link (map 1:E9–F8)

Distances from Appalachia parking area (1306')

to Memorial Bridge (1425'): 0.7 mi., 100 ft., 25 min.

to Cliffway (2170'): 2.0 mi., 850 ft., 1 hr. 25 min.

to Lowe's Path (2475'): 2.7 mi., 1150 ft., 1 hr. 55 min.

to Israel Ridge Path (2800'): 4.0 mi., 1500 ft., 2 hr. 45 min.

to Castle Ravine Trail, lower junction (3125'): 5.1 mi., 1800 ft., 3 hr. 25 min.

to Castle Trail (4025'): 6.0 mi., 2700 ft., 4 hr. 20 min.

to Caps Ridge Trail (3800'): 7.6 mi. (12.2 km.), 2850 ft. (rev. 400 ft.), 5 hr. 15 min.

Great Gulf Trail (WMNF)

This trail begins at the parking area on NH 16, about 1.5 mi. south of its junction with Pinkham B (Dolly Copp) Rd. near Dolly Copp Campground. It follows the West Branch of the Peabody River through the Great Gulf, climbs up the headwall, and ends at a junction with the Gulfside Trail 0.5 mi. below the summit of Mt. Washington. Ascent on the headwall is steep and rough. Except for first 1.6 mi. this trail is in the Great Gulf Wilderness; camping is prohibited above the junction with the Sphinx Trail, and below that point it is limited to designated trailside sites or sites at least 200 ft. away from the trail.

Leaving the parking lot, the trail leads north on an old road then turns left and descends slightly to cross the Peabody River on a suspension bridge. It then ascends to a junction at 0.3 mi. with the former route from Dolly Copp Campground, now called the Great Gulf Link Trail. The Great Gulf Trail turns sharp left here and follows a logging road along the northwest bank of the West Branch of the Peabody River, at first close to the stream and later some distance away from it. An alternate route of the trail for skiing diverges right at 0.6 mi. and rejoins at 1.0 mi., where the main trail turns sharp left. At 1.6 mi. the Hayes Copp Ski Trail diverges right, the Great Gulf Trail soon crosses into the Great Gulf Wilderness, and the Osgood Trail diverges right at 1.8 mi.; Osgood Campsite is 0.9 mi. from here via the Osgood Trail. The Great Gulf Trail returns to the West Branch and follows it fairly closely for 0.7 mi., then climbs to the high gravelly bank called the Bluff, where there is a good view of the gulf and the mountains around it. The trail follows the edge of the Bluff, then at 2.7 mi. the Osgood Cutoff (which is part of the Appalachian Trail) continues straight ahead while the Great Gulf Trail descends sharp left; for a short distance this trail is also part of the Appalachian Trail. In 50 yd. it crosses Parapet Brook (no bridge), then climbs to the crest of the little ridge that separates Parapet Brook from the West Branch, where the Madison Gulf Trail enters right, coming down from the vicinity of Madison Hut through Madison Gulf. The two trails coincide for a short distance, descending to cross the West Branch on a suspension bridge and ascending the steep bank on the south side. Here, the Madison Gulf Trail branches left, taking the Appalachian Trail designation with it, while the Great Gulf Trail turns right, leading up the south bank of the river past Clam Rock, a huge boulder on the left, at 3.1 mi.

At 3.9 mi. the Great Gulf Trail crosses Chandler Brook, and on the far bank the Chandler Brook Trail diverges left and ascends to the Mt. Washington Auto Rd. The Great Gulf Trail continues close to the river, passing in sight of the mouth of the stream that issues from Jefferson Ravine on the north, to join the Six Husbands Trail (right) and Wamsutta Trail (left) at 4.5 mi. At 5.2 mi. the trail climbs up ledges beside a cascade and continues past numerous other attractive cascades in the next 0.2 mi. After crossing over to the northwest bank of the West Branch (may be difficult), it soon crosses the brook that descends from Sphinx Col and at 5.6 mi. reaches the junction where the Sphinx Trail, leading to the Gulfside Trail, diverges right. Camping is prohibited above this junction. The Great Gulf Trail soon crosses again to the southeast bank of the West Branch, passing waterfalls, including Weetamoo Falls, the finest in the gulf. There are remarkable views up the gulf to Mt. Adams and Mt. Madison. The trail crosses an eastern tributary and, after a slight ascent, reaches Spaulding Lake (4228 ft.) at 6.5 mi. from NH 16 and about 1.4 mi. by trail from the summit of Mt. Washington.

The Great Gulf Trail continues on the east side of the lake, and a little beyond begins to ascend the steep headwall. The trail runs south and then southeast, rising 1600 ft. in about 0.8 mi. over fragments of stone, many of which are loose. The way may be poorly marked, because snow slides may sweep away cairns, but paint blazes are usually visible on the rocks. The trail generally curves a little to the left until within a few yards of the top of the headwall; then, bearing slightly right, it emerges from the gulf and ends at the Gulfside Trail near the Cog Railway. It is 0.4 mi. from here to the summit of Mt. Washington by the Gulfside Trail.

Great Gulf Trail (map 1:F10–F9)

Distances from parking area on NH 16 (1350')

to Osgood Trail (1850'): 1.8 mi., 500 ft., 1 hr. 10 min.

to Osgood Cutoff (2300'): 2.7 mi., 950 ft., 1 hr. 50 min.

to Madison Gulf Trail, south junction (2300'): 2.8 mi., 1000 ft., 1 hr. 55 min.

to Six Husbands and Wamsutta Trails (3100'): 4.5 mi., 1800 ft., 3 hr. 10 min.

to Sphinx Trail (3625'): 5.6 mi., 2350 ft., 4 hr.

to Spaulding Lake (4228'): 6.5 mi., 2950 ft., 4 hr. 45 min.

to Gulfside Trail junction (5925'): 7.5 mi. (12.1 km.), 4650 ft., 6 hr. 5 min.

to Mt. Washington summit (6288') via Gulfside Trail and Crawford Path:
   7.9 mi. (12.7 km.), 5000 ft., 6 hr. 25 min.

Great Gulf Link Trail (WMNF)

This trail was formerly a segment of the Great Gulf Trail. It leaves Dolly Copp Campground at the south end of the main camp road, which is a dead end. The trail enters the woods, and in 0.1 mi. turns sharp left onto an old logging road that has cross-country ski markers in both directions. It follows the logging road south along the west bank of the Peabody River, passing some interesting pools, and at 0.7 mi. it passes a junction with a branch of the Hayes Copp Ski Trail on the right. It ends at a junction with the Great Gulf Trail, which comes in on the left from the parking lot on NH 16 and continues straight ahead into the gulf.

Great Gulf Link Trail (map 1:F10)

Distance from Dolly Copp Campground (1250′)

to Great Gulf Trail (1375′): 1.0 mi. (1.6 km.), 150 ft., 35 min.

Madison Gulf Trail (AMC)

This trail begins on the Mt. Washington Auto Rd. a little more than 2 mi. from the Glen House site, opposite the Old Jackson Road. It first crosses a low ridge then descends gently to the West Branch, where it meets the Great Gulf Trail, then ascends along Parapet Brook to the Parapet, where it ends at a point 0.3 mi. from Madison Hut. From the Auto Rd. to its departure from the Great Gulf Trail, the Madison Gulf Trail is part of the Appalachian Trail and therefore blazed in white; the rest is blazed in blue. It is almost entirely within the Great Gulf Wilderness.

Caution: The section of this trail on the headwall of Madison Gulf is one of the most difficult in the White Mtns., going over several ledge outcrops, bouldery areas, and a chimney with loose rock. The steep slabs may be slippery when wet, and several ledges require scrambling and the use of handholds—hikers with short arms may have a particular problem reaching the handholds. Stream crossings may be very difficult in wet weather. The trail is not recommended for the descent, for hikers with heavy packs, or in wet weather. Allow extra time, and do not start up the headwall late in the day. The ascent of the headwall may require several hours more than the estimated time; parties frequently fail to reach the hut before dark on account of slowness on the headwall.

This trail is well marked, well protected from storms, and has plenty of water. Combined with the Old Jackson Road, it is the shortest route (7.1 mi.) from Pinkham Notch Visitor Center to Madison Hut via the Great Gulf, but not usually the easiest; there are several reasonable alternative routes, though none of them is without drawbacks. The route via the Osgood Cutoff and Osgood Trail, 7.5 mi. long, is steep in parts but has no hard brook crossings or difficult scrambles; however, it is very exposed to weather in the upper part, even if the rough but more sheltered Parapet Trail is used to bypass Mt. Madison's summit. The route via the Buttress Trail is 8.4 mi. long, and has two significant brook crossings and somewhat more weather exposure than the Madison Gulf Trail, though substantially less than the Osgood-Parapet route. In any event, for parties traveling to the hut from the Great Gulf side, there is no way to avoid the 0.3-mi. walk to Madison

Hut across the windswept col between Madison and Adams, except by going over the summit of Madison where conditions may well be much worse. Therefore choice of route comes down to a trade-off among the factors of distance, weather exposure, brook crossings, and rock scrambles; hikers must consider which factors they feel better prepared to deal with, taking current and expected conditions into account. The main advantage that the Madison Gulf Trail has in bad weather, compared to the Buttress Trail, is that the brook crossings on the Madison Gulf Trail, while they may be difficult, are unlikely to be impassable, whereas those on the Buttress Trail may be impossible to cross without an unacceptable risk of drowning. However, in rainy conditions the deep streams and steep slippery ledges on the Madison Gulf Trail would pose great difficulty. In sum, hikers who are not prepared for this level of challenge would be well advised to change their plans rather than attempt any of the direct routes between Pinkham Notch Visitor Center and Madison Hut in adverse conditions, and even in favorable conditions the Madison Gulf Trail must be treated with serious caution and vigilance.

The Madison Gulf Trail leaves the Auto Rd. above the 2-mi. mark, opposite the Old Jackson Road junction, and enters the Great Gulf Wilderness. In 0.2 mi. a side path branches right in a little pass west of Lowe's Bald Spot and climbs 0.1 mi. to this little ledgy knob, an excellent viewpoint. The Madison Gulf Trail bears left and ascends over a ledge with a limited view, then descends, first rapidly for a short distance, then easily, crossing many small brooks. The trail curves into the valley of the West Branch of the Peabody River and continues descending gently until it meets the Great Gulf Trail on the south bank at 2.1 mi. The two trails now run together, descending the steep bank to the West Branch, crossing a suspension bridge to the north bank, and climbing to the crest of the little ridge that divides Parapet Brook from the West Branch. Here the Great Gulf Trail continues straight ahead, leading to NH 16 or (via the Osgood Cutoff) to the Osgood Trail for Mt. Madison and Madison Hut. The Madison Gulf Trail turns left up the narrow ridge and continues between the two streams until it enters its former route near the bank of Parapet Brook at 2.5 mi. At 2.8 mi. it crosses one channel of the divided brook, runs between the two for 0.1 mi., then crosses the other to the northeast bank. It follows the brook bank for a little way; then it turns right, away from the brook, then turns left and ascends along the valley wall at a moderate grade, coming back to the brook at the mouth of the branch stream from Osgood Ridge. From here it follows Parapet Brook rather closely, and at 3.5 mi. crosses the brook for the first of three times in less than 0.5 mi., ascending to the lower floor of the gulf where it reaches Sylvan Cascade, a fine waterfall, at 4.1 mi.

The Madison Gulf Trail then ascends to the upper floor of the gulf, where it crosses numerous small brooks. From the floor it rises gradually to Mossy Slide at the foot of the headwall, then ascends very rapidly alongside a stream, which becomes partly hidden among the rocks as the trail rises. The trail then reaches the headwall of the gulf and climbs very steeply, with some difficult scrambles on the ledges. As it emerges on the rocks at treeline, it bears right and the grade moderates, and soon it ends at the Parapet Trail. For the Parapet (0.1 mi.) and Madison Hut (0.3 mi.), turn left; for the Osgood Trail via the Parapet Trail, turn right.

Madison Gulf Trail (map 1:F9)

Distances from Mt. Washington Auto Rd. (2625′)

to Great Gulf Trail (2300′): 2.1 mi., 200 ft. (rev. 500 ft.), 1 hr. 10 min.

to foot of Madison Gulf headwall at Sylvan Cascade (3900′): 4.1 mi., 1800 ft., 2 hr. 55 min.

to Parapet Trail (4850′): 4.8 mi. (7.7 km.), 2750 ft., 3 hr. 45 min.

to Madison Hut (4825′) via Parapet and Star Lake Trails: 5.2 mi., 2800 ft., 4 hr.

Distance from Pinkham Notch Visitor Center (2032′)

to Madison Hut (4825′) via Old Jackson Road and Madison Gulf, Parapet, and Star Lake Trails: 7.1 mi. (11.4 km.), 3500 ft., 5 hr. 20 min.

Chandler Brook Trail (AMC)

This steep and rough but wild and beautiful trail passes many cascades as it climbs from the Great Gulf Trail to the Auto Rd. just above the 4-mi. post. Lying on a very steep slope, its brook crossings can quickly become difficult in rainy weather. It is almost entirely within the Great Gulf Wilderness.

It diverges south from the Great Gulf Trail 3.9 mi. from NH 16, just above its crossing of Chandler Brook, and follows the brook rather closely, crossing three times, passing fine waterfalls that can be seen from the trail. From the last crossing it runs southeast, rising over a jumbled mass of stones and keeping west of interesting rock formations. The trail enters the Auto Rd. near a ledge of white quartz at the Horn, 0.3 mi. above the 4-mi. post. (Descending, look for this white ledge, which is close to the Auto Rd. The trail is marked by cairns here and is visible from the road.)

Chandler Brook Trail (map 1:F9)

Distance from Great Gulf Trail (2800')

to Mt. Washington Auto Rd. (4125'): 0.9 mi. (1.4 km.), 1300 ft., 1 hr. 5 min.

Wamsutta Trail (AMC)

This steep and rough but wild and beautiful trail begins on the Great Gulf Trail and ascends to the Auto Rd. just above the 6-mi. marker and opposite the Alpine Garden Trail, with which it provides routes to Tuckerman Junction, Lakes of the Clouds Hut, and other points to the south. It is almost entirely within the Great Gulf Wilderness. The trail was named for Wamsutta, the first of six successive husbands of Weetamoo, a queen of the Pocasset tribe, for whom a beautiful waterfall in the Great Gulf is named.

Leaving the Great Gulf Trail opposite the Six Husbands Trail, 4.5 mi. from NH 16, the trail crosses a small stream, then ascends gradually. Soon it climbs the very steep and rough northerly spur of Chandler Ridge. Passing a quartz ledge on the right, the trail continues steeply to a small, open promontory on the crest of the spur, which offers a good view, at 0.9 mi. It then ascends gradually through woods, passing a spring on the right. Continuing along the ridgecrest at a moderate grade, the trail emerges at the treeline and climbs to a point near the top end of the winter shortcut of the Auto Rd. After turning right along this road, it ends in another 100 yd. at the Auto Rd. just above the 6-mi. post.

Wamsutta Trail (map 1:F9)

Distances from Great Gulf Trail (3100')

to outlook on promontory (4350'): 0.9 mi., 1250 ft., 1 hr. 5 min.

to Mt. Washington Auto Rd. (5305'): 1.7 mi. (2.7 km.), 2200 ft., 1 hr. 55 min.

Sphinx Trail (AMC)

This steep and very rough but wild and beautiful trail runs from the Great Gulf Trail below Spaulding Lake to the Gulfside Trail in Sphinx Col, between Mt. Jefferson and Mt. Clay. This trail is particularly important because it affords the quickest escape route for anyone overtaken by storm in the vicinity of Sphinx Col. It diverges east from the Gulfside Trail 40 yd. north of the lowest point in the col, running through a grassy, rock-walled corridor, and descends to the Great Gulf Trail. Once below the col, the hiker is quickly protected from the rigor of west and northwest winds. For a considerable part of its length this trail climbs very steeply; there is a long section of very slippery rocks in a brook bed, very tedious particularly on the descent, and some of the scrambles on the ledges in the upper part are challenging. The trail's name is derived from the profile of a rock formation seen from just below the meadow where water is found. This trail is almost entirely within the Great Gulf Wilderness.

The trail branches northwest from the Great Gulf Trail 5.6 mi. from NH 16, near the crossing of the brook that flows down from Sphinx Col through the minor ravine between Mt. Clay and Mt. Jefferson. It soon turns due west and ascends close to the brook, first gradually, then very steeply, passing several attractive cascades and pools. For about 100 yd. it runs directly in the brook bed, where the rocks are extremely slippery. At 0.6 mi., at the foot of a broken ledge with several small streams cascading over it, the trail turns left away from the brook and angles up across two more small brooks. It climbs a small chimney where views out from the scrubby slope start to appear, then scrambles up ledges with several rock pitches of some difficulty. About 100 yd. above the chimney, after a slight descent, the trail crosses a small meadow where there is usually water under a rock just downhill to the north of the trail. The trail then climbs steeply up a rocky cleft, ascends easily over the crest of a small rocky ridge, and descends into a slight sag. It finally climbs to the ridgecrest and traverses a grassy passage at the base of a rock wall to the Gulfside just north of Sphinx Col.

Sphinx Trail (map 1:F9)

Distance from Great Gulf Trail (3625′)

to Gulfside Trail (4975′): 1.1 mi. (1.7 km.), 1350 ft., 1 hr. 15 min.

Six Husbands Trail (AMC)

This steep and very rough but wild and beautiful trail provides magnificent views of the inner part of the Great Gulf. It diverges from the Great Gulf Trail 4.5 mi. from NH 16, opposite the Wamsutta Trail, and climbs up the north knee of Jefferson, crosses the Gulfside Trail, and ends at the Mount Jefferson Loop a short distance northeast of the summit. It is very steep and is not recommended for descent except to escape bad conditions above treeline. Up to the Gulfside Trail junction, it is entirely within the Great Gulf Wilderness. The name honors the six successive husbands of Weetamoo, queen of the Pocasset tribe.

Leaving the Great Gulf Trail, it descends directly across the West Branch, avoiding side paths along the stream. In times of high water this crossing may be very difficult, but there may be a better crossing upstream. The trail climbs easily northward across a low ridge to join Jefferson Brook, the stream that flows from Jefferson Ravine, and ascends along its southwest bank. At 0.5 mi. the Buttress Trail branches right and crosses the stream. The Six Husbands Trail swings away from the brook (last sure water) and runs through an area containing many large boulders. Soon it begins to attack the very steep main buttress, the north knee of Jefferson, passing by one boulder cave and through another. At 1.0 mi. it ascends a steep ledge on a pair of ladders, then climbs under an overhanging ledge on a second pair, with a tricky spot at the top that might be dangerous if wet or icy. In another 100 yd. it reaches a promontory with a fine view, and begins a moderately difficult scramble up the crest of a rocky ridge.

At 1.3 mi. the trail reaches the top of the knee approximately at treeline, and the grade moderates. Across the bare stretches the trail is marked by cairns. At 1.7 mi. the Edmands Col Cutoff branches right, leading in 0.5 mi. to Edmands Col, and the trail becomes steeper as it begins to climb the cone of Mt. Jefferson. Soon it passes over a talus slope that is usually covered well into July by a great drift of snow, conspicuous for a considerable distance from viewpoints to the east. Marked by cairns, the trail crosses the Gulfside Trail and continues west toward the summit of Mt. Jefferson, joining the Mount Jefferson Loop 0.1 mi. below the summit.

Six Husbands Trail (map 1:F9)

Distances from Great Gulf Trail junction (3100′)

   to Buttress Trail (3350′): 0.5 mi., 250 ft., 25 min.

   to Edmands Col Cutoff (4925′): 1.7 mi., 1850 ft., 1 hr. 45 min.

   to Gulfside Trail (5325′): 2.0 mi., 2250 ft., 2 hr. 10 min.

   to Mount Jefferson Loop (5625′): 2.3 mi. (3.6 km.), 2550 ft., 2 hr. 25 min.

Buttress Trail (AMC)

This trail leads from the Six Husbands Trail to the Star Lake Trail near Madison Hut, and is the most direct route from the upper part of the Great Gulf to Madison Hut. It is mostly well sheltered until it nears the hut, and grades are moderate; in bad weather, or for hikers with heavy packs, or for descending, it is probably the best route from the lower part of the gulf to the hut, in spite of the somewhat greater distance. (See Madison Gulf Trail, the principal alternative, for a discussion of the options.) It is almost entirely within the Great Gulf Wilderness.

The trail diverges north from the Six Husbands Trail 0.5 mi. from the Great Gulf Trail, and immediately crosses Jefferson Brook (last sure water), the brook that flows out of Jefferson Ravine. It bears right (east) in 0.1 mi., and climbs diagonally across a steep slope of large, loose, angular fragments of rock (care must be taken not to dislodge the loose rocks). At the top of this talus slope there is a spectacular view up the Great Gulf, and to the steep buttress of Jefferson's north knee rising nearby across a small valley. The trail continues east, rising gradually along a steep, wooded slope, then at 0.5 mi. it reaches a ridge corner and swings left (north) and runs across a gently sloping upland covered with trees, passing a spring (reliable water) on the left at 1.0 mi. At 1.2 mi. the trail passes through a boulder cave formed by a large boulder across the path, then reaches the foot of a steep ledge, swings left, and climbs it. At 1.4 mi. the trail swings right after passing between two ledges; the ledge on the right provides a fine view. The trail now ascends less steeply on open rocks above the scrub line, crosses a minor ridge, and descends moderately. After passing under an overhanging rock, it re-enters high scrub that provides shelter almost all the way to the junction with the Star Lake Trail, which is reached in the gap between the Parapet and Mt. Quincy Adams, just southwest of Star Lake and 0.3 mi. from Madison Hut.

Buttress Trail (map 1:F9)

Distances from Six Husbands Trail junction (3350')

to Star Lake Trail (4900'): 1.9 mi. (3.1 km.), 1600 ft., 1 hr. 45 min.

to Madison Hut (4825') via Star Lake Trail: 2.2 mi. (3.6 km.), 1600 ft., 1 hr. 55 min.

Osgood Trail (AMC)

This trail runs from the Great Gulf Trail, 1.8 mi. from the Great Gulf Wilderness parking area on NH 16, up the southeast ridge of Mt. Madison to the summit, then down to Madison Hut. The upper 1.7 mi. is very exposed to the weather. Made by Benjamin F. Osgood in 1878, this is the oldest trail now in use to the summit of Mt. Madison. Above the Osgood Cutoff it is part of the Appalachian Trail. The section of the trail that formerly ran from the Great Gulf Trail to the Mt. Washington Auto Rd. has been abandoned. The Osgood Trail begins in the Great Gulf Wilderness, but for most of its length it is just outside the boundary (in fact, it constitutes the northern section of the eastern boundary of the Great Gulf Wilderness).

This trail leaves the Great Gulf Trail and ascends at an easy to moderate grade. At 0.3 mi. it crosses a small brook, follows it, recrosses, and bears away from it to the left. At 0.8 mi. the Osgood Cutoff comes in from the left, and a spur path leads right over a small brook (last sure water) and continues about 100 yd. to Osgood Campsite. From this junction to Madison Hut, the Osgood Trail is part of the Appalachian Trail.

At 1.4 mi. the trail begins to climb a very steep and rough section, then at about 1.6 mi. it gradually but steadily becomes less steep, and the grade is easy by the time the trail emerges on the crest of Osgood Ridge at the treeline at 2.1 mi. Ahead, on the crest of the ridge, 10 or 12 small, rocky peaks curve to the left in a crescent toward the summit of Mt. Madison; the trail, marked by cairns, follows this ridgecrest. At 2.8 mi. from the Great Gulf Trail, the Osgood Trail reaches Osgood Junction in a small hollow. Here, the Daniel Webster–Scout Trail enters on the right, ascending from Dolly Copp Campground, and the Parapet Trail diverges left on a level path marked by cairns and passes around the south side of the cone of Madison with little change of elevation, making a very rough but comparatively sheltered route to Madison Hut.

From Osgood Junction the Osgood Trail climbs over a prominent crag, crosses a shallow sag, and starts up the east ridge of Madison's summit cone, where it is soon joined on the right by the Howker Ridge Trail. Hikers planning to descend on the Howker Ridge Trail must take care to distinguish that trail from beaten side paths that lead back to the Osgood Trail. The Osgood Trail ascends to the summit of Mt. Madison at 3.3 mi., where the Watson Path enters on the right, then follows the crest of the ridge past several large cairns, drops off to the left (south), and continues to descend westward just below the ridgecrest and above the steep slopes falling off into Madison Gulf on the left. Soon it crosses to the north side of the ridge and descends steeply, and, 30 yd. before it reaches Madison Hut, the Pine Link joins on the right.

Osgood Trail (map 1:F10–F9)

Distances from Great Gulf Trail (1850′)

   to Osgood Cutoff (2486′): 0.8 mi., 650 ft., 45 min.

   to Osgood Junction (4822′): 2.8 mi., 3000 ft., 2 hr. 55 min.

   to Mt. Madison summit (5366′): 3.3 mi., 3550 ft., 3 hr. 25 min.

   to Madison Hut (4825′): 3.8 mi. (6.1 km.), 3550 ft. (rev. 550 ft.), 3 hr. 40 min.

Osgood Cutoff (AMC)

This link trail, a part of the Appalachian Trail, provides a convenient shortcut from the Great Gulf and Madison Gulf Trails to the Osgood Trail. It is entirely within the Great Gulf Wilderness. This trail leaves the Great Gulf Trail on the Bluff, continuing straight ahead where the Great Gulf Trail turns sharp left to descend to Parapet Brook. The Osgood Cutoff climbs moderately for 0.2 mi. to its former junction with the Madison Gulf Trail, then turns sharp right and runs nearly on contour east across several small brooks to the Osgood Trail at its junction with the spur path to Osgood Campsite, where there is reliable water.

Osgood Cutoff (map 1:F9)

Distance from Madison Gulf Trail (2300')
   to Osgood Trail (2486'): 0.6 mi. (1.0 km.), 200 ft., 25 min.

Daniel Webster–Scout Trail (WMNF)

This trail, cut in 1933 by Boy Scouts from the Daniel Webster Council, leads from Dolly Copp Campground to the Osgood Trail at Osgood Junction, 0.5 mi. below the summit of Mt. Madison. It begins on the main campground road 0.9 mi. south of the campground entrance on the Pinkham B (Dolly Copp) Rd., with adequate parking available on the left in another 0.1 mi. For most of its length its grades are moderate and its footing is somewhat rocky but not unusually rough; however, the upper part of this trail is very steep and very exposed to the weather.

The trail starts out through a section of open woods with some very large trees, soon crosses the Hayes Copp Ski Trail (here a grassy logging road), and swings northwest almost to the bank of Culhane Brook. Veering away from the brook just before reaching it, the trail climbs moderately up the east slope of Madison, mostly angling upward and carefully avoiding a more direct assault on the steeper parts of the mountainside. At 2.0 mi. it reaches the base of a little buttress, where the forest changes rather abruptly from hardwoods to evergreens. It winds steeply up this buttress to its top, switchbacks upward a bit farther, then resumes its moderate ascent, angling northwest across the steep slope, becoming steeper and rockier. At 2.9 mi. it begins a very steep and rough climb nearly straight up the slope with ever-increasing amounts of talus and decreasing amounts of scrub, where views begin to appear and improve. At 3.2 mi. the trail reaches the treeline and moderates somewhat, though it is still steep. As it approaches the ridgecrest, it turns left and ascends directly up the slope for the last 100 yd. to Osgood Junction and the Osgood Trail.

Daniel Webster–Scout Trail (map 1:F10–F9)

Distances from Dolly Copp Campground (1250')

 to foot of little buttress (2800'): 2.0 mi., 1550 ft., 1 hr. 45 min.

 to Osgood Junction (4822'): 3.5 mi., 3600 ft., 3 hr. 35 min.

 to Mt. Madison summit (5366') via Osgood Trail: 4.1 mi. (6.6 km.), 4100 ft., 4 hr. 5 min.

Parapet Trail (AMC)

This trail, marked with cairns and blue paint, runs at a roughly constant elevation around the south side of the cone of Mt. Madison, from the Osgood and Daniel Webster–Scout Trails at Osgood Junction to the Star Lake Trail between the Parapet and Madison Hut. Although above timberline and extremely rough, particularly in its eastern half, in bad weather the Parapet Trail is mostly sheltered from the northwest winds. The rocks can be very slippery, the trail may be hard to follow if visibility is poor, and the extra effort of rock-hopping more than expends the energy saved by avoiding the climb of about 500 ft. over the summit of Mt. Madison. Therefore it is probably a useful bad-weather route only if strong northwest or west winds are a major part of the problem.

From Osgood Junction the trail rises very slightly, marked by cairns across the open rocks; at the start care must be taken to distinguish its cairns from those ascending the ridgecrest on the right, which belong to the Osgood Trail. At 0.8 mi. the Madison Gulf Trail enters left at the bottom of a little gully, and the Parapet Trail ascends a ledge and then makes a sharp right turn at 0.9 mi., where a spur path leads left 30 yd. onto the Parapet, a ledge that commands excellent views over the Great Gulf and Madison Gulf to the mountains beyond. The Parapet Trail then runs north, passing above Star Lake, and joins the Star Lake Trail 0.1 mi. south of Madison Hut.

Parapet Trail (map 1:F9)

Distances from Osgood Junction (1822')

 to Madison Gulf Trail (4850'): 0.8 mi., 150 ft. (rev. 100 ft.), 30 min.

 to Star Lake Trail (4900'): 1.0 mi. (1.5 km.), 200 ft., 35 min.

 to Madison Hut (4825') via Star Lake Trail: 1.1 mi. (1.8 km.), 200 ft., 40 min.

Pine Link (AMC)

The Pine Link ascends Mt. Madison from the highest point of the Pinkham B (Dolly Copp) Rd., almost directly opposite the private road to the Horton Center on Pine Mtn., 2.4 mi. from US 2 at the foot of the big hill west of Gorham and 1.9 mi. from NH 16 near Dolly Copp Campground. It is an interesting trail that provides an unusual variety of views from its outlook ledges and from the section above the treeline on Madison's northwest slope. Combined with the upper part of the Howker Ridge Trail, it provides a very scenic loop. In general it is not unusually steep, but the footing is often rough and consumes an unusual amount of attention and energy in comparison to most trails of similar steepness. The part above the treeline is continuously exposed to the full force of northwest winds for about 0.7 mi. and might be difficult to follow if visibility is poor, and also requires a considerable amount of fairly strenuous rock-hopping. The result is that the trail generally proves more challenging than its statistical details might indicate.

The trail first ascends the northwest slope of a spur of Howker Ridge, climbing by a series of short steep pitches interspersed with level sections. At 1.0 mi. it crosses a flat, swampy area and ascends another steep pitch, then climbs to the ridgecrest of the spur and follows it. At 1.7 mi. it passes an overgrown outlook with restricted views from the south side of the trail, the result of a 1968 fire. At 1.9 mi., just before the trail descends into a sag, a spur path leads left 20 yd. to a bare crag with fine views up to Madison and out to the Carters. At 2.4 mi., after a fairly long section of trail that has a brook running in and out of it, the Pine Link turns right and joins the Howker Ridge Trail in a shady little glen. Turning left at this junction, the Pine Link coincides with the Howker Ridge Trail. The two trails pass over a ledgy minor knob (a "Howk") that offers a good view and then descend from the ledge down a steep cleft to a wet sag. After passing a small cave on the right of the trail, the Pine Link branches right at 2.8 mi. at the foot of the most prominent Howk. The fine viewpoint at the top of this crag is only about 0.1 mi. above the junction and is well worth a visit. From the junction the Pine Link runs nearly level across a wet area, then rises moderately on the slope above Bumpus Basin, crossing several small brooks. Climbing out of the scrub at 3.3 mi., it runs above the treeline with fine views and great exposure to the weather. After crossing the Watson Path at 3.5 mi. (0.3 mi. below the summit of Mt. Madison), the Pine Link descends gradually, frequently crossing jumbles of large rocks that require strenuous rock-hopping, to the Osgood Trail 30 yd. from Madison Hut.

Pine Link (map 1:E10–F9)

Distances from Pinkham B (Dolly Copp) Rd. (1650′)

to Howker Ridge Trail, lower junction (3850′): 2.4 mi., 2300 ft., 2 hr. 20 min.

to Watson Path (4950′): 3.5 mi., 3500 ft., 3 hr. 30 min.

to Madison Hut (4825′): 4.0 mi. (6.5 km.), 3600 ft. (rev. 200 ft.), 3 hr. 50 min.

Howker Ridge Trail (RMC)

This wild, rough, very scenic trail was built by Eugene B. Cook and William H. Peek, although the lower part no longer follows the original route. It leads from the Pinkham B (Dolly Copp) Rd. at the Randolph East parking area, 0.2 mi. south of US 2, to the Osgood Trail near the summit of Mt. Madison. It is an interesting trail with a great variety of attractive scenery and woods, passing three fine cascades in the lower part of the trail and offering excellent outlooks at different altitudes higher up. Howker Ridge is the long, curving northeast ridge of Mt. Madison that partly encloses the deep, bowl-shaped valley called Bumpus Basin. The trail follows the crest of the ridge, on which there are four little peaks called the Howks. The ridge gets its name from a Howker family that once had a farm at its base.

Coinciding with the Randolph Path, the trail quickly crosses the railroad grade, and 30 yd. beyond diverges left (southeast) where the Randolph Path turns right (west). (Logging activity has disrupted this part of the trail somewhat in recent years, and trail markings must be observed and followed with great care.) It crosses a recent logging road near a yarding area, then enters a shallow gully and turns right, going up through it. At 0.4 mi. it reaches the bank of Bumpus Brook and follows it, passing Stairs Fall, a cascade on a tributary that enters Bumpus Brook directly across from the viewpoint. The trail continues along the brook, passing a small rocky gorge called the Devil's Kitchen and other interesting pools and cascades. At Coosauk Fall the Sylvan Way enters on the right, and in less than 0.1 mi. the Kelton Trail diverges on the right. At 1.0 mi. the Howker Ridge Trail crosses Bumpus Brook at the foot of Hitchcock Fall, then climbs steeply up the bank on the other side, levels off, descends slightly, and reaches a junction with a spur trail that leads right 40 yd. to the Bear Pit, a natural cleft in the ledge that forms a traplike box. The main trail climbs steeply through conifer woods, then moderates, reaching a rocky shoulder and descending into a slight sag. It resumes climbing and passes over a ledgy ridgecrest called Blueberry Ledge—now far too overgrown to produce many blueberries—then continues up the ridge. It continues to climb, steeply at first and then moderately as it approaches the crest of the first Howk, a long, narrow, densely wooded ridge capped by a number of small peaks. Following the ridge at easy grades, it passes a good though limited outlook ahead to Mt. Madison and crosses the ledgy but viewless summit of the first Howk at 2.3 mi., then descends steeply for a short distance. After crossing through a long, fairly level sag, the trail climbs seriously again, and at 3.0 mi. it passes over the ledgy summit of the second Howk, where there are fine views up to Mt. Madison and out to the Carter Range to the east and the Crescent and Pliny Ranges to the north and northwest. Descending into the woods again, it passes through the shady glen where the Pine Link enters on the left; there is water down this trail in less than 100 yd.

From this junction the two trails coincide for 0.3 mi., ascending over one of a group of several small, ledgy knobs that constitute the third Howk, affording another good view. Descending a steep cleft to a wet sag, the trail passes a small cave to the right of the path and then ascends to a junction where the Pine Link branches right. Bearing slightly left, the Howker Ridge Trail climbs rather steeply up ledges to the open summit of the highest, most prominent Howk (4315 ft.) at 3.6 mi., where there are fine views in all directions. The trail descends back into the scrub, climbs over another minor crag, and passes through one last patch of high scrub before breaking out above treeline for good. The ensuing section of trail is very exposed to northwest winds and may be difficult to follow in poor visibility; however, if the trail is lost in conditions that do not dictate a retreat below the treeline, it is easy enough to reach the Osgood Trail simply by climbing up to the ridgecrest, as the Osgood Trail follows that crest closely. From the treeline the trail climbs steeply up the rocks, generally angling a bit to the left and aiming for the notch between the most prominent visible crag and the lower crag to its left. As it approaches the ridgecrest it turns more to the right, heading for the most prominent visible crag, and enters the Osgood Trail about 100 yd. above a small sag and 0.2 mi. below the summit of Mt. Madison.

On the descent, at the junction of the Howker Ridge and Osgood Trails, care must be taken to avoid beaten paths that lead back into the Osgood Trail. On leaving the junction one should keep well to the left, descending only slightly, until the RMC sign a short distance down the path has been sighted.

Howker Ridge Trail (map 1:E9–F9)

Distances from Pinkham B (Dolly Copp) Rd. (1225′)

to Hitchcock Fall (1875′): 1.0 mi., 650 ft., 50 min.

to first Howk (3425'): 2.3 mi., 2200 ft., 2 hr. 15 min.

to Pine Link, lower junction (3850'): 3.1 mi., 2750 ft. (rev. 150 ft.), 2 hr. 55 min.

to Osgood Trail (5100'): 4.2 mi. (6.8 km.), 4100 ft. (rev. 50 ft.), 4 hr. 10 min.

to Mt. Madison summit (5366') via Osgood Trail: 4.5 mi., 4350 ft., 4 hr. 25 min.

Kelton Trail (RMC)

This path runs from the Howker Ridge Trail just above Coosauk Fall to the Brookside just below Salmacis Fall, from which the Watson Path and Valley Way can be quickly reached. It passes several fine viewpoints, notably the Upper Inlook.

The trail branches right from the Howker Ridge Trail 0.8 mi. from the Pinkham B (Dolly Copp) Rd. It climbs steeply with some slippery sections to Kelton Crag, then ascends toward the fingerlike north spur of Gordon Ridge, reaching an upper crag at the edge of a very old burn. From both these crags there are restricted views; there is usually water between them on the right. Ascending, the trail reaches the Overlook at the edge of the old burn, where there are good views north and east. It then runs west to the Upper Inlook (outlook to the west) at 0.9 mi., where the Inlook Trail enters right from Dome Rock. The Kelton Trail then runs south, nearly level but rough in places, through dense woods. It crosses Gordon Rill (reliable water) and Snyder Brook, and enters the Brookside 0.1 mi. below the foot of Salmacis Fall.

Kelton Trail (map 1:E9)

Distances from Howker Ridge Trail (1700')

to Kelton Crag (2075'): 0.3 mi., 400 ft., 25 min.

to Inlook Trail (2732'): 0.9 mi., 1050 ft., 1 hr.

to the Brookside (2750'): 1.7 mi. (2.7 km.), 1100 ft., 1 hr. 25 min.

Inlook Trail (RMC)

This path ascends the ridge that leads northwest from the end of the fingerlike north spur of Gordon Ridge, offering excellent views from the brink of the line of cliffs that overlook Snyder Brook and culminate in Dome Rock. It begins at the junction of the Randolph Path and the Brookside on the east bank of Snyder

Brook. It ascends, steeply at the start, soon reaching the first of several "inlooks" up the valley of Snyder Brook to Mt. Madison, Mt. John Quincy Adams, and Mt. Adams. After passing Dome Rock, which offers an excellent view north from the tip of the finger, the trail continues up to the Upper Inlook near the crest of the finger, where it ends at its junction with the Kelton Trail.

Inlook Trail (map 1:E9)

Distances from Randolph Path (1900′)

   to Dome Rock (2662′): 0.6 mi., 750 ft., 40 min.

   to Kelton Trail (2732′): 0.7 mi. (1.1 km.), 850 ft., 45 min.

The Brookside (RMC)

This trail follows Snyder Brook, offering views of many cascades and pools. It begins at the junction with the Inlook Trail and the Valley Way, at the point where the Valley Way leaves the edge of the brook 0.9 mi. from the Appalachia parking area, and climbs along the brook to the Watson Path a short distance north of Bruin Rock.

The Brookside begins by continuing straight about 30 yd. above its junction with the Beechwood Way, where the Valley Way turns uphill to the right. After a short washed-out section the Randolph Path joins on the right, and the two trails cross Snyder Brook together on the Carolyn Cutter Stevens Memorial Bridge. Here the Randolph Path turns left, the Inlook Trail leaves straight ahead, and the Brookside turns right, continuing up the bank of the brook. At 0.3 mi. the Brookside recrosses the brook and climbs along the west bank at a moderate grade, rising well above the brook, with occasional views through the trees to cliffs on the valley wall on the other side of the brook. Returning gradually to brook level, it comes to the junction with the Kelton Trail, which enters from the left at 1.2 mi. Above this point the Brookside becomes steeper and rougher (though recent intensive trail work has significantly improved the footing), and again runs close to the brook, passing Salmacis Fall and continuing along a wild and beautiful part of the brook, with cascades and mossy rocks in a fine forest. It then climbs away from the brook and finally ascends sharply to the Watson Path a short distance north of Bruin Rock.

The Brookside (map 1:E9)

Distance from the Valley Way and Inlook Trail (1900′)

   to Watson Path (3250′): 1.7 mi. (2.7 km.), 1350 ft., 1 hr. 30 min.

Watson Path (RMC)

The original Watson Path, completed by Laban M. Watson in 1882, led from the Ravine House to the summit of Mt. Madison. The present path begins at the Scar Trail, leads across the Valley Way to Bruin Rock, and then follows the original route to the summit. It is an interesting route to Mt. Madison, but it is steep and rough, and, on the slopes above treeline, exposed to the full fury of northwest winds in a storm. The cairns above treeline are not very prominent, and the trail may be hard to follow when visibility is poor. Therefore, in bad weather it is potentially one of the most dangerous routes on the Northern Peaks.

Branching from the Scar Trail 0.3 mi. from the Valley Way, it runs level, turning sharp left at 0.1 mi. and crossing the Valley Way at 0.2 mi., at a point 2.4 mi. from the Appalachia parking area via the Valley Way. This first section is seldom used and is rather difficult to follow. After crossing the Valley Way, the trail continues at an easy grade, passing the junction with the Brookside on the left just before reaching Bruin Rock—a large, flat-topped boulder on the west bank of Snyder Brook. In another 80 yd. the Lower Bruin branches to the right toward the Valley Way, and the Watson Path crosses the brook at the foot of Duck Fall. The trail soon attacks the steep flank of Gordon Ridge on a very steep and rough footway. At 1.0 mi. it emerges from the scrub onto the grassy, stony back of the ridge, crosses the Pine Link at 1.4 mi., and ascends to the summit of Mt. Madison over rough and shelving stones.

Watson Path (map 1:E9–F9)

Distances from Scar Trail (3200′)

to Valley Way (3175′): 0.2 mi., 0 ft., 5 min.

to Pine Link (4950′): 1.4 mi., 1750 ft., 1 hr. 35 min.

to Mt. Madison summit (5366′): 1.7 mi. (2.7 km.), 2200 ft., 1 hr. 55 min.

Distance from Appalachia parking area (1306′)

to Mt. Madison summit (5366′) via Valley Way and Watson Path: 4.1 mi. (6.6 km.), 4050 ft., 4 hr. 5 min.

Valley Way (WMNF)

This is the most direct and easiest route from the Appalachia parking area to Madison Hut, well sheltered almost to the door of the hut. In bad weather it is the safest route to or from the hut. It was constructed by J. R. Edmands in his unmistakable style in 1895–97, using parts of earlier trails constructed by Laban Watson and Eugene Cook.

The trail, in common with the Air Line, begins at Appalachia and crosses the former railroad grade to a fork, where the Valley Way leads to the left and the Air Line to the right across the power-line clearing into the woods. Just into the woods, the Maple Walk diverges left, and at 0.2 mi. Sylvan Way crosses. The trail enters the WMNF at 0.3 mi., and at 0.5 mi. the Fallsway comes in on the left, soon departs on the left for Tama Fall and the Brookbank, then re-enters the Valley Way in a few yards—a short but worthwhile loop.

The Valley Way leads nearer Snyder Brook and is soon joined from the right by the Beechwood Way. About 30 yd. above this junction the Brookside continues straight, while the Valley Way turns right and climbs 100 yd. to the crossing of the Randolph Path at 0.9 mi., then climbs at a comfortable grade high above Snyder Brook. At 2.1 mi. the Scar Trail branches right, leading to the Air Line via Durand Scar, an excellent outlook on the Scar Loop only about 0.2 mi. above the Valley Way, well worth the small effort required to visit it. At 2.4 mi. the Watson Path crosses, leading left to the summit of Mt. Madison. The Valley Way angles up the rather steep slopes of Durand Ridge at a moderate grade considerably above the stream. At 2.8 mi. the Lower Bruin enters left, coming up from Bruin Rock and Duck Fall. At 3.1 mi. a short side path on the right leads to the recently reopened Valley Way Campsite. Soon the trail passes a spring to the right of the trail. At 3.3 mi. the Upper Bruin branches steeply right, leading in 0.2 mi. to the Air Line at the lower end of the Knife-edge.

Now the Valley Way steepens and approaches nearer to Snyder Brook. High up in the scrub, the path swings to the right, away from the brook, then swings back toward the stream and emerges from the scrub close to the stream, reaching a junction with the Air Line Cutoff 50 yd. below the hut. It ends in another 10 yd. at a junction with the Gulfside and Star Lake Trails.

Valley Way (map 1:E9–F9)

Distances from Appalachia parking area (1306′)

to Randolph Path crossing (1953′): 0.9 mi., 650 ft., 45 min.

to Watson Path crossing (3175′): 2.4 mi., 1900 ft., 2 hr. 10 min.

to Upper Bruin junction (4150′): 3.3 mi., 2900 ft., 3 hr. 5 min.

to Madison Hut (4825′): 3.8 mi. (6.1 km.), 3550 ft., 3 hr. 40 min.

to Mt. Madison summit (5366′) via Osgood Trail: 4.2 mi. (6.8 km.), 4100 ft., 4 hr. 10 min.

Lower Bruin (RMC)

This short trail branches right from the Watson Path on the west bank of Snyder Brook, where the Watson Path crosses the brook at Duck Fall. It ascends rapidly, passes through a campsite area, and turns right uphill away from the brook. It soon turns left and continues to climb rather steeply, then becomes gradual and ends at the Valley Way. In the reverse direction, care should be taken to turn left into the campsite area rather than following a beaten path down to the brook.

Lower Bruin (map 1:E9)

Distance from Watson Path (3325')

to Valley Way (3584'): 0.2 mi. (0.3 km.), 250 ft., 15 min.

Upper Bruin (RMC)

This short but steep trail and its companion, the Lower Bruin, are the remnants of the original trail to Mt. Adams from Randolph. It branches to the right from the Valley Way 3.3 mi. from Appalachia and climbs to the Air Line near the treeline, 3.1 mi. from Appalachia.

Upper Bruin (map 1:F9)

Distance from Valley Way (4150')

to Air Line (4400'): 0.2 mi. (0.3 km.), 250 ft., 15 min.

Air Line (AMC)

This trail, completed in 1885, is the shortest route to Mt. Adams from a highway. It runs from the Appalachia parking area up Durand Ridge to the summit. The middle section is rather steep, and the sections on the knife-edged crest of Durand Ridge and above treeline are very exposed to weather but afford magnificent views.

The trail, in common with the Valley Way, begins at Appalachia and crosses the former railroad grade to a fork near the edge of the power-line clearing, where the Air Line leads right and Valley Way left. In 40 yd., just after the Air Line enters the woods, the Link and the Amphibrach diverge right. The Air Line crosses the Sylvan Way at 0.2 mi. and the Beechwood Way and Beechwood Brook at 0.6 mi. At 0.8 mi. from Appalachia the Short Line diverges right, and at 0.9 mi. the Air Line enters the Randolph Path, coincides with it for 15 yd., then diverges left uphill. At 1.6 mi. there may be water in a spring 30 yd. left (east) of the path (sign). From here the path becomes steeper for 0.5 mi., then eases up and reaches an old and now completely overgrown clearing known as Camp Placid Stream (water unreliable) at 2.4 mi., where the Scar Trail enters on the left, coming up from the Valley Way.

At 3.0 mi. the Air Line emerges from the scrub, and at 3.1 mi. the Upper Bruin comes up left from the Valley Way. The Air Line now ascends over the bare, ledgy crest of Durand Ridge known as the Knife-edge, passing over crags that drop off sharply into King Ravine on the right and descend steeply but not precipitously into Snyder Glen on the left. At 3.2 mi., just south of the little peak called Needle Rock, the Chemin des Dames comes up from King Ravine. The Air Line now climbs steadily up the ridge toward Mt. Adams. From several outlooks along the upper part of this ridge, one can look back down the ridge for a fine demonstration of the difference between the U-shaped glacial cirque of King Ravine on the left (west), and the ordinary V-brook valley of Snyder Glen on the right (east). At 3.5 mi. the Air Line Cutoff diverges left (southeast) to Madison Hut, which is visible from this junction in clear weather.

Air Line Cutoff (AMC). This short branch path provides a direct route 0.2 mi. (10 min.) long, fully sheltered by scrub, from the Air Line high on Durand Ridge to the Valley Way just below Madison Hut. Water can be obtained on this trail not far from the Air Line.

The Air Line now departs a little from the edge of the ravine, going left of the jutting crags at the ravine's southeast corner, and rises steeply. Since there is no single well-beaten footway in this section, following the trail in poor visibility requires great care. At 3.7 mi. it passes the Gateway of King Ravine, where the King Ravine Trail diverges right and plunges between two crags into that gulf. Here there is a striking view of Mt. Madison. In 60 yd. the path enters the Gulfside Trail, turns right, and coincides with it for 70 yd. on the high plateau at the head of the ravine. Then the Air Line diverges to the left (southwest), passing northwest of Mt. Quincy Adams, up a rough way over large, angular stones to the summit of Mt. Adams, where it meets Lowe's Path and the Star Lake Trail.

Air Line (map 1:E9–F9)

Distances from Appalachia parking area (1306′)

to Randolph Path (2000′): 0.9 mi., 700 ft., 50 min.

to Scar Trail (3700′): 2.4 mi., 2400 ft., 2 hr. 25 min.

to Chemin des Dames (4475′): 3.2 mi., 3150 ft., 3 hr. 10 min.

to Air Line Cutoff (4800′): 3.5 mi., 3500 ft., 3 hr. 30 min.

to Gulfside Trail (5125′): 3.7 mi., 3850 ft., 3 hr. 45 min.

to Mt. Adams summit (5799′): 4.3 mi. (6.9 km.), 4500 ft., 4 hr. 25 min.

to Madison Hut (4825′) via Air Line Cutoff: 3.7 mi. (6.0 km.), 3550 ft., 3 hr. 40 min.

Scar Trail (RMC)

This trail runs from the Valley Way 2.1 mi. from Appalachia to the Air Line at Camp Placid Stream, an old overgrown clearing 2.4 mi. from Appalachia. It provides a route to Mt. Adams that includes the spectacular views from Durand Ridge while avoiding the steepest section of the Air Line, and it also has excellent outlooks of its own from Durand Scar, reached by the Scar Loop.

The trail ascends moderately and divides 0.2 mi. above the Valley Way. The Scar Loop, an alternative route to the right, climbs up a natural ramp between two sections of rock face, turns sharp left, and 40 yd. above the loop junction reaches Durand Scar, which commands excellent views both up and down the valley of Snyder Brook; those up to Adams and Madison are especially fine. The Scar Loop then scrambles up the ledge, passes another fine outlook up the Snyder Brook valley toward Mt. Madison, and descends slightly to rejoin the main path 0.4 mi. above the Valley Way.

The main Scar Trail, which is easier but misses the best views, bears left at the loop junction. In 0.1 mi. it turns sharp right as the Watson Path diverges left, then climbs across a small brook to the upper loop junction where the Scar Loop re-enters. From here the trail winds its way up the mountainside to the Air Line with mostly moderate grades and good footing.

Scar Trail (map 1:E9)

Distances from Valley Way (2811′)

to Durand Scar (3200′) via Scar Loop: 0.2 mi., 400 ft., 20 min.

to Watson Path (3200′) via main trail: 0.3 mi., 400 ft., 20 min.

to Air Line (3700′) via either main trail or loop: 1.0 mi. (1.6 km.), 900 ft., 55 min.

Distance from Appalachia parking area (1306′)

to Mt. Adams summit (5799′) via Valley Way, Scar Trail or Scar Loop, and Air Line: 5.1 mi. (8.2 km.), 4550 ft., 4 hr. 50 min.

Star Lake Trail (AMC)

This trail leads from Madison Hut to the summit of Mt. Adams, much of the way angling up the steep southeast side of Mt. John Quincy Adams. It is often more sheltered from the wind than the Air Line, but it is steep and rough, especially in the upper part where it rock-hops a great deal of large talus and then tackles some fairly challenging rock scrambles on the steep section just below the summit ridge. It may also be difficult to follow when descending.

The trail runs south from the hut, rising gently, and at 0.2 mi. the Parapet Trail branches to the left, passing east of Star Lake and leading to the Parapet and to the Madison Gulf and Osgood Trails. The Star Lake Trail passes along the west shore of the lake, and beyond it at 0.3 mi. the Buttress Trail diverges left and descends into the Great Gulf. The Star Lake Trail ascends southwest on the steep southeast slope of Mt. Quincy Adams, leaving the scrub and passing a good spring below the trail. It becomes progressively steeper and rougher as it angles up the steep, rocky slope, and the rocks become larger and require more strenuous hopping. Approaching the crest of a minor easterly ridge, it turns right and climbs very steeply with some fairly difficult scrambles to the top of the shoulder, then ascends moderately along the ridgecrest to the summit of Adams, where it meets Lowe's Path and the Air Line.

Star Lake Trail (map 1:F9)

Distances from Madison Hut (4825′)

  to Buttress Trail (4900′): 0.3 mi., 100 ft., 10 min.

  to Mt. Adams summit (5799′): 1.0 mi. (1.6 km.), 1000 ft., 1 hr.

Short Line (RMC)

This graded path, leading from the Air Line to the King Ravine Trail below Mossy Fall, was made in 1899–1901 by J. Rayner Edmands. It offers direct access to the Randolph Path and to King Ravine from the Appalachia parking area.

The Short Line branches right from the Air Line 0.8 mi. from Appalachia. At 0.5 mi. it unites with the Randolph Path, coincides with it for 0.4 mi., then branches left and leads south up the valley of Cold Brook toward King Ravine, keeping a short distance east of the stream. At 2.7 mi. from Appalachia, the path joins the King Ravine Trail just below Mossy Fall.

Short Line (map 1:E9)

Distances from Air Line junction (1825')

    to Randolph Path, lower junction (2275'): 0.5 mi., 450 ft., 30 min.

    to Randolph Path, upper junction (2500'): 0.9 mi., 700 ft., 50 min.

    to King Ravine Trail (3150'): 1.9 mi. (3.1 km.), 1350 ft., 1 hr. 40 min.

King Ravine Trail (RMC)

This trail through King Ravine was constructed as a branch of Lowe's Path by Charles E. Lowe in 1876. It is very steep and rough on the headwall of the ravine, but it is one of the most spectacular trails in the White Mtns., offering an overwhelming variety of wild and magnificent scenery. It is not a good trail to descend on account of steep, rough, slippery footing, and extra time should be allowed in either direction due to the roughness—and the views. The trip to the floor of the ravine is well worth the effort even if you do not choose to ascend the headwall. Though the King Ravine Trail begins on Lowe's Path, a more direct route to the most scenic part of the trail leads from Appalachia via the Air Line and Short Line.

The King Ravine Trail diverges left from Lowe's Path 1.8 mi. from US 2 and rises over a low swell of Nowell Ridge. At 0.8 mi. it crosses Spur Brook below some cascades known as Canyon Fall, and in another 0.2 mi. it crosses the Randolph Path at its junction with the Amphibrach, a spot called the Pentadoi. Skirting the east spur of Nowell Ridge, it enters King Ravine and descends slightly, crosses a western branch of Cold Brook, goes across the lower floor of the ravine, and crosses the main stream. At 1.8 mi., near the foot of Mossy Fall (last sure water), it is joined by the Short Line, the usual route of access from the Appalachia parking area. Just above this fall, Cold Brook, already a good-sized stream, gushes from beneath the boulders that have fallen into the ravine.

So far the path has been fairly gradual, but in the next 0.3 mi. it rises about 500 ft. and gains the upper floor of the ravine (about 3700 ft.). The grandeur of the views of the ravine from the jumbled rocks that the trail passes around amply rewards the trip to this area, even if one does not continue up the headwall. The Chemin des Dames, leading very steeply up to the Air Line, branches sharp left at 2.2 mi. The King Ravine Trail turns sharp right here and then divides in another 10 yd. An alternate route called the Subway—more interesting but very strenuous—leads to the right from this junction; it is one of the celebrated features of White Mtn. trails, winding through boulder caves over and under boulders ranging up to the size of a small house. The main path, called the Elevated, leads to the left avoiding many of the boulder caves, and is thus much easier; it also offers some good views of the ravine. The paths rejoin after 220 yd. on the Subway or 140 yd. on the Elevated, and soon the Great Gully Trail diverges right, then the King Ravine Trail divides again. The left fork is the main trail and the right is a loop path, about 30 yd. shorter than the main trail, that leads to boulder caves near the foot of the headwall; these caves have ice that remains throughout the year. After the paths rejoin at about 0.7 mi. from the Short Line junction, the ascent of the headwall begins. It is very steep and rough, rising about 1100 ft. in 0.5 mi. over large blocks of rock marked with cairns and paint. It climbs to the Gateway, where the trail emerges from the ravine between two crags and immediately joins the Air Line just below its junction with the Gulfside Trail. From the Gateway there is a striking view of Mt. Madison. Madison Hut is in sight and can be reached by taking the Gulfside Trail left. The summit of Mt. Adams is 0.6 mi. away via the Air Line.

King Ravine Trail (map 1:E9–F9)

Distances from Lowe's Path (2575')

to Randolph Path and the Amphibrach (2925'): 1.0 mi., 350 ft., 40 min.

to Short Line (3150'): 1.8 mi., 700 ft. (rev. 100 ft.), 1 hr. 15 min.

to foot of King Ravine headwall (3825'): 2.5 mi., 1400 ft., 1 hr. 55 min.

to Air Line (5100'): 3.1 mi. (5.0 km.), 2700 ft., 2 hr. 50 min.

Distance from Appalachia parking area (1306')

to summit of Mt. Adams (5799') via Air Line, Short Line, King Ravine Trail, and Air Line: 4.6 mi. (7.4 km.), 4600 ft., 4 hr. 35 min.

Chemin des Dames (RMC)

This trail leads from the floor of King Ravine up its east wall and joins the Air Line just above the treeline. It is the shortest route out of the ravine, but is nevertheless very steep and rough, climbing about 750 ft. in 0.4 mi. over gravel and talus, some of which is loose; it is also a difficult trail to descend.

Leaving the King Ravine Trail just before the point where the Subway and Elevated divide, it winds through scrub and boulders to the east side of the ravine, where it climbs steeply over talus through varying amounts of scrub, permitting plentiful though not constant views. About halfway up the steep slope it passes through a boulder cave called Tunnel Rock. Above this there are many fine views out across King Ravine and up to the towering crags of Durand Ridge. High up, the trail angles to the right across the top of a small slide and along the base of a rock face, reaching the Air Line in a little col.

Chemin des Dames (map 1:F9)
Distance from King Ravine Trail (3700′)
   to Air Line junction (4450′): 0.4 mi. (0.6 km.), 750 ft., 35 min.

Great Gully Trail (RMC)

This remarkably wild and beautiful trail provides an alternative route between the floor of King Ravine and the Gulfside Trail, reaching the latter at Thunderstorm Junction. It is extremely steep and rough, and, like the other trails in the ravine, especially difficult to descend. It is well marked but lightly used, and must be followed with some care. It has one particularly difficult scramble, and should not be attempted in wet or icy conditions. On this shady north slope large snowdrifts may cover the trail well into June.

Leaving the King Ravine Trail just past the point where the Subway and Elevated rejoin, the Great Gully Trail leads across a region damaged by an avalanche, and at 0.3 mi. it reaches (but does not cross) the brook that flows down the gully. At the base of an attractive high cascade the trail turns right, away from the brook, and climbs up rocks to the spine of a narrow ridge and to a promontory with a spectacular view. The trail then passes under an overhanging rock on a ledge with a high sheer drop close by on the left, forcing the faint of heart to crawl on their bellies, possibly dragging their packs behind them. After negotiating this pitch the climber is rewarded with a fine view of the cascade. Here the trail turns sharp right and climbs to another viewpoint, then crosses the brook above the cascade at a spot where *Arnica mollis,* an herb of the Aster family sought by Thoreau on his trips to the mountains, grows in profusion. The trail continues to climb steeply to the treeline, then begins to moderate as it runs almost due south across a grassy area marked by cairns that might be hard to follow in poor visibility, and finally meets the Gulfside and Lowe's Path at Thunderstorm Junction.

Great Gully Trail (map 1:F9)
Distance from King Ravine Trail (3775′)
   to Gulfside Trail (5490′): 1.0 mi. (1.6 km.), 1700 ft., 1 hr. 20 min.

The Amphibrach (RMC)

This trail runs from the Appalachia parking area to Memorial Bridge, then swings south and parallels Cold Brook to the five-way junction with the Randolph Path and King Ravine Trail known as the Pentadoi. The trail takes its unusual name from the marking that was used when it was first made, about 1883: three blazes—short, long, and short—arranged vertically. It is a good alternative approach to King Ravine or to any point reached via the Randolph Path or the Link—and also, via the Beechwood Way, to points reached by the Short Line, the Air Line, or the Valley Way. Its moderate grade and relative smoothness make it comparatively less difficult when descent after dark is necessary. It is, in fact, one of the kindest trails to the feet in this region.

The Amphibrach, coinciding with the Link, diverges right from the Air Line 100 yd. south of Appalachia, just after entering the woods beyond the power-line clearing, and runs west, fairly close to the edge of this clearing. At 0.6 mi. it enters a logging road and bears left, then the Beechwood Way diverges left and, just east of Cold Brook, the Sylvan Way enters left. Cold Brook is crossed at 0.7 mi. on the Memorial Bridge, dedicated to the pioneer path makers of the Randolph Valley. Here there is a fine view upstream to Cold Brook Fall, which can be reached in less than 100 yd. by the Sylvan Way or by a spur from the Amphibrach. Just west of the brook the Amphibrach diverges left and the Link continues straight ahead.

The Amphibrach now follows the course of Cold Brook, ascending west of the stream but generally not in sight of the water. In 20 yd. from the junction a side trail branches left 50 yd. to the foot of Cold Brook Fall. Soon the Amphibrach enters the WMNF. At 1.8 mi. the Monaway crosses, leading right to the Cliffway and left to Coldspur Ledges, pleasant flat ledges at the confluence of Cold and Spur Brooks reached about 80 yd. from this junction. The Amphibrach soon crosses Spur Brook on the rocks and then bears away to the left (east), ascending the tongue of land between the two brooks, climbing moderately. At 2.2 mi. it crosses the Cliffway, which leads right (west) less than 0.2 mi. to picturesque Spur Brook Fall. Becoming a bit rougher, the Amphibrach continues upward to join the King Ravine Trail a few steps below the Pentadoi.

The Amphibrach (map 1:E9)

Distances from Appalachia parking area (1306′)

to Memorial Bridge (1425′): 0.7 mi., 100 ft., 25 min.

to Monaway (2200′): 1.8 mi., 900 ft., 1 hr. 20 min.

to Randolph Path and King Ravine Trail (2925′): 2.6 mi. (4.2 km.), 1600 ft., 2 hr. 5 min.

Cliffway (RMC)

This path begins on the Link, 2.0 mi. from the Appalachia parking area, and runs across the Amphibrach to the Randolph Path, 2.1 mi. from Appalachia. Many of its former viewpoints from the cliffs and ledges of the low swell of Nowell Ridge are now overgrown, but White Cliff still offers an excellent view of the Randolph Valley and the Pliny and Crescent Ranges to the north. The trail has generally easy grades, but though well marked it is very lightly used, and care may be required to follow it.

Leaving the Link, the Cliffway climbs gradually with several turns to the fine viewpoint at White Cliff, where it turns sharp right. Here the Ladderback Trail diverges left along the cliff top.

Ladderback Trail (RMC). This short link trail—named for Ladderback Rock, a large boulder in the woods—connects the Monaway to the Cliffway at White Cliff, permitting a short loop hike including White Cliff and the overgrown Bog Ledge and King Cliff. It is rough and must be followed with great care. It leaves White Cliff and in a short distance, as it turns sharp right, it is joined from the left by Along the Brink, a path only 20 yd. long that parallels the Ladderback Trail a few steps closer to the brink of White Cliff. The Ladderback Trail then descends past Ladderback Rock to the Monaway 0.2 mi. (5 min.) from White Cliff.

At 1.0 mi., after ascending a zigzag course, the Cliffway crosses overgrown Bog Ledge, where a tantalizing glimpse of King Ravine barely filters through the trees, then descends sharply for a short distance and turns left through a boggy area. It then turns sharp left again and soon meets the Monaway at the edge of overgrown King Cliff. The Monaway continues straight, while the Cliffway turns sharp right and drops down a small broken ledge that resembles a ruined stairway, then runs nearly level across a moist area to Spur Brook at the base of picturesque Spur Brook Fall. It then climbs beside the fall, crosses Spur Brook above the fall, and runs across the Amphibrach to the Randolph Path at the west end of Sanders Bridge over Cold Brook.

Cliffway (map 1:E9)

Distances from the Link (2170')

  to White Cliff (2484'): 0.7 mi., 300 ft., 30 min.

  to Spur Brook Fall (2550'): 1.7 mi., 450 ft., 1 hr. 5 min.

  to Randolph Path (2575'): 2.1 mi. (3.4 km.), 450 ft., 1 hr. 15 min.

Monaway (RMC)

This short link trail affords the shortest route from the Randolph area to the Cliffway at White Cliff or King Cliff. It begins on the Amphibrach just below that trail's crossing of Spur Brook. At this junction, a short segment of the Monaway leads downhill (east) about 80 yd. to pleasant Coldspur Ledges at the confluence of Cold and Spur Brooks. The main part of the Monaway runs uphill (west) from the Amphibrach at a moderate grade, passes a junction on the right at 0.3 mi. with the Ladderback Trail to White Cliff, then swings south and meets the Cliffway near overgrown King Cliff. Turn left here for Spur Brook Fall or continue straight to Bog Ledge and White Cliff.

Monaway (map 1:E9)

Distance from the Amphibrach (2200′)
  to Cliffway (2550′): 0.4 mi. (0.6 km.), 350 ft., 25 min.

Spur Trail (RMC)

This trail leads from the Randolph Path, just above its junction with the King Ravine Trail, to Lowe's Path just below Thunderstorm Junction. It ascends the east spur of Nowell Ridge near the west edge of King Ravine, passing Crag Camp (cabin). At several points below the treeline there are fine outlooks into King Ravine, and above the treeline views into King Ravine and up to Madison and Adams are continuous and excellent. The lower part is steep and rough, while the upper part runs completely in the open, very exposed to weather.

The Spur Trail diverges south from the Randolph Path about 100 yd. west of its junction with the King Ravine Trail, on the west bank of Spur Brook, and climbs rather steeply along Spur Brook past attractive cascades and pools. At 0.2 mi. a short branch path leads left 90 yd. to Chandler Fall, where the brook runs down a steep, smooth slab of rock. At 0.3 mi. the Hincks Trail to Gray Knob (cabin) diverges right, and the Spur Trail crosses to the east side of the brook, the last water until Crag Camp. It ascends the spur that forms the west wall of King Ravine, passing a side path that leads left 10 yd. to the Lower Crag, a good outlook to the ravine and Mts. Madison and Adams. At 0.9 mi. it reaches the Upper Crag, where it passes Crag Camp and soon reaches the junction on the right with the Gray Knob Trail, which leads west 0.4 mi. to Gray Knob.

The trail continues to climb quite steeply up the ridge, but not so near the edge of the ravine. At 1.1 mi. a side path (sign, hard to see on the descent) leads left 100 yd. to Knight's Castle, a spectacular perch high up on the ravine wall.

Here the Spur Trail passes into high scrub, and in another 0.2 mi. it breaks out above the treeline, commanding excellent views; those to King Ravine are better in the lower portion, while those to Madison and Adams are better higher up. The grade moderates as it joins Nowell Ridge, ascending well to the east of the crest. It finally merges with Lowe's Path 100 yd. below the Gulfside Trail at Thunderstorm Junction.

Spur Trail (map 1:E9–F9)

Distances from Randolph Path (2950′)

  to Crag Camp (4247′): 0.9 mi., 1300 ft., 1 hr. 5 min.

  to Lowe's Path (5425′): 2.0 mi. (3.2 km.), 2500 ft., 2 hr. 15 min.

  to Mt. Adams summit (5799′) via Lowe's Path: 2.4 mi., 2850 ft., 2 hr. 40 min.

Hincks Trail (RMC)

This short link trail connects the Spur Trail and Randolph Path to Gray Knob cabin. It is fairly steep and rough. It diverges right from the Spur Trail immediately before the crossing of Spur Brook, about 0.3 mi. above the Randolph Path. Soon it comes to the edge of Spur Brook near a pleasant little cascade over mossy rocks, then winds rather steeply up the valley, passing through several patches of woods damaged by wind, to Gray Knob.

Hincks Trail (map 1:E9–F9)

Distance from Spur Trail (3450′)

  to Gray Knob (4375′): 0.7 mi. (1.1 km.), 950 ft., 50 min.

Gray Knob Trail (RMC)

This trail connects three of the four RMC camps (Crag Camp, Gray Knob, and the Perch) with each other. It also links the upper parts of the Spur Trail and Lowe's, Randolph, and Israel Ridge paths, affording in particular a route from Crag Camp and Gray Knob to Edmands Col without loss of elevation. Grades are mostly easy but the footing is frequently rough, and south of Lowe's Path it has substantial weather exposure, although some sheltering scrub is usually close by.

Leaving the Spur Trail 25 yd. west of Crag Camp, it climbs over a knoll with limited views, then passes a side path on the right leading down 25 yd. to a good piped spring. It traverses a rough slope nearly on the level; then, soon after passing a spring (left), it ascends a short pitch to Gray Knob cabin (left) at 0.4

mi., where the Hincks Trail enters on the right. The Gray Knob Trail then runs almost level, passing a short spur (may be obscure) right to an outlook up to the crag for which the cabin is named. It continues past the Quay, a shortcut path on the right that runs 50 yd. to Lowe's Path at a fine outlook ledge. The Gray Knob Trail crosses Lowe's Path at 0.5 mi. and almost immediately enters scrub of variable height, offering a mixture of shelter and weather exposure with nearly constant views, and begins to climb moderately. At 0.8 mi. the Perch Path diverges right. The Gray Knob Trail continues to climb moderately up the slope, then levels off and runs nearly on contour to the Randolph Path just before its junction with the Israel Ridge Path.

Gray Knob Trail (map 1:F9)

Distances from Spur Trail (4250')

to Lowe's Path (4400'): 0.5 mi., 150 ft., 20 min.

to Randolph Path (4825'): 1.7 mi. (2.7 km.), 600 ft., 1 hr. 10 min.

Perch Path (RMC)

This path runs from the Gray Knob Trail across the Randolph Path and past the Perch (lean-to) to the Israel Ridge Path. It diverges right from the Gray Knob Trail 0.3 mi. south of Lowe's Path, then descends moderately and crosses the Randolph Path at 0.3 mi. It soon passes a small brook, then the Perch and its tent platforms, and runs nearly level to the Israel Ridge Path at a sharp curve.

Perch Path (map 1:F9)

Distances from Gray Knob Trail (4550')

to the Perch (4313'): 0.4 mi., 0 ft. (rev. 200 ft.), 10 min.

to Israel Ridge Path junction (4300'): 0.5 mi. (0.8 km.), 0 ft., 15 min.

Lowe's Path (RMC)

This trail, cut in 1875–76 by Charles E. Lowe and Dr. William G. Nowell from Lowe's house in Randolph to the summit of Mt. Adams, is the oldest of the mountain trails that ascend the peaks from the Randolph Valley. It begins on the south side of US 2, 100 yd. west of Lowe's Store, at which cars may be parked (small fee). It is perhaps the easiest way to climb Mt. Adams, with mostly moderate grades, good footing, and excellent views, but it still has considerable exposure to weather in the part above the treeline.

Leaving US 2, Lowe's Path follows a broad woods road for 100 yd., then diverges right at a sign giving the history of the trail. It crosses a snowmobile trail, the former railroad grade, and then the power lines, and ascends through woods at a moderate grade, heading at first southwest and then southeast, and crossing several small brooks. At 1.7 mi. the Link crosses, and at 1.8 mi. the King Ravine Trail branches left. Lowe's Path continues to ascend, and at 2.4 mi. it passes just to the right of the Log Cabin. Here the Log Cabin Cutoff runs left 0.2 mi. to the Randolph Path, and the Cabin-Cascades Trail to the Israel Ridge Path in Cascade Ravine leaves on the right. Water (reliable) is found at the Log Cabin. The path now begins to ascend more seriously and crosses the Randolph Path at 2.7 mi. At this junction the Randolph Path, angling up to the right, is more obvious than Lowe's Path, which climbs straight ahead up some rocks. Lowe's Path climbs steeply up to the crest of Nowell Ridge, then moderates. At a fine outlook ledge at 3.2 mi., the short path called the Quay diverges left to Gray Knob Trail, and 30 yd. farther the Gray Knob Trail crosses. The cabin at Gray Knob is 0.1 mi. left (east) by either route.

Soon the trail breaks out of the scrub, and from here onward it is above treeline and completely exposed to wind. Views are very fine. At 4.1 mi., after the steady ascent up Nowell Ridge, the trail reaches the crag known as Adams 4 (5355 ft.), descends into a little sag, then rises moderately again, keeping to the left (east) of Mt. Sam Adams. The Spur Trail joins on the left 100 yd. below Thunderstorm Junction, the major intersection with the Gulfside at 4.4 mi., where the Great Gully Trail also enters on the left. Lowe's Path climbs moderately up the jumbled rocks of the cone of Mt. Adams, passing the junction where the Israel Ridge Path enters right at 4.5 mi. Climbing almost due east, it reaches the summit of Mt. Adams at 4.7 mi., where it meets the Air Line and Star Lake Trail.

Lowe's Path (map 1:E9–F9)

Distances from US 2 near Lowe's Store (1375′)

to the Link (2475′): 1.7 mi., 1100 ft., 1 hr. 25 min.

to King Ravine Trail (2575′): 1.8 mi., 1200 ft., 1 hr. 30 min.

to Log Cabin (3263′): 2.4 mi., 1900 ft., 2 hr. 10 min.

to Randolph Path (3600′): 2.7 mi., 2250 ft., 2 hr. 20 min.

to Gray Knob Trail (4400′): 3.2 mi., 3050 ft., 3 hr. 10 min.

to Adams 4 summit (5355′): 4.1 mi., 4000 ft., 4 hr. 5 min.

to Gulfside Trail (5490′): 4.4 mi., 4150 ft., 4 hr. 15 min.

to Mt. Adams summit (5799′): 4.7 mi. (7.6 km.), 4450 ft., 4 hr. 35 min.

Cabin-Cascades Trail (RMC)

One of the earliest trails constructed by the AMC (1881), the Cabin-Cascades Trail leads from the Log Cabin on Lowe's Path to the Israel Ridge Path near the cascades on Cascade Brook, descending almost all the way. It is generally rough with one rather steep, very rough section.

The trail begins at Lowe's Path 2.4 mi. from US 2, opposite the Log Cabin. It runs gradually downhill, with minor ups and downs, crossing the Mystic Stream at 0.3 mi. At 0.7 mi. it enters Cascade Ravine and descends a steep pitch, passing a rocky outlook with a good view to the Castles and Mt. Bowman rising over Israel Ridge. It then begins the final steep, rough descent to Cascade Brook, ending at the Israel Ridge Path just above its upper junction with the Link. The first and highest cascade can be reached by descending on the Israel Ridge Path 60 yd. to the Link, then following it downward to the left another 60 yd. to the ledges at the top of the cascade. The second cascade can be seen by following the Israel Ridge Path about 150 yd. upward.

Cabin-Cascades Trail (map 1:E9–F9)

Distance from Lowe's Path (3263')

  to Israel Ridge Path (2825'): 1.0 mi. (1.6 km.), 0 ft. (rev. 450 ft.), 30 min.

Israel Ridge Path (RMC)

This trail runs to the summit of Mt. Adams from the Castle Trail, 1.3 mi. from US 2 at Bowman (which is 1.0 mi. west of Lowe's Store). It was constructed as a graded path by J. Rayner Edmands beginning in 1892. Although hurricanes and slides have severely damaged the original trail, and there have been many relocations, the upper part is still one of the finest and most beautiful of the Randolph trails. Some brook crossings may be difficult in high water.

From Bowman follow the Castle Trail for 1.3 mi. Here, the Israel Ridge Path branches left and at 0.1 mi. crosses to the east bank of the Israel River. It follows the river, then turns left up the bank at 0.4 mi., where the Castle Ravine Trail diverges right and continues along the river. The Israel Ridge Path bears southeast up the slope of Nowell Ridge into Cascade Ravine, and at 1.2 mi. the Link enters left. The trails coincide for 50 yd., and then the Link diverges right to cross Cascade Brook. The highest of the cascades can be reached by following the Link 60 yd. downhill to the right. In another 60 yd. the Cabin-Cascades Trail enters left from the Log Cabin. The Israel Ridge Path now enters virgin growth. From this point to the treeline, the forest has never been disturbed by lumbering, though slides and windstorms have done much damage.

The path continues to ascend on the north side of Cascade Brook to the head of the second cascade at 1.4 mi., where it crosses the brook, turns right downstream for a short distance, then turns left and climbs. It ascends steeply up Israel Ridge, sometimes also called the Emerald Tongue, which rises between Cascade and Castle Ravines. At 2.2 mi., after a long sidehill section along the east side of the ridge, the path turns sharp left (east) where the Emerald Trail diverges right to descend steeply into Castle Ravine. Emerald Bluff, a remarkable outlook to the Castles and Castle Ravine that is well worth a visit, can be reached from this junction in less than 0.2 mi. by following the Emerald Trail and a spur path that turns right before the main trail begins its steep descent. The Israel Ridge Path angles up a rather steep slope, then turns right at 2.4 mi. where the Perch Path enters left (east), 0.1 mi. from the Perch. The main path ascends south to the treeline, where it joins the Randolph Path at 2.8 mi. The junction of the Gray Knob Trail with the Randolph Path is 80 yd. to the left (north) at this point. For 0.1 mi. the Israel Ridge and Randolph Paths coincide, then the Israel Ridge Path branches to the left and, curving east, ascends the southwest ridge of Mt. Adams and joins the Gulfside Trail at 3.3 mi., near Storm Lake. It coincides with the Gulfside for 0.5 mi., running northeast past Peabody Spring to the Adams–Sam Adams col. At 3.8 mi., with the cairn at Thunderstorm Junction in sight ahead, the Israel Ridge Path branches right from the Gulfside Trail, and at 3.9 mi. enters Lowe's Path, which leads to the summit of Mt. Adams at 4.1 mi. The cairns between the Gulfside Trail and Lowe's Path are rather sketchy, so in poor visibility it might be better to follow Lowe's Path from Thunderstorm Junction to the summit.

Israel Ridge Path (map 1:E8–F9)

Distances from Castle Trail (1900′)

   to Castle Ravine Trail (2100′): 0.4 mi., 200 ft., 20 min.

   to the Link (2800′): 1.2 mi., 900 ft., 1 hr. 5 min.

   to Perch Path (4300′): 2.4 mi., 2400 ft., 2 hr. 25 min.

   to Randolph Path, lower junction (4825′): 2.8 mi., 2950 ft., 2 hr. 55 min.

   to Gulfside Trail (5225′): 3.3 mi., 3350 ft., 3 hr. 20 min.

   to Mt. Adams summit (5799′): 4.1 mi. (6.7 km.), 3900 ft., 4 hr.

   to Edmands Col (4938′) via Randolph Path: 3.5 mi., 3050 ft., 3 hr. 15 min.

Emerald Trail (RMC)

This steep, rough, wild trail connects the Israel Ridge Path with the Castle Ravine Trail, passing Emerald Bluff, a fine viewpoint to the Castles and Castle Ravine. The short section between the Israel Ridge Path and Emerald Bluff is uncharacteristically gradual and easy. The path is lightly used and must be followed with some care. Emerald Bluff can be visited from US 2 by a wild, scenic loop hike using the Castle Ravine Trail, Emerald Trail, and Israel Ridge Path.

This trail leaves the combined Castle Ravine Trail and Link 0.2 mi. from their lower junction and descends slightly across a channel of Castle Brook, then climbs a very steep and rough slope. As the trail levels off on the crest of Israel Ridge just south of Emerald Bluff, it turns sharp right. Here a side path turns left and leads 50 yd. to the viewpoint on Emerald Bluff. The main trail runs at easy grades to the Israel Ridge Path 0.2 mi. below its junction with the Perch Path.

Emerald Trail (map 1:F9)

Distances from Castle Ravine Trail and the Link (3225′)

to Emerald Bluff (4025′): 0.5 mi., 800 ft., 40 min.

to Israel Ridge Path (4050′): 0.6 mi. (1.0 km.), 850 ft., 45 min.

Castle Ravine Trail (RMC)

This scenic, challenging trail diverges from the Israel Ridge Path 1.7 mi. from US 2 at Bowman and leads through wild and beautiful Castle Ravine to the Randolph Path near Edmands Col. While it is reasonably well sheltered except for the highest section, parts of the trail are very rough, especially where it crosses a great deal of unstable talus on the headwall, which makes footing extremely poor for descending or when the rocks are wet. It is well marked but lightly used, and must be followed with some care—particularly on the headwall, where winter avalanches may remove the markings. Some of the brook crossings may be very difficult at moderate to high water, and the ravine walls are very steep, making rapid flooding likely during heavy rain. Except for very experienced hikers, it would almost certainly prove to be a very difficult escape route from Edmands Col in bad-weather conditions.

From Bowman follow the Castle Trail and then the Israel Ridge Path to a point 1.7 mi. from Bowman. Here the Israel Ridge Path turns left up a slope, while the Castle Ravine Trail leads straight ahead near the river. It crosses to the west bank (difficult at high water and not easy at other times) and soon reaches a point abreast of the Forks of Israel, where Cascade and Castle Brooks unite to form the Israel River. The trail crosses to the east bank of Castle Brook, passes a fine cascade, and recrosses to the west bank. In general it follows the route of an old logging road, now almost imperceptible. After entering Castle Ravine, the trail crosses to the east bank and climbs at a moderate grade well above the brook. At 1.5 mi. the Link enters from the left, and the two trails coincide, passing at 1.7 mi. the junction with the Emerald Trail left (north) from Israel Ridge. After crossing to the southwest side of the brook in a tract of enchanted cool virgin forest beloved of *Musca nigra,* the Link diverges right for the Castle Trail at 1.8 mi., while the Castle Ravine Trail continues up the ravine close to the brook, crossing it several times and once using its bed for a short distance. It recrosses Castle Brook near the foot of the headwall, close to where the stream emerges from under the mossy boulders that have fallen into the ravine, then winds through a rocky area where water can often be heard running underground. The trail then turns left and mounts the steep slope, and at 2.1 mi. it passes under Roof Rock, a large flat-bottomed boulder that would provide some shelter in a rainstorm.

Rising very steeply southeast with very rough footing, the trail soon winds up a patch of bare rocks marked by small cairns and dashes of paint, where there are good views up to the Castles and down the valley northward to the Pliny Range. It re-enters the scrub at a large cairn, and in 100 yd. it re-emerges from the scrub at the foot of a steep slope of very loose rock (use extreme care, particularly when descending). It climbs very steeply to the top of the headwall, marked by cairns and paint on rocks, then ascends gradually in a grassy little valley with little evident footway and sparsely placed cairns, passing Spaulding Spring and joining the Randolph Path (sign) on the rocks to the left of the grassy valley, 0.1 mi. north of Edmands Col.

Descending, follow the Randolph Path north from Edmands Col to the small grassy valley, then descend along it until the line of cairns is found leading down the headwall.

Castle Ravine Trail (map 1:E8–F9)

Distances from Israel Ridge Path (2100')

    to the Link, lower junction (3125'): 1.5 mi., 1050 ft., 1 hr. 15 min.

    to Roof Rock (3600'): 2.1 mi., 1500 ft., 1 hr. 50 min.

    to Randolph Path (4900'): 2.8 mi. (4.5 km.), 2800 ft., 2 hr. 50 min.

Castle Trail (AMC)

This trail follows the narrow, serrated ridge that runs northwest from Mt. Jefferson, providing magnificent views in a spectacular setting. The part that traverses the Castles is rough with some difficult rock scrambles. In bad weather it can be a dangerous trail due to long and continuous exposure to the northwest winds at and above the Castles. The path was first cut in 1883–84, but most of it has since been relocated.

The Castle Trail begins at Bowman on US 2, 3 mi. west of the Appalachia parking area and 4.2 mi. east of the junction of US 2 and NH 115. Park on the north side of the former railroad grade.

The trail crosses the former grade and follows the right-hand driveway for 150 yd. to where the trail enters the woods on the right (sign). It then traverses an open logged area where the footway may be obscured by brush. At 0.3 mi. it enters the WMNF, crosses a power line, and soon reaches the bank of the Israel River. Here the trail turns sharp left and runs along the bank for 60 yd., then crosses the river (may be difficult at high water) at 0.4 mi. On the far side the trail turns left and parallels the stream for 100 yd., then bears right up a bank and rises at an easy grade through a hardwood forest.

At 1.3 mi. the Israel Ridge Path branches left (east) toward the brook. The last sure water is a short distance along this trail. The Castle Trail continues to rise above the brook on the northeast flank of Mt. Bowman, and at 1.5 mi. it turns sharp right away from the brook. Now climbing up the slope at a steeper angle, it ascends a long series of rock steps, passes a very large boulder on the left at 2.2 mi., and becomes much steeper for the next 0.3 mi. At 2.5 mi. it enters a blowdown area near the crest of the ridge connecting Mt. Bowman and the Castellated Ridge and becomes almost level. Soon it ascends easily with excellent footing through open woods with abundant ferns, and gradually becomes steeper again as it climbs the main ridge below the Castles to a densely wooded shoulder with a sharp, ragged crest. Here it winds along the steep slopes near the ridgecrest to a little gap at 3.5 mi., where the Link crosses, coming up from Castle Ravine on the left and leading off to the Caps Ridge Trail on the right.

The ridge becomes very narrow and the trail becomes steep and rough with some fairly difficult scrambles. After passing over two ledges with a good outlook from each, it reaches treeline and climbs to the foot of the first and most impressive Castle, a pair of 20-ft. pillars, at 3.8 mi. The view is very fine. The trail leads on past a slightly higher but less impressive Castle, runs through a small col filled with scrub that would provide reasonable shelter in a storm, and continues to ascend over several higher but lesser crags as the Castellated Ridge blends into the main mass of Mt. Jefferson. At 4.5 mi. the Cornice crosses, leading northeast to the Randolph Path near Edmands Col and south to the Caps Ridge and Gulfside Trails. The Castle Trail ascends moderately over the rocks and joins the Mount Jefferson Loop in a small flat area just north of the summit crag.

Castle Trail (map 1:E8–F9)

Distances from Bowman (1500′)

to Israel Ridge Path (1900′): 1.3 mi., 400 ft., 50 min.

to the Link junction (4025′): 3.5 mi., 2550 ft., 3 hr.

to first Castle (4450′): 3.8 mi., 2950 ft., 3 hr. 20 min.

to Mt. Jefferson summit (5716′): 5.0 mi. (8.1 km.), 4200 ft., 4 hr. 35 min.

Caps Ridge Trail (AMC)

The Caps Ridge Trail makes a direct ascent of Mt. Jefferson from the height-of-land (3008 ft.) on the road through Jefferson Notch, the pass between Mt. Jefferson and the Dartmouth Range. This is the highest trailhead on a public through-road in the White Mtns., making it possible to ascend Mt. Jefferson with much less elevation gain than on any other trail to a Presidential peak over 5000 ft., except for a few trails that begin high on the Mt. Washington Auto Rd. However, the Caps Ridge Trail is steep and rough with numerous ledges that require rock scrambling and are slippery when wet, and the upper part is very exposed to weather. Therefore the route is more strenuous than might be anticipated from the relatively small distance and elevation gain. (One should take note that it is not easier to ascend Mt. Washington via the Caps Ridge Trail than via the Jewell Trail, because the descent from Monticello Lawn to Sphinx Col mostly cancels out the advantage of the higher start.)

The south end of Jefferson Notch Rd. is located directly opposite Mt. Clinton Rd. at a crossroads on Base Rd. (the road that runs from US 302 to the Cog Railway). The north end is on Valley Rd. in Jefferson (which runs between US 2 and NH 115). The high point in the notch is about 5.5 mi. from Valley Rd. on the north and 3.4 mi. from Base Rd. on the south. Jefferson Notch Rd. is a good gravel road, open in summer and early fall, but due to the high elevation it reaches, snow and mud disappear late in spring and ice returns early. Drive with care, since it is winding and narrow in places, and watch out for logging trucks. The southern half is usually in better condition than the northern half, which is often very rough (but still sound).

The trail leaves the parking area and crosses a wet section on log bridges, then ascends steadily up the lower part of the ridge. At 1.0 mi. there is an outcrop of granite on the right that provides a fine view, particularly of the summit of Jefferson and the Caps Ridge ahead. There are several potholes in this outcrop; such potholes are normally formed only by torrential streams, and such streams occur on high ridges like the Ridge of the Caps only during the melting of a glacier, so these potholes indicate to geologists that the continental ice sheet once covered this area.

About 100 yd. beyond this outcrop, the Link enters from the left, providing a nearly level but rough path that runs 1.6 mi. to the Castle Trail just below the Castles, making possible a very scenic though strenuous loop over the Caps and Castles. The Caps Ridge Trail follows the narrow crest of the ridge, becoming steeper and rougher as it climbs up into scrub, and views become more and more frequent. At 1.5 mi. the trail reaches the lowest Cap after a steep scramble up ledges, and it runs entirely in the open from here on. The trail ascends very steeply up the ridge to the highest Cap at 1.9 mi., then continues to climb steeply as the ridge blends into the summit mass. At 2.1 mi. the Cornice enters left, providing a very rough route to the Castle Trail and Edmands Col, and then diverges right in 20 yd., providing an easy shortcut to Monticello Lawn and points to the south. The Caps Ridge Trail continues east, keeping a little south of the crest of the ridge, to the summit of Mt. Jefferson, then descends east 40 yd. to the base of the little conical summit crag, where it meets the Mount Jefferson Loop just above its junctions with the Castle and Six Husbands Trails.

Caps Ridge Trail (map 1:F8–F9)

Distances from Jefferson Notch Rd. (3008′)

to the Link (3800′): 1.1 mi., 800 ft., 55 min.

to lower Cap (4422′): 1.5 mi., 1400 ft., 1 hr. 25 min.

to upper Cap (4830′): 1.9 mi., 1800 ft., 1 hr. 50 min.

to Cornice (5025′): 2.1 mi., 2000 ft., 2 hr. 5 min.

to Mt. Jefferson summit (5716′): 2.5 mi., 2700 ft., 2 hr. 35 min.

to junction with Mount Jefferson Loop (5700′): 2.6 mi. (4.1 km.), 2700 ft., 2 hr. 40 min.

to Gulfside Trail (5325′) via Cornice: 2.5 mi., 2300 ft., 2 hr. 25 min.

to Mt. Washington summit (6288′) via Cornice, Gulfside Trail, and Crawford Path: 5.2 mi. (8.4 km.), 3700 ft. (rev. 400 ft.), 4 hr. 25 min.

for loop over Caps and Castles (via Caps Ridge Trail, Castle Trail, Link, and Caps Ridge Trail): 6.7 mi. (10.8 km.), 2850 ft., 4 hr. 25 min.

Boundary Line Trail (WMNF)

This trail connects the Jefferson Notch Rd., 1.4 mi. south of the Caps Ridge Trail, to the new parking area on the Cog Railway Base Rd., 1.1 mi. from its junction with the Jefferson Notch Rd. It thus provides a shortcut between the trailheads of the Caps Ridge Trail and the Jewell Trail or the Ammonoosuc Ravine Trail (Section 1), though it is lightly used and often poorly marked, and must be followed with care. It diverges left (north) from the Jewell Trail 0.4 mi. from the Base Rd. parking lot and runs north, nearly level, closely following the straight boundary line between two unincorporated townships. At 0.5 mi. it crosses Clay Brook, then continues to its end at the Jefferson Notch Rd.

Boundary Line Trail (map 1:F8)

Distance from Jewell Trail (2525′)

to Jefferson Notch Rd. (2525′): 0.9 mi. (1.4 km.), 50 ft. (rev. 50 ft.), 30 min.

Distance from Cog Railway Base Rd. parking area (2500′)

to Caps Ridge Trail (3008′) via Jewell Trail, Boundary Line Trail, and Jefferson Notch Rd.: 2.7 mi. (4.3 km.), 550 ft., 1 hr. 40 min.

Jewell Trail (WMNF)

This trail begins at a parking area on the Cog Railway Base Rd., 1.1 mi. from its junction with Jefferson Notch Rd. and Mt. Clinton Rd. Base Rd. is the road that leads from US 302 to the Cog Railway Base Station at Marshfield. The trail ascends the unnamed ridge that leads west from Mt. Clay and ends at the Gulfside Trail high on the west slope of Mt. Clay, 0.3 mi. north of the Clay-Washington col and 1.4 mi. north of the summit of Mt. Washington. The grade is constant but seldom steep, there are no rock scrambles, and the footing is generally very good below the treeline and only moderately rough and rocky in the last section below the Gulfside. It provides the easiest route to Mt. Washington from the west, featuring a great length of ridge walking above the treeline with fine views, but this part is also greatly exposed to the weather and offers no shelter between the summit and treeline. In bad weather, or if afternoon thunderstorms threaten, it is safer to descend from Mt. Washington via Lakes of the Clouds Hut and the Ammonoosuc Ravine Trail, despite the steep and slippery footing on the latter trail; descent by the Jewell Trail offers much easier footing and thus may be preferred when the weather cooperates. The trail is named for Sergeant Winfield S. Jewell, once an observer for the Army Signal Corps on Mt. Washington, who perished on the Greeley expedition to the Arctic in 1884.

The Jewell Trail enters the woods directly across the road from the parking area, crosses the Ammonoosuc River at 0.1 mi., then swings northeast and ascends at an easy grade. At 0.4 mi. the Boundary Line Trail diverges left, while the Jewell Trail ascends the crest of the low ridge between the Ammonoosuc River and Clay Brook, joining the old route of the trail at 1.0 mi. The old path (sign) can be followed right 0.4 mi. to the Base Station. From the junction the main trail descends slightly to Clay Brook, crosses on a footbridge, then climbs northeast by long switchbacks. At 2.0 mi. it passes through a blowdown patch at the edge of the steep wall of Burt Ravine, where there are interesting though limited views. It then swings somewhat to the north side of the ridge and climbs east, staying well below the ridgecrest until near the treeline. Reaching treeline at about 3.0 mi., it zigzags at a moderate grade with rough, rocky footing up the ridgecrest, which quickly becomes less prominent and blends into the slope of Mt. Clay. At 3.5 mi. the trail swings to the right away from what remains of the ridge and angles up the slope at an easy grade to the Gulfside Trail. For Mt. Washington, follow the Gulfside right. In good weather, the fine views from the cliffs of Mt. Clay can be reached fairly easily by a scramble directly up the rocks above the junction.

Jewell Trail (map 1:F8–F9)

Distances from Cog Railway Base Rd. parking area (2500')

to Clay Brook crossing (2850'): 1.1 mi., 400 ft., 45 min.

to Gulfside Trail (5400'): 3.7 mi. (5.9 km.), 2950 ft., 3 hr. 20 min.

to Mt. Washington summit (6288') via Gulfside Trail: 5.1 mi. (8.2 km.), 3900 ft., 4 hr. 30 min.

Pine Mountain Trail (WMNF)

This new trail is a restoration of an abandoned section of the Pine Link that once linked an old route of the Appalachian Trail in Gorham with the Northern Presidentials via Pine Mtn. The trailhead can be reached by turning west onto Promenade St. from NH 16 at a point 0.1 mi. south of its junction with US 2 at the eastern edge of the Gorham business district. Follow this road past a small cemetery on the right and an equipment shed on the left at 0.5 mi., then a larger cemetery on the right. The road becomes gravel at 0.6 mi. and continues to a gravel pit at 0.7 mi. from NH 16, where cars may be parked (no sign).

The trail first follows an old gravel road that starts on the left side of the pit, then swings right and then left uphill above and behind the open pit, passing through an overgrown section of the pit until it intersects a snowmobile trail along the natural gas pipeline clearing at 0.2 mi. Here trail signs will be found. The trail follows an old road (also a snowmobile trail) for 0.3 mi., bearing left twice. The trail then leaves this road on the right (sign) and passes through a recently logged area, then swings left onto a small ridge (arrow) and ascends. At 1.3 mi. the trail descends briefly, enters the WMNF, and angles up the northwest slope of Pine Mtn., crossing several old logging roads. At 2.1 mi. there is a spur path leading left to a limited view to the north. At 2.3 mi. the grade eases and the trail swings left under utility lines; here an unmarked path ascends to the left along the power-line clearing and in 0.1 mi. reaches the north summit and the Horton Center worship area, where there is an excellent view from a rocky pinnacle called Chapel Rock. Hikers are welcome to enjoy the views and meditate, but are requested to avoid disturbing religious activities that may be in progress there. After crossing the power lines, the main trail bears right and ascends to the old Pine Mountain Trail at 2.4 mi. A right turn here leads to the Pine Mountain Road in 0.1 mi. Turning left, the main trail leads to the summit of Pine Mtn. and the junction with the Ledge Trail.

Pine Mountain Trail (map 5:E10)
Distance from gravel pit on Promenade Rd. (825′)
   to Pine Mtn. summit (2405′): 2.7 mi. (4.3 km.), 1600 ft., 2 hr. 10 min.

Pine Mountain Road

This trail uses the private automobile road to the Horton Center on Pine Mtn. most of the way to the summit of Pine Mtn. (The WMNF has plans to extend the Ledge Trail so that, at some point in the future, hikers will no longer need to use this road.) The road begins a little northwest of the highest point of the Pinkham B (Dolly Copp) Rd., opposite the Pine Link trailhead (where parking is available), 2.4 mi. from US 2 at the foot of the big hill west of Gorham and 1.9 mi. from NH 16 near Dolly Copp Campground. It is closed to public vehicular use and has a locked gate, but is open to the public as a foot trail to the summit; hikers should watch out for automobiles. The Ledge Trail, a foot trail over the top of the south cliff, diverges from the road and runs to the summit; it is frequently used to make a loop over the summit. The views from the summit are fine, both to the much higher surrounding peaks and to the valleys of the Androscoggin, Moose, and Peabody Rivers. The Douglas Horton Center, a center for renewal and education operated by the New Hampshire Conference of the United Church of Christ (Congregational), occupies a tract of 100 acres on the summit. The center consists of six buildings and an outdoor chapel on the more precipitous northeast peak (which has excellent views and can be reached by a spur path from the new Pine Mountain Trail). Although camping is not permitted on this mountain, day-hikers are welcome to use the trails and appreciate the views but should be careful to avoid disturbing religious activities that may be in progress there.

The road runs northeast from Pinkham B Rd. across the col and winds its way up the south and west flanks of the mountain. At 0.9 mi. the Ledge Trail branches right to climb to the summit by way of the south cliff. About 1.6 mi. from Pinkham B Rd., the trail turns to the right off the gravel road and follows the old tractor road, which swings south past a spur on the left to a northeast outlook and ascends easily to the summit, where it meets the Ledge Trail.

Pine Mountain Road (map 1:E10)

Distances from Pinkham B (Dolly Copp) Rd. (1650′)

to Ledge Trail (1800′): 0.9 mi., 200 ft., 35 min.

to Pine Mtn. summit (2405′): 2.0 mi. (3.2 km.), 800 ft., 1 hr. 25 min.

for loop to Pine Mtn. via Ledge Trail with return via Pine Mountain Road: 3.5 mi., 800 ft., 2 hr. 10 min.

Ledge Trail (WMNF)

This trail runs to the summit of Pine Mtn. from the Pine Mountain Road (a private road, closed to public vehicles), making possible an attractive loop with a sporty ascent past excellent views and an easy return. It diverges from the Pine Mountain Rd. 0.9 mi. from the Pinkham B (Dolly Copp) Rd., runs under the south cliff, and then climbs up to the east of the cliff to its top, with beautiful views to the south and west. It then continues to meet the Pine Mountain Road at the summit.

Ledge Trail (map 1:E10)

Distance from Pine Mountain Road (1800′)

to summit (2405′): 0.6 mi. (1.0 km.), 600 ft., 35 min.

Town Line Brook Trail (RMC)

This good but steep path gives access to Triple Falls from Pinkham B (Dolly Copp) Rd., 1.4 mi. southeast of the former railroad grade crossing. Triple Falls are beautiful cascades on Town Line Brook named Proteus, Erebus, and Evans. The watershed is steep and the rainwater runs off very rapidly, so the falls should be visited during or immediately after a rainfall.

Town Line Brook Trail (map 1:E10)

Distance from Pinkham B (Dolly Copp) Rd. (1475')

> *to* the end of the path above Triple Falls (1725'): 0.2 mi. (0.3 km.), 250 ft., 15 min.

Sylvan Way (RMC)

The Sylvan Way departs from the Link and Amphibrach at Memorial Bridge, 0.7 mi. from the Appalachia parking area, and leads over Snyder Brook to the Howker Ridge Trail just above Coosauk Fall. Leaving Memorial Bridge, after 80 yd. it turns left away from Cold Brook at the base of Cold Brook Fall, where a beaten path continues ahead up the brook. The Sylvan Way crosses the Beechwood Way at 0.1 mi., the Air Line at 0.6 mi., and the Valley Way 100 yd. farther. At 0.7 mi., within a space of 30 yd., the Maple Walk enters left, the Fallsway crosses, the Sylvan Way crosses Snyder Brook on ledges 60 yd. above Gordon Fall, and the Brookbank crosses. From here the Sylvan Way ascends gradually, crossing the Randolph Path at 1.1 mi. It then passes through a recently logged area, then enters the WMNF and continues to the Howker Ridge Trail.

Sylvan Way (map 1:E9)

Distance from Memorial Bridge (1425')

> *to* Howker Ridge Trail (1625'): 1.7 mi. (2.7 km.), 250 ft., 1 hr.

Fallsway (RMC)

The Fallsway is an alternative route to the first 0.6 mi. of the Valley Way, following close to Snyder Brook and passing several falls. From the east end of the Appalachia parking area it goes east for 60 yd., then turns right on a gravel road and crosses the former railroad grade and the power lines. Here the Brookbank diverges left as the Fallsway enters the woods and continues straight ahead.

At 0.2 mi. from Appalachia, the path reaches Snyder Brook and soon passes Gordon Fall. In 60 yd. the Sylvan Way crosses and the Maple Walk enters right as the trail continues up the brook in hemlock woods. Lower and Upper Salroc Falls are passed, and soon the Fallsway enters the Valley Way at 0.6 mi., below Tama Fall. In 30 yd. the Fallsway leaves the Valley Way and passes Tama Fall, where the Brookbank enters, and in another 60 yd. the Fallsway ends at the Valley Way.

Fallsway (map 1:E9)

Distance from Appalachia parking area (1306′)

to Valley Way junction above Tama Fall (1700′): 0.7 mi. (1.2 km.), 400 ft., 35 min.

Brookbank (RMC)

The Brookbank diverges from the Fallsway near the former railroad grade and rejoins the Fallsway above Tama Fall. It leaves the Fallsway at the edge of the woods just beyond the power lines, 0.1 mi. from the Appalachia parking lot. It runs parallel to the railroad grade for about 0.1 mi., then crosses Snyder Brook, turns sharp right (south), and enters the woods. It runs up the east side of the brook, passing Gordon Fall, Sylvan Way, Lower and Upper Salroc Falls, and Tama Fall. Above Tama Fall it recrosses the brook and re-enters the Fallsway.

Brookbank (map 1:E9)

Distance from lower junction with Fallsway (1310′)

to upper junction with Fallsway (1675′): 0.7 mi. (1.2 km.), 350 ft., 30 min.

Maple Walk (RMC)

The Maple Walk diverges left from the Valley Way, a few yards from the Appalachia parking area, and runs at easy grades to the junction of the Fallsway and the Sylvan Way just above Gordon Fall.

Maple Walk (map 1:E9)

Distance from Valley Way (1310′)

to Sylvan Way and Fallsway (1400′): 0.2 mi. (0.3 km.), 100 ft., 5 min.

Beechwood Way (RMC)

This path runs from the Link and Amphibrach 0.6 mi. from Appalachia to the Valley Way 0.9 mi. from Appalachia, just below its junctions with the Brookside and the Randolph Path. It follows a good logging road with moderate grades. It leaves the Amphibrach, crosses the Sylvan Way in 100 yd. and then the Air Line at 0.6 mi., and ends at the Valley Way.

Beechwood Way (map 1:E9)

Distance from Link and Amphibrach (1400′)

  to Valley Way (1850′): 0.8 mi. (1.3 km.), 450 ft., 40 min.

SUGGESTED HIKES

For more information on suggested hikes, see p. xxx.

Easy Hikes

Waterfall Hikes. On the north side of the Presidentials the RMC trail system provides access to a number of waterfalls and cascades. While all of these falls are essentially small, unspectacular cascades they do provide pleasant walks along the banks of sparkling, splashing brooks. The dense trail network makes an almost infinite variety of walks possible—it is quite feasible to simply wander until one's capacity for the day is reached. Several easy trips are described below, and more possibilities are listed under Moderate Hikes.

Triple Falls [rt: 0.4 mi., 200 ft., 0:20]. These cascades on Town Line Brook can be visited in a very short trip on the fairly steep Town Line Brook Trail.

Fallsway Loop [lp: 1.5 mi., 400 ft., 0:55]. This easy loop via the Fallsway and Brookbank passes Gordon, Salroc, and Tama Falls.

Lower Howker Ridge Trail [rt: 2.0 mi., 650 ft., 1:15]. The lower part of this trail passes Coosauk and Hitchcock Falls, as well as some smaller falls and the interesting little gorge called Devil's Kitchen.

Moderate Hikes

Pine Mtn. This small ledgy peak at the northeast end of the Presidential Range offers perhaps the best views in the region for the effort required. The main trail is a good gravel road, closed to public vehicular use but open to hiking [rt: 4.0 mi., 800 ft., 2:25]. This is an asset for people looking for smooth footing. Still, many hikers will prefer a shorter and more sporty ascent on the branch trail over the south ledges [lp: 3.5 mi., 800 ft., 2:10].

The Bluff [rt: 5.4 mi., 950 ft., 3:10]. This fairly easy trip follows the Great Gulf Trail along the West Branch of the Peabody River to a viewpoint in the lower gulf.

Dome Rock Loop [lp: 4.0 mi., 1500 ft., 2:45]. This fairly rugged trip offers good views from Dome Rock and several other open ledges. Follow Maple Walk and Sylvan Way to Howker Ridge Trail near Coosauk Fall, ascend the Kelton Trail, then descend the Inlook Trail past Dome Rock and return via Brookside, Valley Way, and either Fallsway or Brookbank. The Kelton and Inlook Trails both have fairly steep sections with rough footing.

Waterfall Hikes. A good trip involving many waterfalls can be made by taking the Amphibrach past Cold Brook Fall, and then making the side trips to the pleasant, broad Coldspur Ledges via the short eastern extension of the Monaway and to Spur Brook Falls via the Cliffway. One can return by the same route [rt: 4.8 mi., 1300 ft., 3:05] or lengthen the trip by continuing to the end of the Amphibrach at the junction called the Pentadoi, then following the Randolph Path down to Valley Way, and soon diverging on either the Fallsway or Brookbank [lp: 5.3 mi., 1700 ft., 3:30].

King Ravine [rt: 6.2 mi., 2400 ft., 4:20]. Although usually regarded as a route to the summit of Mt. Adams, this wild ravine, with its rugged scenery and its fascinating boulders and boulder caves, is a completely worthy objective in its own right. The shortest, easiest route to the ravine floor is via the Air Line, Short Line, and King Ravine Trail. It is also feasible to visit King Ravine as an extension of the waterfalls trip described above, following the Amphibrach to the Pentadoi and the King Ravine Trail from there to the floor of the ravine, then descending on the Short Line to the Randolph Path, Valley Way, and Fallsway or Brookbank [lp: 7.0 mi, 2400 ft., 4:40].

The Howks [rt: 5.8 mi., 2800 ft., 4:20]. This rugged trip affords excellent views from several ledges on the northern ridges of Mt. Madison. Take Pine Link to the Howker Ridge Trail and continue to the open summit of the highest Howk.

Mt. Jefferson via Caps Ridge Trail [rt: 5.0 mi., 2700 ft., 3:50]. The Caps Ridge Trail has some fairly steep, rough sections, but the relatively short distance and elevation gain make this the route of choice to Mt. Jefferson for most hikers.

Strenuous Hikes

Note: On ascents of the Northern Peaks, one should never underestimate the potential severity of above-treeline weather, or the strenuousness of the usual elevation gain of over 4000 ft. Possible routes of ascent are nearly limitless, considering all the side trails and the variations and linkings they permit.

Mt. Madison. The easiest route to Madison is probably via Madison Spring Hut, using the Valley Way and Osgood Trail [rt: 8.4 mi., 4100 ft., 6:15]. The Daniel Webster Scout Trail [rt: 8.2 mi., 4100 ft., 6:10] and the Osgood Trail [rt: 10.2 mi., 4100 ft., 7:10] offer routes of somewhat greater difficulty, rougher and much more exposed to weather. The Howker Ridge Trail is a beautiful, wild route, but is much rougher and requires some care to follow, particularly above treeline [rt: 9.0 mi., 4500 ft., 6:45].

Mt. Adams. There are numerous direct routes to Mt. Adams, such as Lowe's Path [ow: 4.7 mi., 4400 ft., 4:35] and the Air Line [ow: 4.3 mi., 4500 ft., 4:25], not to mention the routes via Madison Hut; the most popular route to the hut combines the Valley Way, Gulfside Trail, and Lowe's Path [ow: 5.0 mi., 4500 ft., 4:30]. The King Ravine Trail (including the variations afforded by the Great Gully Trail and the Chemin des Dames–Air Line combination) provides what are possibly the most scenic routes to the summit, but these are all extremely strenuous. One attractive route that is no more strenuous than the direct trails follows the Valley Way, the Scar Trail and Loop, and the Air Line, thereby including the fine ledge outlook called the Scar and the long, open knife-edged section of Durand Ridge [ow: 5.0 mi., 4300 ft., 4:40]. Another route, perhaps a bit steeper and rougher than the direct routes, follows the Amphibrach, Randolph Path, and Spur Trail to Thunderstorm Junction, passing the Knight's Castle, an unusual and spectacular viewpoint on the brink of King Ravine's cliffs [ow: 5.2 mi., 4300 ft., 4:45].

Mt. Jefferson via Castle Trail [rt: 10:0 mi., 4200 ft., 7:05]. This is a beautiful but strenuous route requiring some fairly difficult ledge scrambling on the spectacular Castles. The loop involving the Caps Ridge and Castle Trails and the Link is scenic and very entertaining, but one must take into account the roughness of the Link with its numerous ankle-twisting holes between rocks and roots, requiring an adequate supply of energy and daylight [lp: 6.7 mi., 2900 ft., 4:50].

Spaulding Lake [rt: 13.0 mi., 3050 ft., 8:00]. This trip follows the Great Gulf Trail past cascades and pools to a tiny pond enclosed by high mountain walls.

Section 3

A Brief History of the White Mountains

According to Ticknor's *White Mountains*, published in 1887, the higher peaks "seem to have received the name of White Mountains from the sailors off the coast, to whom they were a landmark and a mystery lifting their crowns of brilliant snow against the blue sky from October until June."

For more than three centuries Mt. Washington has exerted an almost mystical attraction that has brought to its deep ravines and barren, wind-swept summit a great variety of visitors: rock and ice climbers, hikers and wildflower enthusiasts; botanists, meteorologists, and other scientific investigators; writers such as Nathaniel Hawthorne, Ralph Waldo Emerson, Henry David Thoreau, and John Greenleaf Whittier; artists such as Thomas Cole, Frederic Church, Benjamin Champney, Albert Bierstadt, and Winslow Homer; and tourists by the thousand. This section will recount some of the historical events and the next section will describe a number of the natural features that have contributed to this attraction, so strongly felt by so many people with such diverse interests.

Mt. Washington is the highest mountain in North America east of Hudson Bay, the Great Lakes, and the Mississippi River, except for a dozen great wooded hills in the southern Appalachians, which exceed its elevation by less than 400 feet and lack its rocky ruggedness and its great expanses of bare, rocky land above the treeline. Its only rivals for eminence in New England are Katahdin in north central Maine, rising in splendid solitude from countless lakes and vast forest, and the Franconia Range in the White Mountains, a gothic masterpiece of rock towers and flying buttresses. However, both are a thousand feet lower and far less massive.

To the dominating size of Mt. Washington, add the legendary ferocity of its weather: its record wind of 231 mph, its climate similar to that of northern Labrador, its worst weather conditions comparable to those of Antarctica or of the great mountains of Alaska and the Yukon. And all this is within a day's drive of millions of residents of the temperate zone—"an arctic outpost in the midst of civilization," as F. Allen Burt wrote. Ponder the stories of the dozens of people who have died on the slopes of Mt. Washington, so many of them from foolishly challenging the overwhelming natural forces. Consider, in contrast, the tiny, beautiful, rare plants that flourish in a climate whose worst conditions could kill any one of us in a few minutes. Then add in the fabled skiing on the cone and in Tuckerman Ravine, the rock and ice climbing in Huntington Ravine, and such artifacts of human ingenuity as the Cog Railway.

At first the mountain could only be admired at a distance. The native peoples who first lived in the nearby valleys regarded the mountain as the sacred abode of the spirits, where a human trespasser would be punished for the act of impiety. To the adventurous sailors who sailed along the northern coast in the cold seasons and were the first Europeans to see Mt. Washington, and to the early settlers along the coast, this mountain must have seemed a great mystery, a ghostly white shape that appeared with the approach of winter, looming beyond the coastal hills, and then disappeared with the coming of summer only to appear again in the fall. The mountain was thought to be composed of crystal (quartz) and was thus called the Crystal Hill; later the name White Mountains evolved from the mountain's visibility from great distances when covered with snow.

Even when the mountain was finally ascended, it retained its claim to the visitor's awe. Darby Field, who made the first recorded climb in 1642, reported—clearly under the mountain's influence—the existence of large diamonds and huge sheets of muscovy glass (mica), described an endless lake lying to the north, and provided estimates of distances above treeline far in excess of what dispassionate measurements have since confirmed. John Josselyn wrote in 1772 a description of the view from the summit which, as an example of the power of the wilderness over the first visitors, can scarcely be improved upon: "Beyond these hills northward is daunting terrible, being full of rocky hills as thick as mole hills in a meadow, and cloathed with infinite thick woods." Even Jeremy Belknap, New Hampshire's first historian and leader of a scientific expedition to Mt. Washington in 1784, was led astray by the mountain's influence. On that expedition, Manasseh Cutler attempted a measurement of the mountain's height, but bad weather interfered, and only a crude estimate of 10,000 ft. could be produced. Accurate measurements have since shown that Cutler's estimate was far too high; Belknap, however, had ventured the opinion that Mt. Washington would prove to be even higher.

Today—with civilization firmly ensconced on a summit which has had at various times several hotels, a newspaper, a television station, an automobile road, and a railway—most visitors, even those who are comfortably conveyed to the top by cars or trains, can share the awe and reverence with which the Abenaki regarded the mountain when it was still untrodden, and the astonishment that influenced Field, Josselyn, and Belknap when they explored it.

EARLY EXPLORATION AND SETTLEMENT

Several names, including "Waumbekket Methna" and "Agiochook" or "Agiocochook," have been suggested as "Abenaki" names for Mt. Washington or the White Mountains, but there is no clear authority for any of them. "Christall hill" was apparently common among early visitors and settlers. The name White Mountains was first applied to the range by John Josselyn in his *New England's Rarities Discovered* (1692). There has been some disagreement about the origin of this name, which tends to appear somewhat inappropriate to those who visit the mountains in summer; some attempts have been made to explain the name by some fancied whitish appearance of the gray rocks when seen from a distance. But to anyone who has seen Mt. Washington in winter, when its pure white dome is strikingly visible from many low hills far to the south, the probable origins of the name will be quite apparent.

Far too little is known about the Abenaki, who once inhabited the river valleys and had a major village at Pequawket (near Conway). According to Frederick Kilbourne, they had already been decimated by disease and warfare before the first British settlers moved into the area. The Abenaki, one of the ten major Algonquin nations, occupied most of New Hampshire, including the region around the Presidential Range. Vestiges of their wigwam villages, surrounded by wooden palisades, have been found in the river valleys and intervales. These hunting and fishing people also grew some corn; corn hills and other hints of their agriculture survive, along with earthenware, pipes, and burial mounds. It is generally assumed that none of them attempted to climb Mt. Washington; superstitious fears of mountain spirits are often mentioned, but it is perhaps also true that these practical people found sufficient challenge in the daily struggle for existence in this harsh climate, and saw no need to undertake unnecessary risks.

Although John and Sebastian Cabot had probably seen the White Mountains in 1497–1498, the Italian explorer Verrazano is credited with being the first European to record a sighting of the White Mountains, in his ship's log, on a coastal exploration in 1524. The mountains were not visited until May or June of 1642, when Darby Field made the first known ascent of Mt. Washington, accompanied by two Abenaki. Based on Field's description of his journey, it is believed that he ascended Mt. Washington via Boott Spur. He reported that "within 12 miles of the top was neither tree nor grass, but low savins [shrubs], which they went upon the top of sometimes…within four miles from the top they had no clouds, but very cold." Twelve miles is, of course, several times the actual distance from the treeline to the summit. Field's glowing but wildly inaccurate account of the mineral riches to be had there—the crystals he thought were diamonds—led to several later expeditions, but there were no mineral riches, and the region was left until the turn of the nineteenth century to other explorers, scientists, and naturalists, who found riches indeed—the plants, animals, insects, weather, and geological phenomena discussed earlier.

"It was not until the latter part of the eighteenth century," Kilbourne states, "that the New England colonies were sufficiently established, and the country secure enough from Indian depredations, for the settlement of the remoter regions to be thought of and attempted." The first town in the region, Fryeburg ME, was chartered in 1762 and settled a year later; Conway NH was founded in 1765. Many of the other towns in the region were first settled in the following decade.

The real frontier drama of the region surrounding the Presidential Range, however, lies in the settlement of the towns and, particularly, the mountain country. In this drama the greatest figure—and perhaps a truly tragic one—was Ethan Allen Crawford. Much of the history of the early settlement of Crawford Notch involves Crawford and his wife, Lucy Howe Crawford, and other relatives such as his father, Abel Crawford, and his grandfather, Eleazar Rosebrook. Lucy Crawford wrote a fine book about their life in Crawford Notch, and thus she preserved many stories and details, which would otherwise have been lost.

The notch, which was formerly called the White Mountain Notch but now bears Crawford's name, was discovered about 1771 by a settler named Timothy Nash; one common legend has it that he was pursuing a moose on Cherry Mtn. and climbed a tree to look for landmarks, and thus discovered the notch by accident, while Lucy Crawford states that Nash and Benjamin Sawyer went deliberately to search for a pass through the mountains. As the settlers in the fertile intervales of the upper Connecticut River around Lancaster were in desperate need of a more convenient route for trade with the coastal towns than what the river itself provided, it seems more than likely that a deliberate search produced the discovery of Crawford Notch. Nash and Sawyer fulfilled Governor John Wentworth's requirement of getting a horse through the notch, and were rewarded with a grant of land. This grant included the area where the present-day Mt. Washington Hotel and the Crawford Depot and Highland Center are located. It was many years before a good road was built through this notch, but the settlers passed through on foot and even managed to get horses and their loads through.

In 1792 Eleazar Rosebrook bought from his son-in-law Abel Crawford a parcel of land at the north end of the notch that Abel had bought and had lived on for a while before. Both Rosebrook and Crawford had previously lived in Guildhall VT, on the Connecticut River above Lancaster, but they were apparently the kind of men who preferred not to have many neighbors. Rosebrook and his wife Hannah had come to Guildhall from Grafton MA shortly after the birth of their first child, and then, after the birth of their second child, they made an attempt to establish a farm near present-day Colebrook NH on the Connecticut River, 30 miles north from the nearest fellow settler. Rosebrook's service in the Revolutionary War ended this venture, but the urge to pioneer clearly never deserted him. His son-in-law Abel was of similar temperament; after selling out to Rosebrook "rather than be crowded by neighbors," he moved 12 miles farther south into the wilderness of the notch, where he built what was to become the first Mount Crawford House.

Conventional history emphasizes the actions and accomplishments of the men who settled these wild regions; the contributions of the women are usually ignored, because it is less exciting to recount the endless, grinding hours of household and farm labor, and the repeated childbearing without adequate rest or nutrition—or effective health care—that sent so many settler women to an early grave. Lucy Crawford follows this tradition to a substantial degree—she wrote her book in the first person, as if spoken by Ethan—but she does provide occasional glimpses into the hardships that her pioneer sisters bore with such great restraint. In these days one can drive from Grafton MA to Guildhall VT in four or five hours; in Hannah Rosebrook's time, with poor transportation and the limited leisure available to farmers in the seasons when such travel was possible, the move from Grafton to Guildhall meant a separation from family and friends practically as final as death. During the time when she and her husband were the lone settlers in Colebrook, they possessed but one cow, which for lack of a fence was allowed to run free; often Hannah "in the absence of her husband, shut her dear child up in her cabin and taking her infant in her arms, [did] proceed into the woods in search of her cow....Sometimes she was under the necessity of wading the river to get where the animal was, and then she would return home and find the deserted child safe, and with the infant still in her arms, and followed by the other child, did she milk her cow." (The "infant in her arms," Hannah, became the wife of Abel Crawford and the mother of Ethan

Allen Crawford, while the "deserted child," Mercy, became the mother of Lucy Crawford.)

Later Hannah Rosebrook "used frequently to work a whole week, both night and day, without undressing herself. She would only lie down for a short time with her clothes on, while carding and spinning." This was in the relatively civilized Guildhall; how much more burdensome must have been the conditions in the wild notch. After the move to the notch, "as they were dependent on their neighbors for food, they were obliged to go, or send their children that distance [twelve miles] to obtain it, always feeling anxious for their safety when they were gone, fearing some accident might befall them….Many an hour…she has spent in meditation of her absent children." On the day that Lucy Crawford gave birth to her first child, attended only by the aged grandmother Hannah Rosebrook, she suffered the loss by fire of her home and almost everything except the bed she gave birth in. Such were the daily hardships and occasional harsh blows dealt by life in the wilderness.

The Rosebrooks and the Crawfords farmed, and they worked on improving the roads, occasionally receiving pay for their road work. In 1803, the New Hampshire legislature chartered the Tenth New Hampshire Turnpike, which would cause the construction of a good road (by the standard of that time) through the notch. As the roads improved and the traffic on them increased, a growing number of travelers arrived at the Rosebrook and Crawford farms seeking lodging during their journeys. One of these travelers was Timothy Dwight, then president of Yale. For farmers who lived along the roads of the sparsely settled areas, putting up travelers had always been a source of the hard cash, which was so rare and so necessary for purchasing what the farmers could not produce for themselves. It is not clear that the settlers of Crawford Notch originally intended to become innkeepers, but the income that fell into their hands from this business was welcome in the region where the severe climate and rocky soil made subsistence farming a precarious way to maintain a family. At first the guests were lodged right with the family, but as this business increased, such an arrangement led to very cramped quarters. Soon after the completion of the turnpike through the notch and the consequent increase in traffic, Rosebrook put up a two-story building and furnished it for the comfort of his guests, no doubt in the somewhat rough style of the times—including the inevitable barroom. This was the first building constructed specifically for lodging guests in the region, and thus the first of the White Mtn. hotels, rude though it was. Whether or not he planned it, Eleazar Rosebrook had become the first of the great line of White Mtn. innkeepers.

Meanwhile, 12 miles down the notch, his grandson Ethan Allen Crawford was growing to manhood in the harsh life of the wilderness. Used to very hard labor at an early age, inured to pain and cold, he was well prepared for the physical feats, which would later be required of him. As a young boy, he chopped trees to clear land until his hands swelled and he required poultices on them to be able to sleep at night; he harnessed horses in light clothing in the coldest weather. He grew to be a large man, over six feet in height, whose great strength was renowned even in a day when most men made their living by hard physical labor. At the age of 19, he enlisted as a soldier, and spent several years in the army at Plattsburgh NY. After this he worked at building roads in New York State. In 1816, when Ethan was 24, Rosebrook contracted cancer of the lower lip and asked Ethan to come and care for him. He offered to give his property to Ethan if Ethan would care for him and Hannah, and also assume all of the Rosebrook's debts, a sum of between $2000 and $3000. With some reluctance, Ethan consented. To help care for his grandfather he brought to the notch a first cousin named Lucy Howe. Thus, in one sort space of time, Ethan acquired the property which would become the stage upon which he would earn lasting fame, the woman who would become his wife and record the story of his life, and the debt that he would never be able to repay, which would stalk him all the way to the debtor's prison and an early grave.

Two months after Rosebrook died, Lucy and Ethan were married. The next summer Lucy gave birth to a son, attended only by Hannah Rosebrook. Ethan went out, at their grandmother's request, to catch some trout; when he returned, he found his house in flames, and his wife and newborn son lying out in the open in a bed which, in the process of removing it from the burning house, had three times caught fire, requiring Lucy to smother the flames with her hands. The fire apparently started from a lit candle, which the old grandmother forgetfully left burning on a chair.

Ethan's loss, uninsured, was about $3000. Although he could not have known it then, this catastrophe sealed his financial doom; never, in spite of all his exertions during the next two decades, would he be able to escape the consequences of the financial burdens that had been placed upon him by his grandfather's death and the ruinous fire. In good years, Crawford was able to repay some of his debt, but fires and floods caused him severe loss in other years. Taken together, the inn, his farming, and his activities as a mountain guide were more than adequate to support his family, but they never generated enough hard cash to reduce his debt; in fact, the requirements of this expanding business, in which he had set out with so little premeditation, forced him to borrow even more. Eventually, when he had proved that an inn could be successfully operated in Crawford Notch, competitors took up the business and cut into Crawford's profits, making it impossible for him to make progress out of debt.

Ethan attempted to sell the property in the winter of 1819, but the deal fell through, so he and Lucy set out to make a go of their projects, and were able to accomplish great things in spite of their financial insecurity. In the summer of 1819, noting that several parties had come to climb Mt. Washington, Ethan and Abel Crawford cut a footpath from the notch through the woods to treeline. This was the beginning of the Crawford Path, which is considered to be the oldest continuously maintained mountain footpath in the country. This path was advertised in some newspapers, and visitors began to come to use it, although they were compelled to stay at Abel Crawford's due to Ethan's lack of space. Ethan's patrons at this time consisted mostly of travelers and those transporting goods over the notch road, which had become an important market route; such guests who traveled by necessity and not for pleasure, demanded less comfort. In 1820, Ethan guided to the summit a party which included Philip Carrigain (who made the first reasonably accurate map of the state of New Hampshire in 1816); these men gave names to Mounts Adams, Jefferson, Madison, and Monroe (although the peaks they named Adams and Jefferson have since had their names interchanged).

In 1824, Ethan Crawford finally constructed a building specifically for lodging guests, although in his circumstances this expense caused him some worry. He also made several unsuccessful attempts to provide a comfortable place to spend the night on the summit of Mt. Washington; first he built stone cabins that proved too damp for comfort, then he bought and carried up a tent and an iron stove, but the tent was soon destroyed. During this time, he led many parties to the summit of Mt. Washington, and often had to carry out exhausted climbers on his back. He constructed a camp partway up the mountain, as the distance was too great for most parties to make a complete trip in one day. In 1825, Lucy Crawford made her first ascent of Mt. Washington.

Near the end of the summer of 1826, heavy rains caused great damage to Ethan Allen Crawford's property, and even greater damage to Abel Crawford's property down in the deep valley in the southern portion of the notch area. At the latter place, Ethan's mother stood at a window with a pole, pushing away streamborne debris which was collecting at the corner of the house and might have caused the house to be swept away, occasionally hearing the bleating of their drowning sheep that were carried past the house in the swift current. But the most famous disaster produced by this storm was the destruction of the

Willey family, which became the inspiration for Nathaniel Hawthorne's well-known story "The Ambitious Guest."

Midway between the Rosebrook and Crawford farms, in the heart of Crawford Notch, the Willey House was a lonely refuge for travelers in the wilderness. When the flood occurred, there was naturally great concern for the family, which consisted of the parents, five children, and two hired men. The following day a traveler found the Willey House deserted, as if the family had left in great haste. Over the next several days the bodies of the husband, wife, two children, and the two hired hands were discovered among the debris of a huge landslide. The bodies of three other children were never found. Although it will always be uncertain exactly what happened, it is believed that the family, which had seen smaller slides earlier in the storm and had made plans to escape, fled the house when they heard the landslide amid the storm. But a ledge between the house and the mountain slope protected the dwelling from the slide, which split into two parts that cascaded down on either side; thus, ironically, they ran away from safety directly into the path of the slide. The scar left by the slide is still visible on the face of Mount Willey, which was named for the family; there is a monument at the Willey House site in Crawford Notch State Park.

The flood left Ethan Crawford and his family intact, but it swept away the fruits of several years of hard labor, and made the prospect of his paying off his debts even more remote, since he lost his entire cash crop. It also nearly totally destroyed the turnpike which was the very reason for the existence of Crawford's establishment, but with the help of a donation of $1500, raised by the people of Portland ME, the road was rebuilt. Still Ethan persevered, rebuilt, and even worked on constructing a new road toward the base of Mt. Washington, near the present location of the Cog Railway Base Station, which would make ascents of the mountain in a single day more practical for the average visitor. In 1828 another heavy rain struck, from which the floods again caused great damage to Crawford's property and destroyed the turnpike. At first the directors of the turnpike declined to rebuild, which would have left Crawford isolated, with little business and unable to obtain food without great difficulty, but he was able to secure enough support in the turnpike corporation to proceed with the reconstruction. Still, he was forced to advance $400 from his own money and only got it back four years later. A man who was himself deeply in debt could ill afford to make what was in effect an interest-free loan to the turnpike corporation, but Crawford did what seemed to be required for his own and the public's benefit. Still, he managed to construct with his father a new lodging at the top of the notch, near the present-day Crawford Depot information center, and his brother

Thomas was installed as manager. This was a great service to travelers, and became a popular stopping-place, but again it was a drain on Ethan's financial resources.

By this time Ethan Crawford had begun to find routine ascents of Mt. Washington rather tiresome; however, he still led botanists and others with scientific purposes to the mountain. In fact, he became so familiar with the rare mountain plants, and the places to find them, that he was occasionally asked to collect plants himself and send them off to botanists or museums. In 1831 he guided his most famous guest, Daniel Webster, to the summit. Webster was a native of Franklin NH; he was perhaps the most famous native son of New Hampshire (although he was elected to the Senate from Massachusetts), and the most spellbinding speaker in the country at a time when political oratory was one of the highest forms of public entertainment. Reaching the summit in the clouds, he addressed the mountain thus: "Mt. Washington, I have come a long distance, have toiled hard to arrive at your summit, and now you seem to give me a cold reception."

In 1832 Crawford enlarged his guest lodgings. The expense of building and furnishing this addition was great, but his existing lodgings were frequently overcrowded—even to the point of filling up the family's own quarters. The prospect for increased business seemed promising, and the owners of the stage line put considerable pressure on him to enlarge his accommodations, as their business depended in part on having adequate lodgings for their patrons. However, the increase in business convinced others that a good living might be made in this line of service. A competitor set up an inn within a mile of Crawford's, and offered stage drivers free feed and stabling in order to induce the drivers to bring their passengers to his establishment. The horses that Crawford kept to carry guests to the foot of Mt. Washington, so that they could climb it in a day, were also a constant drain on his resources, as they had to be fed and cared for throughout the year though they were only used for a few short months. Crawford had made it a point of great pride that he always conducted his business openly and honestly and with a strong concern for the public good, and that he had always paid his hired workers fully and on time, no matter what other obligations he might have to leave unpaid. The traditional Yankee sharp practices he forswore might have paid his debts more effectively, but Crawford was a man ruled by public spirit and a stern conscience, and an honesty and a trust in the honesty of others which was sometimes almost naïve.

Through all the years of hardship and hard labor, Ethan and Lucy had been fortunate in having good health; Ethan had occasional rheumatism from having frequently worked in water during his road-building days in New York State, and in 1821 he had suffered an axe wound to his heel that lamed him for some time, but neither he nor Lucy lost more than a few days of work to sickness. This good fortune came to an end in 1834. First, Lucy became ill soon after the birth of her ninth child, was unable to nurse it, and decided to give the child over to her brother and sister-in-law, who had recently lost their own infant. Knowing that the sister-in-law, having nursed the child, would be reluctant to give it back, Lucy consoled herself with the knowledge that the child would be comfortably taken care of. Lucy's illness continued and appeared to be threatening her life. By great fortune, one of their guests that summer was Dr. John Collins Warren, the eminent Boston physician who twelve years later performed the first public operation in the world in which ether was used as an anaesthetic. Dr. Warren treated her, without charge, and apparently effected a cure that local doctors had failed to accomplish.

Next, in the fall of 1834, Ethan suffered a painful injury while riding a horse. This injury, severe in itself, was no doubt exacerbated by the toll taken on his body by the long years of hardship, overwork, and the frequent feats of strength and endurance for which he was famous. Never again would the "Giant of the White Hills" enjoy the physical and mental vigor of which the legends were written, since his ailments, together with the mental strain from his financial troubles, affected his mind as well as his body; Lucy Crawford later described his condition as "a premature decay of mind [which] caused him to wander from his native mind more and more rapidly." During this period he made an unwise agreement to sell his property to a land speculator, and was thus forced to pass up even better deals; by the time the agreement expired, and the sale fell through, the better terms were no longer available. An operation performed by a generous doctor in 1836 finally relieved some of his suffering and improved his condition somewhat, but some creditors had heard of his illnesses and feared that he would die without paying what he owed them; he was therefore put in the Lancaster jail for 25 days, while still in a weakened condition recuperating from his ordeals. Within the year he departed from the notch, leaving his property in the hands of his creditors to be sold. For six years he farmed in Guildhall VT, with the help of his large family, on land once occupied by his grandmother, Hannah Rosebrook.

In 1843 Ethan and Lucy Crawford returned to Crawford Notch, renting a house within a mile of their former mountain home. They still entertained hopes of returning to that scene of their many years of toil and service; in fact, one of Lucy's motives in writing her history was the hope that the book would produce enough profits and public goodwill to restore them to their old home. But it was not to be; Ethan contracted typhoid fever in the fall of 1845 and gradually declined. He died on June 22, 1846, at the age of 54. William Oakes, the botanist that Crawford had guided over the hills to the rare plants, had a marble tombstone placed on Crawford's grave on a knoll overlooking the region where his great deeds had taken place. Lucy Crawford lived for another 23 years.

Ethan and Lucy Crawford had been great pioneers; they had accepted endless labor and hardship. Ethan's services to botanists, mountain climbers, and travelers were great and can be appreciated even today, particularly since the path he and his father built still exists, and is for much of its distance part of the Appalachian Trail. Perhaps less obvious is the service the Crawfords provided to the people of the settlements of the upper Connecticut River Valley; by helping to keep the road through Crawford Notch open and making travel along that route relatively comfortable and safe, they made a tremendous contribution to the economy of the region, undoubtedly making the difference between prosperity and poverty, and perhaps even between survival and failure for many settlers in that fertile but remote area. They broke ground and made the way smoother for many that followed, but they never fully enjoyed the fruits of their labors; in some sense, Ethan was repaid for his great services by a constant burden of debt ending in prison, and died in circumstances in which he must have thought himself to a great degree a failure. Except for his good fortune in marrying a woman who, against all odds, proved to have significant literary ability, his deeds might have faded into the obscurity which has claimed the stories of most of the brave people who settled this wilderness. Thus the Crawfords also stand as examples of the men and women who built the settlements of the New England wilderness, and who are now remembered, if at all, mostly by names, dates, and verses on weathered gravestones. The innkeepers who succeeded the Crawfords within a very short period of time created a little world of luxury which far exceeded anything that the Crawfords could have imagined, but which seems almost tawdry in comparison to the simple and steadfast virtues that governed the lives and works of Ethan and Lucy Crawford.

THE ERA OF THE GRAND HOTELS

By the latter part of the nineteenth century, resort hotels dotted the White Mtn. landscape, served by a rail network bringing vacationers from all over the East. Both the railway and a carriage road climbed Mt. Washington, and there was a thriving seasonal community on the summit to serve the whims of the visiting travelers. In its heyday, the region attracted artists and writers as well as other distinguished visitors, and was considered a chic and opulent watering place.

Early access to the Presidential Range depended, naturally, on the available transportation. The first main road in the region, as mentioned earlier, was the turnpike from the seacoast of Portland ME through Crawford Notch to the upper Connecticut River Valley. The earliest settlers, most notably the Crawfords, did much to keep this road open in spite of floods, landslides, and blizzards, for their livelihoods depended on it. The earliest traffic was commercial, farm produce from the settlements exchanged for finished goods from the long-established towns nearer the coast. Noncommercial visitors tended to be scientists and explorers, not tourists.

Catering to this trade were a half-dozen inns in Crawford Notch. The first, as noted previously, was built by Eleazar Rosebrook on the site of his decade-old homestead at the north end of the notch in 1803. In 1816 Ethan Allen Crawford and his wife Lucy came to take care of Rosebrook, and after his death the following year they ran an inn on the spot until forced out of the notch by illness and debt in 1837. At about the same time that Rosebrook opened his inn, a second way station was opened by Henry Hill at the Willey House site, halfway through the notch, and a third was begun by Abel Crawford, Rosebrook's son-in-law and Ethan Allen Crawford's father, at the south end of the notch. These early inns were not always planned to be such; in many cases, they started with farmers offering lodging to travelers in exchange for scarce hard cash, and gradually developed into full-scale inns as this business increased.

In 1819, Abel and Ethan Crawford cut their first path—now the Crawford Path—over the Southern Peaks, and in 1821 Ethan cut another path in roughly the location used today by the Cog Railway. This ushered in a new era, attracting tourists who came in increasing numbers, not for business but for pleasure, to see the mountains. By 1825 tourists had begun to come to North Conway, which then had five hotels, the first having been opened in 1812. The town was a terminus of a stagecoach line from Center Harbor on Lake Winnipesaukee, which brought travelers from southern New Hampshire and beyond. Business increased steadily in Crawford Notch. Ethan Allen Crawford constructed a new building for lodging guests in 1824, and enlarged it in 1832. With his father he built a new inn between the present Crawford Hostel and the Gate of the Notch, in 1828, which was managed by his brother T. J. Crawford for almost 25 years.

Soon the area began to attract notable visitors whose interests were not directed toward exploration or science. Daniel Webster, as previously mentioned, ascended Mt. Washington with Ethan Allen Crawford in 1831. Nathaniel

Hawthorne, who wrote several stories with White Mtn. settings, including "The Ambitious Guest," first visited the area in 1832. He was only one of the many famous writers to visit these mountains; others were Henry Wadsworth Longfellow, Henry David Thoreau, Ralph Waldo Emerson, Francis Parkman, John Greenleaf Whittier, and William Cullen Bryant. Many artists of national importance also came to the mountains—but for work rather than play—including Thomas Cole and Asher B. Durand of the Hudson River School, and Albert Bierstadt, Benjamin Champney, and John Kensett; many of these painters did important work in the White Mountains. Soon the region was established as a true resort, and people came to the White Mountains summer after summer, staying for several weeks in their favorite hotels, visiting with summertime friends and amusing themselves with the grand mountain scenery.

It would be a great era for the region, an era that would bring a new generation of entrepreneurs, but at first the pattern of hard work with great financial risk and frequent failure persisted. In 1837, after Ethan Allen Crawford had been forced to give up his property, Horace Fabyan purchased it, renamed it as the Mt. Washington House, and ran it for 15 years. In 1845 he built another hotel at the Willey House site, and in 1851 took over management of the Conway House, but in 1853 the Mt. Washington House burned and Fabyan was financially ruined. Abel Crawford's son-in-law, Nathaniel T. P. Davis, assumed the management of Abel's Mount Crawford House, but went heavily in debt to Dr. Samuel A. Bemis, a longtime summer visitor to the region; Bemis finally took over this hotel. All this activity in the hotel business spurred major changes in the routes to Mt. Washington's summit, as the new visitors had to be given the opportunity to enjoy the region's chief natural attraction. In 1839 and 1840 the original Crawford path over the Southern Peaks was rebuilt as a bridle path, and Abel Crawford, at the age of 75, rode the first horse to the summit in 1840. Fabyan improved Ethan Crawford's 1821 path along the present day Cog Railway route so that it could also be used by horses, and in 1845 Davis built his own bridle path, which was perhaps the most arduous construction project of all the Presidential bridle paths. This last path was abandoned around 1853 but was reopened in 1910, and still exists as one of the longest and most strenuous routes to Mt. Washington.

Around mid-century the hotel business started to spread more widely through the region. In Crawford Notch, hotels continued to be built and renovated; they periodically burned down and were rebuilt. Destruction by fire was the almost inevitable fate of these huge wooden buildings. In 1852 the railway was completed from Portland ME to Gorham NH, at the head of Pinkham Notch on the eastern side of the Presidentials, and the Alpine House was built in

Gorham. In the same year, the first real hotel in Pinkham Notch—the Glen House—was constructed near where the present Auto Rd. begins its ascent of Mt. Washington. For many years before this Dolly Copp had put up travelers at the Copp farm several miles to the north of the Glen House site, and had built a thriving business similar to those in Crawford Notch. The railroad also reached Conway from the south at about that time, and as the much more comfortable railroads replaced stagecoaches and horseback rides, many more visitors found the trip to the mountains enjoyable.

Commercial interest was also growing in the summit of Mt. Washington. Until 1852 no permanent building was successfully constructed in that weather-whipped and rocky place, but in that year the first Summit House was built of stones blasted from the mountaintop. The following year the Tip-Top House opened, and this building still stands in spite of a fire in 1915. With two hotels, it is not surprising that a road to the summit was considered desirable; thus the Mt. Washington Road Company was chartered in 1853, with General David O. Macomber as president. The project proved more difficult and expensive than expected, and the company failed in 1855–1856 after four miles had been completed. In 1861 the Mt. Washington Summit Road Company finished the road, the world's first mountain toll road, which rises 4700 feet in 8 miles. The route of that road was substantially the same as the one that the Mt. Washington Auto Rd. uses today, a testimony to the surveying and engineering skill of the earlier era. (For a good description of what can be seen from the Auto Rd., which leaves NH 16 opposite the Glen House site, see Peter Randall's *Mt. Washington.*)

On the other side of the mountain an even more daring engineering project was under way. Its principal sponsor was Sylvester Marsh, who in 1833 had moved from Boston to Chicago, then a village of about 300 people. He sold beef, then invented meatpacking machinery that made him rich. After losing everything in the financial panics during the 1830s, he went into the grain business and became rich again. Retiring from business at the age of 52, he came to the White Mountains looking for a new outlet for his genius and fortune, and thus decided to build the world's first mountain cog railway to the summit of Mt. Washington.

The engineering and planning skill for this project, and possibly even the original idea, came from Herrick Aiken of Franklin NH and his son Walter. Herrick Aiken, a manufacturer of knitting needles, invented the first circular knitting machine for making seamless stockings, and was considered by many to be almost a genius because of his inventions. He looked over a route and made a model for a cog railway, but railroad people dissuaded him from the project.

Marsh's financial and promotional ability finally made the project a reality, and Aiken later built several of the early engines at his factory in Franklin. Many years later, after acrimonious struggles for authority, Walter Aiken took control of the enterprise and made it a profitable business.

When Marsh went to the New Hampshire legislature in 1858 for a charter for his cog railway, the idea was considered so preposterous that he was offered a charter to build a "railway to the moon" if he desired it. Undaunted, in 1866 he began construction, and two years later his railway was open as far as Jacob's Ladder. On July 3, 1869, the first train reached the summit, and a turnpike had been built from Fabyan to the Base Station. However, until 1874, when the main railway line was extended to Fabyan, Crawford Notch was still accessible only by a long and uncomfortable stagecoach ride. "Old Peppersass," Marsh's first locomotive is still on display at the Base Station. (For a good description of what can be seen from the cog railway, see, again, Randall's *Mt. Washington.*)

New development occurred rapidly on the summit of Mt. Washington. In 1862 Col. John R. Hitchcock leased both summit hotels, and when his Alpine House in Gorham burned a decade later, he connected the two summit hotels and at the same time began construction for the new Summit House. In 1870 a train shed was built on the summit, and in 1874 the Signal Station was constructed to house the world's first mountain weather station, which had operated in borrowed buildings since 1870. When the new Summit House was completed in 1873, the old Tip-Top House was turned into a dormitory and later became the first office of "Among the Clouds," the first newspaper printed on top of a mountain. A stage office was constructed in 1878, so that by 1880 there were six buildings on the summit of Mt. Washington. In 1908, fire destroyed the Summit House and all other buildings on the summit of Mt. Washington except the old Tip-Top House. In 1915, a new Summit House opened, after five years in the building, but by then the twentieth century—and a new era in the Presidentials—was well underway.

The 1870s saw the advent of the last great era of hotel-building in the White Mountains, resulting from increasing numbers of visitors brought to the area by an improved transportation system; it lasted until the turn of the century, when the motor car ushered in a new age. In 1876, there was much activity in Crawford Notch: The railway was extended from Fabyan to the Cog Railway Base Station, and two new hotels were built in the vicinity. The harbinger of the end of this era came in 1899, when the first automobile ascended the carriage road; by 1904 an annual automobile race, "The Climb to the Clouds," was being run. The huge and sumptuous Mt. Washington Hotel, built on virgin ground a mile from Fabyan, was completed in 1901–1902. So visible from the road and from many summits, this last survivor of an era of grandeur may seem the epitome of the White Mtn. hotel, but in fact the era had already come near its end when the Mt. Washington Hotel was built. It gained its greatest fame when, in 1944, it was the site of the international financial conference that set up the World Bank and the International Monetary fund. Today, it is the last of the great hotels of the region, the only one that has not been torn down or burned to the ground. In recent years it has been extensively renovated and winterized and operates year round as part of a major resort at Bretton Woods. It survives as a monument to a short but opulent period in the region's history.

THE ERA OF THE LOGGING BARONS

The history of the logging in the White Mountains begins in 1867, when the New Hampshire legislature passed a law permitting the governor to sell all of the state's public lands to pay for school maintenance. The governor quickly did so, at very low prices, and much of this land was later bought up by a half-dozen lumber barons who systematically clear-cut large forested areas in the White Mountains between 1875 and 1915, stripping the mountain slopes and starting forest fires with their spark-spewing steam locomotives. A fascinating account of this era is contained in C. F. Belcher's *Logging Railroads of the White Mountains*. It was the wanton destruction of the forests, more than anything else, that caused the sense of outrage among White Mtn. visitors and residents that inspired the movement toward conservation and preservation in the twentieth century.

By 1907, 650 million board feet were being cut in the region each year to satisfy the demand caused by the building boom in New England. Also, techniques for making paper from spruce pulpwood by the sulphite process became reasonably sophisticated near the end of the nineteenth century, so trees that would otherwise have been regarded as having little economic value—particularly those typical of higher slopes—were now enthusiastically cut. A forestry study of the period indicates that "New Hampshire was the most intensively lumbered state, per acre of wooded area, of any of the states."

River driving was tried as a method of getting logs to the mill; this had been successful in the lowlands where rivers were large, but the mountain rivers and streams were generally too small and rocky, and were useful for only a short time in the spring. The railroad, then, became the principal mode of transportation for the lumber companies. Each laid its own tracks into the wilderness it had purchased, until most of the White Mtn. region bore a network of active and abandoned rail lines. When an area was logged out, the tracks were usually taken up and moved to the next area to be stripped of timber. When the trains were not hauling out logs, they sometimes took excursion parties in on their flat-cars. The ruins of old lumber camps, now mostly clearings, are still visible in many parts of the region, and many of the abandoned railroad beds and logging roads were used for hiking trails.

Compared to other areas of the White Mountains, the Presidential Range was relatively unscathed by timber harvesting, probably because its slopes rose so quickly from the valley that they lacked the fine stands of large trees that grew on lower, gentler slopes. One railroad line ran from Whitefield up the south branch of the Israel River to service the logging in the area northwest of the Northern Peaks, where the gentler terrain produced finer stands of timber. This operation reached into the great northwest ravines of the Presidential Range. From the south, lines ran from the Saco valley below Crawford Notch up the Rocky Branch and the Dry River, the long valleys south and southeast of Mt. Washington.

However, the damage caused by lumbering was still sufficient to provoke determined criticism throughout New England. The devastation in the Zealand valley, just west of Crawford Notch and within a few miles of the site of Ethan Allen Crawford's inn, was described as follows in an editorial titled "The Trail of the Sawmill" in the *Boston Transcript* of July 20, 1892:

"The beautiful Zealand Valley is one vast scene of waste and desolation; immense heaps of sawdust roll down the slopes to choke the stream and, by the destructive acids distilled from their decaying substance, to poison the fish; smoke rises night and day from fires which are maintained to destroy the still accumulating piles of slabs and other mill debris."

Other criticisms of the timber industry in New Hampshire at the time were even more strident, with one account comparing the destruction to that of the Holy Land around Jerusalem.

Completing the devastation of many areas were forest fires, mostly caused by lightning or the timber harvesters' spark-belching locomotives, which ignited dry slash left after lumbering. In 1903 such fires destroyed more than 10% of the White Mtn. forests. Altogether 554 serious fires were reported to the authorities during the first eight months of that year. The most notorious fire occurred in the same Zealand valley in 1903, leaving devastation that was described by Ernest Russell in *Collier's*:

"Today, however, it is a dull brown waste of lifeless, fire-eaten soil and stark white boulders. All about lie the great blackened stumps and tangled roots of what were once majestic trees. It is as if the contents of some vast cemetery had been unearthed in that little valley."

An observant visitor today can detect the traces of these fires in many places, including the Rocky Branch valley, which suffered fires in three successive years, the last in 1914. However, most of these areas are well on their way to recovery; in some places, particularly around Zealand valley, beautiful stands of white birch have grown up on slopes that were once left hideous by the fires.

Such events were obviously a grave threat to the White Mountains as a summer resort area, since its appeal to visitors depended on its scenic beauty. In 1888 the historian Francis Parkman had made an early plea for the preservation of White Mtn. forests because of their importance to the beauty of the mountains sought by visitors. Writing in the February 1893 issue of *Atlantic Monthly*, Julius H. Ward proclaimed his view that the White Mountains were "worth infinitely more for the purpose of a great national park than for the temporary supply of lumber which they furnish to the market.

THE TWENTIETH CENTURY

By the turn of the century there was a strong public sentiment in favor of a forest preserve maintained by the U.S. government where conservation, through selective timber harvesting, would be practiced. The Society for the Protection of New Hampshire Forests (SPNHF) was founded in 1901 to pursue this aim, and in 1903 the New Hampshire legislature passed a bill favoring such a preserve. That same year, the New Hampshire resolution was introduced into Congress as a bill, but it met with intense political opposition; many in Congress felt that the government had no constitutional authority to spend money for such a purpose. Much legislative maneuvering during several congressional sessions was needed to get what came to be known as the Weeks Act finally passed in 1911. It had started as a specific bill to protect the White Mountains, introduced by and named after Massachusetts Congressman (later US Senator and then Secretary of War under President Harding) John Wingate Weeks, a native of Lancaster NH; it ended up, because of the legislative compromises needed to get it enacted, as a general doctrine in which the government asserted its right to protect the headwaters of navigable rivers and to acquire watersheds for that purpose. In 1912 the commission empowered to apply the new law purchased more than 30,000 acres on the northern slopes of the Presidentials. By 1914 the total acreage exceeded 224,000, approximately one-third of the area within the purchase boundary; acquisitions included the all-important Mt. Washington, except for the summit area. In 1912 the state of New Hampshire purchased a 6000-acre tract in the heart of Crawford Notch and made it into a state park.

A strong force behind passage of the Weeks Act was the Appalachian Mountain Club, an organization founded in 1876 by a Massachusetts Institute of Technology professor (and later director of the Harvard Observatory), E. C. Pickering, "for the advancement of the interests of those who visit the mountains of New England and adjacent regions, whether for the purpose of scientific research or summer recreation." One of its first efforts had been to take over maintenance of some of the footpaths that had been cut in the Presidentials and nearby ranges over the past half-century by guides and explorers. In the 1920s the AMC hired a professional trail crew, the first of its kind in the country. Now made up of seasonal and full-time employees, the AMC crew continues to maintain about 375 miles of trail in the White Mountains, as well as about 20 back-country shelters and campsites. An important part of the trail system in New Hampshire is the Appalachian Trail (AT), a long-distance hiking trail from Maine to Georgia first conceived in the 1920s and completed in the 1930s; in the White Mountains (east of Kinsman Notch) the AT was made up from existing trails of the AMC. The AT is now administered by the Department of the Interior, and maintained principally by a number of volunteer organizations coordinated by the Appalachian Trail Conference. The AMC and its various New England chapters are responsible for more than 275 miles of the AT in the Northeast.

Along the AT in New Hampshire are eight mountain huts, the only alpine-style hut system in this country. The system began with a shelter constructed on Mt. Madison by the AMC in 1888 to provide protection for hikers caught in inclement weather. This hut was later enlarged, and a second was built on the flank of Mt. Washington in 1915 at Lakes of the Clouds. Today a string of eight, each a day's hike from the next, traverses the White Mountains, running from Carter Notch to Lonesome Lake, west of Franconia Notch. There is also a base camp at Pinkham Notch, at the foot of Mt. Washington. The original intent of the hut system was to enable hikers, in a time before lightweight backpacking equipment was available, to walk this entire scenic area with only a knapsack on their backs, thus making it accessible to many who could not otherwise enjoy its beauty. At first only shelters from the weather, the huts are now equipped with bunks and serve meals; a large part of the huts' supplies is packed in on the backs of young hut crew members. The huts also dispense information, provide educational programs, and serve as a base for search-and-rescue operations.

Shortly after the turn of the century, the new mobility provided to the average person by the automobile brought an end to the era of the grand hotels, although many of them managed to stay in operation until after World War II. New patterns of tourism were arriving. As Frederick Kilbourne described it in 1916: "The advent of the automobile, with its almost immediate leap into general use for touring, greatly to the regret of many, including some landlords, has largely transformed in character the summer hotel and tourist business in the White Mountains, as well as elsewhere. While the volume of travel has increased, the majority of the visitors to the region are now of the transient variety, making in most cases but a fleeting stay at any one place and consisting largely of those who are 'doing' the Mountains in their 'motor-car.'"

Now motorists stopped at the resort hotels for a meal, or perhaps to stay overnight; at most they stayed a few days, using the hotel as a jumping-off point for visiting nearby sights. The summer-long sojourn, when people returned year after year to spend weeks or even months at the same hotel, gradually became less and less common, and the large establishments suffered, especially those off the major scenic highway routes. Today the visitors backpack, or stay in motels or campgrounds, or own condominiums or vacation homes in the mountains. The volume of passenger traffic on trains also declined steadily, until shortly after World War II the railroads began to drop passenger service; one or two now remain as scenic attractions. With the new modes of transporting and sheltering visitors have come new tourist attractions; "theme" parks and ski areas that now try to stay open all year with gondola rides or alpine slides.

One serious effect of these changes in vacation patterns, from the hiker's point of view, is the decline of some of the local trail systems, which depended greatly on the pride and attachment felt for "our trails" by people who returned to the same place year after year; they came to regard these trails, in a sense, as a part of themselves. The conditions created by this process are acute and very obvious today, as some of the fine trail networks that once provided varied walks, without the crowds that the major trunkline trails draw, are now sinking into oblivion.

Skiing came to the mountains in the 1920s, at first practiced by a few hardy individuals who were looking for a winter sport more thrilling than snowshoeing—a sport that most of them also practiced. When mechanized tows were invented, and skiers no longer had to climb up the mountain in order to enjoy the exhilarating swoop down the slopes, the sport's popularity increased very rapidly. Perhaps the last important role of the railroads in recreational passenger transportation was played by the ski trains that once left Boston every weekend. One important twentieth-century trend in the region, which owed much to the boom in alpine skiing, was its use by visitors throughout the year. Kilbourne noted that in the nineteenth century, only the hardy inhabitants and a few intrepid mountaineering enthusiasts could be found anywhere near the Presidential Range in winter. However, the phenomenal growth of downhill skiing in New England, and more recently of ski touring, has made the region a four-season resort area today. For this reason the AMC now keeps three of its huts open on a caretaker basis throughout the winter, and Pinkham Notch Visitor Center is an important base for winter ice climbers, snowshoers, and ski tourers, as well as summer hikers and rock climbers.

The most renowned winter sport in the Presidentials is the spring skiing in Tuckerman Ravine. There, skiable snow often lasts well in May; once winter avalanche danger has subsided, ambitious skiers hike up the two miles from Pinkham, then climb the precipitous headwall for each run, since there is no lift. A few places are safe for average skiers, but the headwall has sections that can severely challenge the most expert skier. The acme of this tradition was the three Inferno Races from the summit of Mt. Washington to Pinkham, sponsored by the Dartmouth Outing Club in the 1930s.

The growth of tourism and developed recreation, along with increased use of the backcountry, has often brought pressure for kinds of development that are viewed as destructive by those who want to preserve the wild and scenic values of the woods and mountains. As early as 1915, plans were made for a second scenic railway to the summit of Mt. Washington; as surveyed, this railroad would have required a tunnel through the Castellated Ridge and one and a half loops around the summit cone. Fortunately (or so most people probably feel today), the promoters ran into financial problems unrelated to this project and were unable to get it started. In the 1930s the Works Progress Administration drew up plans for a scenic highway crossing all the Presidential peaks, similar to those that now exist in the southern Appalachians, and got as far as sending surveying crews into the field. This plan met bitter opposition and died. Today, controversies come from ski areas that want to expand both in area and in summer activities, and housing developments, particularly for condos and other vacation homes. Southwest of the Presidential Range, in Franconia Notch, a parkway was completed after more than a decade of struggle and compromise between those who wanted a superhighway and those who wanted to protect the scenic values of New England's most famous notch.

During the modern era the White Mountain National Forest has become the dominant institution in the White Mtn. region. Organized under the authority of the Weeks Act of 1911, the WMNF grew steadily as lands were acquired from lumber companies and other private owners, and it now totals about 770,000 acres. Approximately 85% of the land within the designated purchase boundary is now part of the forest, a very high percentage among national forests. Because it is situated so close to the East Coast population centers, the WMNF is one of the ten most heavily used national forests in the country. It is estimated that 200,000 people visit the summit of Mt. Washington each year, on foot or by the Cog Railway or Auto Rd.

This great and rather sudden popularity has led to concern about overcrowding and degradation of the backcountry. The development of lightweight backpacking equipment in the 1960s and 1970s contributed to a tremendous increase in the use of backcountry; efforts to educate hikers and campers in the means of preserving the natural values of the wild country, including the development of the "clean camping" ethic, have helped to minimize campers' impact on the land, but it has still been necessary to prohibit or limit camping in some areas (see Forest Protection Areas). Tent platforms are provided at several backcountry sites to limit the areas where the ground cover will be damaged by the pitching of tents. In the Great Gulf Wilderness the old shelters were removed because their sites had been overused and abused. Careful backcountry users have helped to make possible a relatively low level of restriction on camping throughout the WMNF.

A major recent development has been the designation of areas as Wilderness, which is done by Congress on the recommendation of the Forest Service with advice from other groups. This process started when the Great Gulf area was officially designated a Wild Area by the WMNF in 1959, and was then included in the new Wilderness system when Congress passed the Wilderness Act in 1964. The Presidential Range-Dry River Wilderness was added in 1974, and since then the Pemigewaset Wilderness, Sandwich Range Wilderness, and Caribou-Speckled Mountain Wilderness have been added. (See Introduction, White Mountain National Forest, for more on Wilderness Areas.) The Wilderness program has engendered a lively debate, which is likely to retain its vigor for some time, between those who would like to see the areas kept available for a wider variety of uses and those who support as much Wilderness as possible because they fear lumbering, road-building, and other development detrimental to the present wild character of the lands.

It is safe to predict that Mt. Washington will continue to attract large numbers of people with very diverse interests to this region, and that problems will arise that will require imaginative solutions in order to preserve, as far as possible, the variety and the quality of the experiences that these people come in search of.

Section 4
Natural History

GEOLOGY

Viewing the massive Presidential Range, with its broad plateaus and deeply carved cirques, many visitors have been moved to wonder how all this came to be. Although the mountains are a common symbol of permanence—by the standard of a human lifetime they are indeed virtually unchanging—like people they are born, flourish, and then die, eventually to be replaced by new mountains. What mountains may someday stand where Mt. Washington now rises we cannot know, but the history of the Presidential Range lies encrypted in the kinds of rocks and their arrangement.

Any explanation of geological history is subject to modification or even complete replacement as new methods of research are devised and new discoveries are made. Thus, all accounts of the formation of the Presidential Range are based on theories that are subject to change as knowledge advances. The discussion that follows is primarily based on a geological booklet, "The Geology of the Mt. Washington Quadrangle," which presents the most widely accepted accounts of the development of the Presidential Range. ("The Geology of the Mt. Washington Quadrangle" and "The Geology of the Crawford Notch Quadrangle" provide very useful and detailed discussions of the geology of the Presidential Range area, written for readers without geological training. They are available from the NH Department of Resources and Economic Development, PO Box 856, Concord NH 03301.) Also presented is an alternative and somewhat iconoclastic theory of recent geological history drawn from Will F. Thompson's three-part article "The Shape of New England Mountains," which was published in the AMC's magazine *Appalachia* in 1960 and 1961.

The history of the bedrock of the Presidential Range, inferred from the known patterns of the rock that can be studied today, is thought to have begun about 500 million years ago in a shallow inland sea that is believed to have covered this region. Over countless centuries, due to erosion of land to the east, a sheet of mud and sand many thousands of feet thick accumulated at the bottom of the sea, which continued to exist because its floor gradually sank as the sediment layers grew thicker and heavier. The rock that was formed from these sediments is no longer part of the Presidential Range, having been converted to quartzite and forced out of the area by subsequent activity, and is found today only to the northwest of the Presidentials.

Next came a period of volcanic activity in the land to the east; great quantities of volcanic ash and debris were carried into the sea and probably filled it completely. The depth of this sheet of volcanic material eventually amounted to about a mile; subsequently altered by heat and pressure, this material, called the Ammonoosuc volcanics, now crops out along the lower northern edge of the Presidentials and presumable underlies much of the range.

Then, about 400 million years ago, seas once again covered the region, depositing many more layers of sediment on top of the previous ones. About 390 million years ago, these sediments (known as the Littleton Formation) were squeezed and folded under great heat and pressure, metamorphosing the shale and sandstone of the sea floor into gneiss, schist, and quartzite. The latter two rocks, which have proved relatively resistant to weathering, are the primary components of the crest of the Presidential Range today—as well as such lower but locally prominent peaks as Moosilauke, Stinson, the southern Kearsarge, and Grand Monadnock. Granite, which is often thought of as the principal component of the White Mountains, is often much less durable than the schists and quartzites; some varieties of granite, particularly those found around Mt. Chocorua and Mt. Osceola, become so "rotten" after exposure to weathering that they can be crumbled in the hand. Many of the rocks found at the higher elevations of the Presidential Range exhibit definite layering and folding which discloses the nature of their development. Recent chemical analysis, which attempts to deduce the temperature and pressure at which rocks were formed by studying their constituent minerals, indicates that the squeezing and folding of the Littleton Formation probably occurred about seven miles below the surface.

Then, about 360 million years ago, molten rock welled up into the region; the resulting granite rocks are found to the west, around Jefferson Notch, and to the north, around Randolph Station (near the Randolph East trailhead). Since then the rocks that form the bedrock of the Presidential Range have changed little—although other rocks were probably deposited by volcanic action on top of them and then worn away—but glaciers, wind, frost, and running water have greatly changed the surface, breaking down and removing great amounts of rock. At the estimated rate of about two feet per 10,000 years, the seven miles of rock which is thought to have overlain the present Presidential ridgecrest could have been eroded in 200 million years. It is believed that some of this eroded rock was recycled into the formation of the Catskill Mountains in New York.

The Presidential Range may never have been substantially higher than now, since the land tended to rise as erosion lightened the overlayer of rocks. The generally accepted theory is that the land was eroded to a rolling plain surmounted by a number of hills that are now the Presidential peaks. Then the land rose gradually, and as it did streams carved deep valleys in the rocks around the peaks, sparing the region of the peaks themselves because of its resistant schist and quartzite cap. This remnant of a once extensive plain is called the Presidential upland. This explanation is suggested by the relatively gentle slopes above treeline, so much in contrast to the steep slopes that descend from the treeline down; as its proponents point out, it takes little effort for a visitor on the upper slopes of the Presidentials to imagine a vast plain continuing outward.

However, in the series of articles on "The Shape of New England Mountains," Will F. Thompson challenged the eroded-plain theory and advanced a far different explanation for the contrast in the steepness of slopes above and below treeline. The area above treeline was commonly thought to be geologically inactive, for large rocks observed above treeline were almost without exception covered by lichens on all their exposed surfaces; thus it was concluded that these boulders could not have moved in recent times. But Thompson argued that all this proved was that the rocks were not rolling along the ground; he advanced the theory that they were being borne along downhill on a mantle of soil where frost action was very vigorous. This process tended to level the ground wherever it took place, and it occurred primarily above treeline because there the winter winds blew the snow cover away, allowing very cold air to sink deep into the soil through gaps between the boulders. This cold air remained well into the summer, making the temperature below ground much colder than average temperature records suggested, and producing the vigorous frost action required to move the mantle of soil and the rocks resting on top of it.

Glacial action is evident throughout the Presidential Range, which has been completely covered by a glacier at least once, and probably several times. Glacial till—a claylike accumulation bearing fragments of rock different from those normally found on the range—has been found in excavations made near the summit. Erratics—boulders of different composition that local rocks, carried by the glacier from other areas—have been discovered almost on the summit of Mt. Washington; rocks from the Pliny Range, several miles to the north, have been found high in the Presidentials. In addition, potholes made by torrential streams have been found on high ridges (for example, the ledge mentioned in the

Caps Ridge Trail description), and scratches and grooves made by rocks embedded in the ice can still be seen on many ledges, allowing geologists to plot the direction of flow of the ice. The major notches of the Presidential Range, Crawford and Pinkham, have the distinctive U-shape of a glacier carved valley, with a flat floor and steep walls, showing that they were gouged out by a continental glacier which was compressed as it passed through these narrow defiles.

Among the most striking features of the Presidential Range are the glacial cirques, such as the Great Gulf and Tuckerman and King ravines, U-shaped gorges with steep walls and gently sloping floor, which contrast with the V-shaped valleys cut by the mountain streams. These cirques were carved by small local glaciers formed from snowdrifts which built up in times of unusual cold on the east side of the range, where prevailing winds deposit the snow which they blow off the upper plateau, and also on the north side, where lesser drifts are sheltered from the sun. The discovery of rounded rocks with glacial scratches high in Tuckerman Ravine, and the lack of moraines—the characteristic tongues of rock debris found in areas where the foot of a glacier melts away—seemed to confirm the commonly held opinion that no local glaciers could have occurred after the retreat of the last continental glacier, about 12,000 years ago.

Thompson, however, argued that the rocks high in Tuckerman Ravine were rounded and scratched by boulders brought to the edge of the ravine from above by frost action and then swept down over the edge by winter avalanches. He also argued that debris that might have formed moraines would have been carried away as quickly as it appeared by processes similar to those which moved the soil and boulders above treeline. Then, on the basis of evidence collected at Katahdin in Maine, nearby and with similar climatic conditions, he argued that it is probable that Presidential Range cirques have borne small glaciers in relatively recent times, and that a relatively small decrease in average annual temperature might convert Tuckerman's famous Snow Arch snowfield—some of which is often present in August—into a real glacier again.

Whether either of these theories accurately explains the present state of the Presidential Range has not been settled, and indeed we can never know with absolute certainty the causes which produced this magnificent scenery.

CLIMATE

The severity of the weather on Mt. Washington is legendary, and statistics can be quoted almost without limit to prove that the legend is based on cold numerical fact. A few such items follow.

The year-round average wind velocity is a brisk 35 mph. In winter, hurricane-force winds (75 mph or higher) are common; they blow an average of 104 days a year. Gusts of over 100 mph have been recorded in every month of the year and gusts of over 150 mph in every month from September to May. On April 12, 1934, the wind reached 231 mph on the summit of Mt. Washington, the highest wind velocity ever recorded except in tornadoes.

The average annual temperature on the summit of Mt. Washington is a chilly 27° F. The summit temperature has never risen above 72° F.; the record low is –47° F. It is below zero 65 days of the year on the average, and in June of 1945 a temperature of –8° F. was recorded.

Precipitation on the summit each year usually amounts to the equivalent of more than 70 inches of water. Much of this falls as snow, which averages 195 inches annually. The winter of 1968–69 saw the heaviest snowfall on record—over 47 feet. More than 4 feet came in one 24-hour period, a record for US weather observatories.

Fog and clouds are also quite common on the summit of Mt. Washington, occurring, on the average, on 305 days a year. Visitors can expect the summit to be socked in 55% of the time, according to weather observatory records. Occasionally a lenticular (lens-shaped) cloud—formed when moisture in the air condenses as it passes over the peak and then evaporates again as the wind descends the other slope—can be seen directly over the summit.

The combination of low temperature, high wind, and much precipitation creates a unique climate on the Presidential Range summits, an area that has been called an arctic island in the midst of the temperate zone. The mountains lie at the intersection of two major North American storm tracks, one sweeping up the coast from the Gulf of Mexico and the other a polar track traversing central Canada, the Midwest, and the St. Lawrence River Valley. The disturbances created when these two tracks cross are enhanced in power by their steep rise over the mountains.

It is no wonder, then, that the mountain has attracted many scientists. The Mt. Washington Weather Observatory, the first of its kind in the world, was initiated in 1870 and has been staffed permanently on a year-round basis since the 1930s, accumulating the detailed knowledge we now have of the climate on the summit. During World War II, all three major military services tested cold-weather equipment and clothing on Mt. Washington, and more recently the Air Force used the site to perform icing tests on engines and propellers.

Despite the summit buildings, the road, and the railroad, Mt. Washington is far from domesticated, and the other Presidential peaks remain mostly uncivilized. The combination of cold, wind, and rain or snow often creates a chilling effect that can freeze exposed flesh in minutes in winter and can kill at any time of the year; some claim that this weather is the equal in severity of any on earth. More lives have been lost on Mt. Washington than on any other peak in North America, mostly due to hypothermia, the uncontrolled loss of body heat.

PLANTS AND ANIMALS

Note: No consistent attempt is made here to systematically provide identification information for the species discussed.

The short White Mtn. summer, from June through August, is characterized by variety, color, and abundance of life. But from September until mid-May quite a different set of conditions—including shortened days, high winds, intense cold, rain, snow, and ice—severely challenges those members of the natural community that do not migrate. The necessity of surviving the brutal climate on the Presidential Range—and even, to a lesser degree, on its lower slopes—exerts a powerful influence on every species that makes its home there. Adaptation, often to a radical extent, is required in order for them to survive through to yet another summer's growth.

Climbing to the crest of the Presidential Range from the surrounding valleys, one passes through a series of zones whose climate and vegetation are characteristic of regions progressively farther north; on the high lawns, for example, one is in an area ecologically comparable to northern Labrador. The elevations at which these zones begin and end vary in response to a number of climatic factors, including exposure to weather and amount of available sunlight; often past disturbances—such as fires, landslides, or logging—cause local variations. The general pattern, however, is evident throughout the range. Given the wide climatic variation between the base and the summit ridges of the Presidential Range, it would require a very large book to discuss all the plants and animals that live there. One study of the alpine zone alone lists 110 plant and 95 insect species. However a general description of the various plants and animal communities of the range is possible.

The hardwood forest: Most trails start in a forest dominated by the northern hardwoods, where the most common large trees are American beech and several birches and maples. The beech and the various types of birch are the easiest to identify. The beech is recognized by its smooth light-gray bark on younger trees or upper limbs. A single large beech is often surrounded by numerous pole-size trees that have sprouted from the older tree's roots, making it almost possible to map the root system by the location of these sprouts. The white (or paper) birch has shiny white bark, which tends to peel off in strips, on its mature trunk and limbs; young trees and limbs are bronze in color. The gray birch is a smaller tree, often growing in clumps of three to five, with prominent black horizontal scars on white bark that does not peel in large strips. The yellow (or silver) birch is a large tree with lustrous silvery yellow bark that peels off in narrow translucent strips. The quaking aspen, best identified by its generally smooth gray-green bark, is a common resident on the borders of marshes and beaver ponds. Birches and aspens are fast growing but cannot tolerate shade; birches in particular are often found in pure stands where a disturbance, such as a fire, has opened up the forest floor to full sunlight.

Maples are a major component of the hardwood forest. The sugar maple is a large tree with gray bark, darker than the beech. The bark of young trees has irregular cracks, while that of older ones is often deeply furrowed. Three smaller maples are also commonly found in the White Mountains. The red maple, recognized by its gray bark (smooth when young and scaled when older) and conspicuous red twigs, grows very well in swampy soil that would be too moist for many other trees. The striped maple (or moosewood) is a small, shrubby tree, which grows well beneath a canopy of other hardwoods; its leaves are very large and its furrowed dark-brown or green bark sports vertical white stripes, more obvious on smaller trunks and branches, which give the tree its name. The mountain maple. is bushy, often forming thickets; its thin, slightly fissured bark is a light reddish brown, and its hairy green to red-brown twigs reveal a brown pith when broken.

Conifers are also common in this zone: red spruce is found throughout the zone, hemlocks grow in some of the lower valleys, and a few fine stands of red pines may be seen on some of the lower southern ledges of the range. Perhaps the most unusual tree in the woods is the tamarack, which sheds its needles each fall—the only deciduous conifer in the White Mountains. Tamaracks are slender with reddish, scaly bark, and bear small spherical cones that stand upright on the branch. Tamarack and black spruce commonly grow together in swamps and peat bogs at elevations of up to 4000 ft., and a winter hiker coming on a mixed stand of tamarack and black spruce is likely to think that the tamaracks are dead.

There are also numerous smaller trees and shrubs, including the striped and mountain maples discussed above. The American mountain ash—not an ash at all, but a relative of the apple tree—is fairly common above 2000 ft.; it produces clusters of bright red fruits about the size of blueberries, which often remain on the tree until mid-winter unless eaten by birds. The hobblebush, which grows in cool, moist woods up to about 3000 ft., is a straggling shrub less than ten feet tall with large oval leaves. Its branches often take root where they touch the ground and may trip an unwary traveler—thus the name. In spring it produces showy white flowers—composed of small fertile flowers surrounded by large sterile flowers—which turn into clusters of bright red to purple berries in late summer and fall. Hobblebush buds are favorite deer food and make the shrub simple to identify in winter, since they are brown, furry, and always in pairs, suggesting rabbit ears.

In fact, variety is the primary characteristic of this region, whose gentler weather provides at least a little suitable habitat for a great many species, in contrast to the higher regions where the severity of the weather greatly restricts the number of species that can survive. But the lower-slope forest community must still contend with severe winter conditions. Although protected from the extremes found on exposed ridges, these plants are also subjected to storms, high winds, and cold. Herbaceous or woody, they must remain dormant for seven months a year. Trees in the forest canopy cannot wait winter out beneath a blanket of snow, and almost invariably show scars from the high winds that send limbs crashing into one another and from storms that overload branches with ice and snow. The loss of a limb opens the door to attack by fungus or insects and can permanently weaken the tree. Violent gusts can make the entire tree a victim of windthrow. Smaller trees, particularly birches, may be bowed or snapped off by ice loading.

This type of woodland, with its high, open canopy of trees and its abundance of shrubs growing in the rich humus of the forest floor, covers much of northern New England. In high summer very little sunlight penetrates to the forest floor, so small plants have had to adopt several strategies in order to flourish. Some sprout as soon as the snow is gone—some even start as soon as sunlight begins to filter through the snowdrifts—then flower as quickly as possible, and complete their annual cycle before the leaves of their larger neighbors choke off their access to the sun, the ultimate source of all energy for plant growth. This strategy is adopted by the familiar flowers of the spring woodlands: yellow violet, spring beauty, red and painted trilliums, bellwort, and trout lily (also called dogtooth violet, but it is not a violet).

The trout lily also shows another common strategy: It sends up leaves for several years, carefully hoarding in its root the tiny amounts of extra food that it is able to photosynthesize each year, until it finally has saved enough to flower and manufacture seeds. It is not uncommon to find a small area completely covered by trout lily leaves without a single plant large enough to flower. With such a strategy plants are able to make use of more shady spots, and avoid the risks of late-spring snowfalls and frosts to which the early bloomers expose themselves.

Once leaves fill the upper canopy, the common flowering plants are the perennials and the shade-tolerant species: Canada mayflower, clintonia (whose blue berries in late summer are far more conspicuous than its flowers), twisted stalk, pink lady's slipper (and often its white variant), bunchberry, starflower, wild sarsaparilla, Indian cucumber, foamflower, and false Solomon's seal. In wet areas Indian poke, jewelweed, and tall meadow-rue are sometimes abundant, and such uncommon but magnificent plants as the purple-fringed orchis provide an occasional treat. In late summer, asters, goldenrods, and joe-pye weeds are frequently seen. Ferns and mosses, which are not flowering plants, are also shade-tolerant and very common in the deep woods.

It is interesting to note that the common summer flowers of lawns, fields, and roadsides—daisies, dandelions, buttercups, common yarrow, red and yellow hawkweed, black-eyed Susans, and most clovers—are not natives to the region but immigrants. Except for black-eyed Susan, an invader from the west, they are not even native to North America. These larger, fast-growing species, mostly annuals, are seldom found in the mountains except along logging roads and in overgrown clearings—and sometimes near the AMC huts. Their huge requirements for sunlight make it impossible for them to grow in the deep woods, and they proliferate only where human activities have created openings; prior to large-scale human intervention, there was no ecological niche for such plants in the White Mountains. Fortunately for hikers, poison ivy is likewise intolerant of shade, so this noxious native species is seldom found in the White Mountains.

Flitting among the trees and shrubs of the northern hardwood forest will be warblers, thrushes, vireos, rose-breasted grosbeaks, and redstarts. Chipmunks and red squirrels, the latter frequently heard and seen scolding the intruding hiker from a tree, are the mammals most likely to be encountered. The engineering feats of beaver are visible in many ponds, and sometimes trails are flooded by this energetic animal. Rabbits and deer abound, though their tracks in winter are seen far more often than the animals themselves in any season. Porcupines and raccoons, learning to profit from human presence, often become major pests. Moose have steadily increased their numbers over the last two decades, so hikers have a much improved chance of meeting this huge, ungainly living symbol of the north woods, which has not yet been taught to fear humans. Bears are fairly common, but they make a mostly successful effort to stay out of sight—except for the semi-civilized individuals who have learned that hikers often carry food and can be persuaded to relinquish it, and who sometimes become pests at popular campsites. Bears are normally dangerous only when surprised or threatened. Toads are ubiquitous, and garter snakes, wood frogs, and red-spotted newts are also common. There are many small rodents, but these shy nocturnal beasts are seldom seen, although they are frequently heard at night helping themselves to campers' food.

The boreal forest: As the trails attain an elevation of 2500 to 3000 ft., the trees change to those of the boreal forest, which is composed primarily of red spruce, balsam fir, and paper birch. At some of the high trailheads, one begins in this forest. The transition between these zones is often slow, with the boreal species taking over gradually, but occasionally a sharp boundary can be seen. The variety of species decreases markedly with increasing elevation. In the course of evolution, deciduous trees found it more energy-efficient to put out new leaves each spring than to maintain them through the winter. In the fall, they withdraw what nutrients and organic molecules they can from the leaves before letting them go. These chemicals—most notably chlorophyll—are broken down and sent to the roots to be stored. Our spectacular autumn colors result from the predominance of anthocyanin pigments left in the leaves after the chlorophyll is gone. By November the deciduous forest has lost most of its summer foliage; the loss of leaves deprives the naturalist of the easiest means of distinguishing one tree from another, so identifying species in the winter requires attention to bark, twigs, buds, and overall growth form. As elevation increases and growing season becomes shorter, most deciduous trees are unable to photosynthesize enough food to replace their full set of leaves each year. The major exception is the paper birch, whose fast growth—much faster than the conifers—allows it to take advantage of any opening. The presence of a stand of nearly pure white birch at higher elevations is an almost certain sign of a forest fire many years ago. Eventually the birches age and the smaller conifers that have grown up between them take over; new birches cannot grow in the shade of the old ones. The conifers, which are adapted to very slow growth patterns, and whose needles are relatively resistant to damage by freezing and can therefore be used for several years, have an overwhelming advantage on the higher slopes. Since these trees maintain their foliage during the winter, loss of water through the needles is a real danger; the cold winter winds contain very little moisture and have a strong drying effect, and surface and ground water is generally frozen. To protect against moisture loss, the surfaces of evergreen leaves and stems are covered with a thick waxy or resinous coating as the tree prepares for winter; the needle-like leaf form also exposes less surface area from which water can evaporate.

Under the dense growth of evergreens only shade-tolerant species and the most patient perennials can survive. The highly acid soils derived from evergreen needles also limit species diversity. Goldthread, which has evergreen leaves and thus wastes less hard-earned energy, is one of the principal species of the deep shade. Wood sorrel often covers large areas; its cloverlike leaves, tart and refreshing, are often chewed by hikers. Clintonia, bunchberry, Canada mayflower, and other species take advantage of breaks in forest cover, including trailsides.

Birds include juncos and a number of northern warblers—black-throated blues and greens, Canadas, and magnolias. In addition to the mixed forest species, a number of birds prefer this habitat, among them the winter wren, Swainson's thrush, hermit thrush, myrtle warbler, and kinglet. Here the white-throated sparrow, called in its assertive voice for "Old Sam Peabody, Peabody, Peabody," provides the most distinctive of all bird songs. Here also are found two of the species that are most likely to engage a hiker's attention. The spruce grouse, a fairly large bird, lacks natural enemies and is not afraid of humans. The male is slate gray with a red patch over the eye, the female is brown. If you meet one, it will probably watch you curiously until you get to within ten yards of it, and then amble casually off into the woods. In late June or early July a female may well burst out of the woods directly at you, and hop down the trail ahead as if her wing were broken. Listen for the low cheep of her chicks, and be careful not to step on them! Another friendly bird is the gray jay, also called the Canada jay or whisky jack. This bird is a northern species, and the high evergreen forests are at its extreme southern limit, but one or two often inhabit peaks of about 4000 ft. elevation where they appear to live off the generosity of passing hikers. They will frequently eat off one's hand, and they often snatch food left on rocks whether intended for them or not. You need not search for them, since if they are present they will undoubtedly come around to inspect you (and your provisions).

Treeline: As one ascends and the climate becomes more severe, the average size of the trees tends to decrease fairly steadily until, as treeline—aptly called by ecologists a zone of tension—is approached at 4000 to 4500 ft., they rapidly become smaller and more thickly spaced. Trees growing in exposed areas have their top branches trained by the prevailing winds. The tops of these "flagged" trees show branches pointing downwind in the shape of a pennant. Here some plant species make their final appearance, although most that have survived this high can also grow in sheltered spots above treeline.

At treeline, the last stunted trees—the same ones that grow 50 to 70 feet tall only a thousand feet lower on the slope—are shaped by the increasing rigors of wind and snow into low mats of tangled branches called *krummholz* (a German word meaning "crooked wood"), which may be a century or more old. They are occasionally found quite high above treeline in sheltered spots, usually where snowdrifts form, or in the lee of boulders or in natural depressions in the terrain. The location of treeline seems to be primarily influenced by climate. On the north-facing slopes exposed to prevailing winter winds from the northwest, treeline is lower; on the eastern and southern slopes, where snow accumulates in the lee of the peaks, it is higher. (Southern slopes also usually receive more sunlight during the growing season.) However, the causes that determine the exact elevation of treeline—which occurs in the Presidential Range at roughly half the elevation of treeline in the Rockies—have yet to be fully explained.

The alpine zone: Some of the most severe weather in the world occurs above treeline in the Presidential Range; the combination of frequent fog and cloud cover, cool summer temperatures, heavy precipitation, and high winds create an island of arctic tundra in the temperate zone, with a climate similar to that of Labrador, north of the continental treeline. This area, the largest continuous above-treeline alpine zone in the eastern United States, runs for 8.5 miles from Mt. Madison to Mt. Eisenhower and has an area of approximately 7.5 square miles. In the alpine zone itself, it is too harsh for full-sized trees, so the plants that predominate are low-lying heaths, grasses, rushes, sedges, lichens, mosses, and the tiny but beautiful mountain wildflowers. Above treeline, there are probably about 110 species of higher plants, of which 75 are true alpine plants that only grow in this zone. The other 35 are native to the boreal forest, but survive at higher elevations in the krummholz mats. Three of the alpine plants are endemic—that is, they only exist in a small geographic area. The dwarf cinquefoil, which only grows in one area in the White Mountains, is the most famous of these; alpine avens and a variety of bluet occur here and on a few islands in the Canadian Atlantic.

Low posture is universal among plants of the alpine zone. Close to the ground, the winter gales are buffered by friction from the land surface. The fact that a given species will grow taller in the lee of a large boulder than on nearby open ground attests to the limitations wind places on growth. Smaller leaf area or loss of leaves in the fall helps to protect against wind damage and desiccation. On plants that retain their leaves through the winter, waxy or hairy surfaces also help to prevent loss of moisture and make leaves more resistant to abrasion by wind-blown snow crystals. Scientists believe that many of the alpine plants migrated south ahead of the advancing continental ice sheet, then, as the climate became milder and the glaciers receded, these plants migrated upslope, were eliminated by competition in gentler climates, and survived only in this climatic island where their competitors could not live. Consequently, these species, and other similarly adapted ones, are found only on other alpine islands in New England and the Adirondacks, and in Labrador far to the north.

Despite common adaptive strategies, there is no single key to survival. Within the alpine zone, local areas differ greatly in their exposure to wind and sun, snowdepth, and soil moisture. It is a combination of these and other factors—called a microclimate—which determines what vascular plants can grow in a particular location. Different species that habitually grow under similar conditions may be grouped into plant communities. Let us look at four distinct communities and their adaptations to the severe climate.

The hiker who ascends beyond treeline will first encounter the *krummholz community* of dwarf black spruce and balsam fir, tightly intergrown mats from 4 inches to 8 feet in height. By growing in this manner, each tree can provide a degree of shelter from the wind for its neighbors; together, they often shelter a considerable community of smaller plants. Snow, which limits the growing season of these evergreens, provides a beneficial service in return. The plants can not grow while covered with snow, but in the eight-month winter the snow that drifts into the krummholz patches provides a protective blanket, insulating them from the wind, low temperatures, and excessive drying out at a time when their roots cannot take up water from the frozen ground. Beneath the snow it remains at roughly the temperature at which the snow fell, as much as 40° to 50° F. warmer than the outside air. The height of a krummholz patch is directly controlled by the depth of drifted snow which that patch is able to accumulate, since new growth that protrudes above the following winter's snow will be killed. The growth of individual trees is therefore primarily horizontal rather than vertical, often extending only downwind from the original stalk. Different patches vary greatly in height due to variations in local topography. On the lee side of a boulder or other topographic high point, trees will grow flush with the height of the obstacle, gradually tapering off as the area downwind becomes more exposed. In a local depression, the krummholz will grow with small trees around the perimeter and taller trees in the center so as to form a roughly level surface with the surrounding slopes. If part of a patch is cut, the bordering trees will likely retain less snow and will die back during the winter; therefore, the cutting of a campsite in krummholz usually has a disastrous effect on the surrounding vegetation, perhaps destroying a hundred years of growth.

A second alpine community that depends upon drifted snow for protection during the winter is the *snowbank community,* composed of both woody and herbaceous plants, most of which are deciduous. These plants establish themselves at the base of cliffs, in depressions or in the lee of rocks and other windbreaks—particularly krummholz patches—at elevations ranging from 4800 to 5800 ft. Plants common in such communities are heaths, sedges, grasses, goldenrods, alpine bluet, Canada mayflower, clintonia (bluebead lily), Indian poke, and goldthread. The herbaceous members of the snowbank community are among the last to begin growing in the spring, since they must wait until their winter insulation has melted before they can begin their growing season, although some species—most strikingly Indian poke—may actually begin to push up through the snow when enough light filters through the melting snowdrift.

On moist, gentle slopes above 5400 ft. is found a third community, the *sedge meadow,* which is almost completely dominated by the Bigelow sedge, a rather broad-leaved species with a purplish fruit stalk. Both of these features may be recognizable in winter, since sedges are found in more exposed areas that do not collect a great deal of snow; though the plants may be covered by rime or groundwater ice, the dry leaves and stalks often protrude. In preparation for winter, sedges withdraw chlorophyll and other organic molecules into their root systems, allowing only skeletal brown leaves to take the full force of the weather. They develop a more extensive root system than the alpine plant communities, which provides a suitable anchor for the leafy sedges against high winds. The sedge meadow also includes some mosses and mountain sandwort; downslope, this community may expand to include large clumps of rushes and low heath shrubs, and lower still is a heath-rush community, which includes three-forked rush, mountain cranberry, alpine bilberry, and three-toothed cinquefoil.

The fourth group, the rugged *diapensia community,* grows on rocky and wind-swept slopes and ridges at the limits of habitable terrain. Only the nonvascular lichens, which can withstand almost complete desiccation, exist under harsher conditions. Diapensia has thick, waxy leaves and grows in very tight cushionlike mats one inch or less in height, which help to hold what moisture may reach the thin, rocky soil on which these plants grow during the summer months. Completely exposed to winter weather, individual plants have only their neighbors to help them resist damage and uprooting. Members of this community include mountain cranberry, Lapland rosebay, alpine azalea, and bearberry willow. All have the ability to withstand intense cold without the insulation provided to more sheltered communities by snow. Diapensia plants have undergone freezing in liquid nitrogen at –210° C. and lived to produce seeds.

The Alpine Garden, Bigelow Lawn, and Monroe Flats (near Lakes of the Clouds) are the most popular locations for viewing the mountain wildflowers that bloom among the rocks each spring. In middle to late June the white diapensia, pink alpine laurel, and purple Lapland rosebay bloom in bright patches on the slopes, along with many other less common or less showy plants. The most accessible area is the Alpine Garden, which can be reached from the Mt. Washington Auto Rd. or from the summit buildings where the Cog Railway stops, as well as by hiking up the mountain. The flowers are protected, as are the other plants in the White Mountain National Forest, and picking or otherwise damaging them is illegal. Preservation of these rare plants depends largely on the care exercised by hikers; be careful to remain on the trails in these areas, and step on rocks rather than vegetation, as damage is repaired very slowly in this severe climate. The habitat of the rarest of the plants, the dwarf cinquefoil, has been closed to all public entry to protect these tiny plants from accidental trampling.

Few animals and birds live in the alpine zone. L. C. Bliss lists nine animals that appear here, mostly small rodents such as mice, shrews, squirrels, woodchucks, porcupines, and chipmunks and also snowshoe rabbits, but most of them are primarily visitors. Only two birds are known to nest above treeline, the slate-colored junco and the white-throated sparrow. However, other birds, such as ravens, hawks, and an occasional eagle, may be seen in the area. Insects are the predominant mobile life form here. One study lists 95 native species, including 61 beetles, although it is difficult to distinguish between those insects occurring naturally and the ones blown up on strong winds from the lowlands. Ten species of black spiders can be seen scurrying among the rocks. Of the 14 species of moths and butterflies that appear here, 3 are endemic. The White Mtn. butterfly, whose larvae feed on the local grasses, lives only above treeline in the White Mountains and can be seen fluttering about the sedge meadows, most frequently in early July. The White Mtn. fritillary and White Mtn. locust are also native species found only in this region.

The Presidential Range is, in fact, one of the finest places to study the ways in which plants and animals adapt to their environment. There is a wealth of understanding and knowledge available to those with the patience to study and observe the inhabitants of this unique area.

Appendix A
Four Thousand Footers

The Four Thousand Footer Club was formed in 1957 to bring together hikers who had traveled to some of the less frequently visited sections of the White Mountains. At that time, such peaks as Hancock, Owl's Head, and West Bond had no trails and were almost never climbed, while other peaks on the list that had trails were seldom climbed, and the problem of over-use was unknown, except in the Presidentials and Franconias. Today the Four Thousand Footer Club is composed of active hikers whose travels in the mountains have made them familiar with many different sections of the White Mountain backcountry, and with the problems that threaten to degrade the mountain experience that we have all been privileged to enjoy. The Four Thousand Footer Committee hopes that this broadened experience of the varied beauties of our beloved peaks and forests will encourage our members to work for the preservation and wise use of wild country, so that it may be enjoyed and passed on to future generations undiminished.

The Four Thousand Footer Committee recognizes three lists of peaks: the White Mountain Four Thousand Footers, the New England Four Thousand Footers, and the New England Hundred Highest. Separate awards are given to those who climb all peaks on a list in winter; to qualify as a winter ascent, the hike must not begin before the hour and minute of the beginning of winter or end after the hour and minute of the end of winter. As of April 2002, these clubs had the following number of officially registered members: White Mountain Four Thousand Footers, 7102 (winter, 271); New England Four Thousand Footers, 1866 (winter, 97); New England Hundred Highest, 523 (winter, 64). To qualify for membership, a hiker must climb on foot to and from each summit on the list. The official lists of the Four Thousand Footers in New Hampshire, Maine, and Vermont are included at the end of this appendix. Applicants for the White Mountain Four Thousand Footer Club must climb all 48 peaks in New Hampshire, while applicants for the New England Four Thousand Footer Club must also climb the 14 peaks in Maine and the 5 in Vermont.

The Four Thousand Footer Committee issued revised lists for these clubs in April 2002. For most climbers the most significant changes will be the substitution of Wildcat "D" for Wildcat "E" and the elevation of Spaulding Mtn. and Mt. Redington in Maine to Four Thousand Footer status.

The New England Hundred Highest Club list differs substantially from the other two because it includes a considerable number of peaks without trails; several of these peaks require advanced wilderness navigation skills of the group leader, and two are on private land where written permission to enter may be required.

If you are seriously interested in becoming a member of one or more of the clubs sponsored by the Four Thousand Footer Committee, please send a self-addressed stamped envelope to the Four Thousand Footer Committee, Appalachian Mountain Club, 5 Joy Street, Boston, MA 02108, and an information packet including application forms will be sent to you. If you are interested in the New England Four Thousand Footer Club and/or the New England Hundred Highest Club, please specify this, since these lists are not routinely included in the basic information packet. After climbing each peak, please record the date of the ascent, companions, if any, and other remarks.

Applicants for any of the clubs need not be AMC members, although the Committee strongly urges all hikers who make considerable use of the trails to contribute to their maintenance in some manner. Membership in the AMC is one of the most effective means of assisting these efforts.

Criteria for mountains on the official list are: (1) each peak must be 4000 ft. high, and (2) each peak must rise 200 ft. above the low point of its connecting ridge with a higher neighbor. The latter qualification eliminates such peaks as Clay, Franklin, North Carter, Guyot, Little Haystack, South Tripyramid, Lethe, Blue, and Jim. All 67 Four Thousand Footers are reached by well-defined trails, although the paths to Owl's Head and Redington and some short spur trails to other summits are not officially maintained.

On the following lists, elevations have been obtained from the latest USGS maps, some of which are now metric, requiring conversion from meters to feet. Where no exact elevation is given on the map, the elevation has been estimated by adding half the contour interval to the highest contour shown on the map; elevations so obtained are marked on the list with an asterisk. The elevations given here for several peaks in the Presidential region differ from those given elsewhere in this book, because the Four Thousand Footer Committee uses the USGS maps as the authority for all elevations, while in the rest of the book the

Bradford Washburn map of the Presidential Range supersedes the USGS maps in the area it covers.

Four Thousand Footers in New Hampshire

Mountain	Elevation		Date Climbed
	(feet)	(meters)	
1. Washington	6288	1916.6	_____
2. Adams	5774	1760	_____
3. Jefferson	5712	1741	_____
4. Monroe	5384*	1641*	_____
5. Madison	5367	1636	_____
6. Lafayette	5260*	1603*	_____
7. Lincoln	5089	1551	_____
8. South Twin	4902	1494	_____
9. Carter Dome	4832	1473	_____
10. Moosilauke	4802	1464	_____
11. Eisenhower	4780*	1457*	_____
12. North Twin	4761	1451	_____
13. Carrigain	4700*	1433*	_____
14. Bond	4698	1432	_____
15. Middle Carter	4610*	1405*	_____
16. West Bond	4540*	1384*	_____
17. Garfield	4500*	1372*	_____
18. Liberty	4459	1359	_____
19. South Carter	4430*	1350*	_____
20. Wildcat	4422	1348	_____
21. Hancock	4420*	1347*	_____
22. South Kinsman	4358	1328	_____
23. Field	4340*	1323*	_____
24. Osceola	4340*	1323*	_____
25. Flume	4328	1319	_____

Mountain	Elevation		Date Climbed
	(feet)	(meters)	
26. South Hancock	4319	1316	_____
27. Pierce (Clinton)	4310	1314	_____
28. North Kinsman	4293	1309	_____
29. Willey	4285	1306	_____
30. Bondcliff	4265	1300	_____
31. Zealand	4260*	1298*	_____
32. North Tripyramid	4180*	1274*	_____
33. Cabot	4170*	1271*	_____
34. East Osceola	4156	1267	_____
35. Middle Tripyramid	4140*	1262*	_____
36. Cannon	4100*	1250*	_____
37. Hale	4054	1236	_____
38. Jackson	4052	1235	_____
39. Tom	4051	1235	_____
40. Wildcat D	4050*	1234*	_____
41. Moriah	4049	1234	_____
42. Passaconaway	4043	1232	_____
43. Owl's Head	4025	1227	_____
44. Galehead	4024	1227	_____
45. Whiteface	4020*	1225*	_____
46. Waumbek	4006	1221	_____
47. Isolation	4004	1220	_____
48. Tecumseh	4003	1220	_____

Four Thousand Footers in Maine

Mountain	Elevation (feet)	(meters)	Date Climbed
1. Katahdin, Baxter Peak	5268	1606	_____
2. Katahdin, Hamlin Peak	4756	1450	_____
3. Sugarloaf	4250*	1295*	_____
4. Crocker	4228	1289	_____
5. Old Speck	4170*	1271*	_____
6. North Brother	4151	1265	_____
7. Bigelow, West Peak	4145	1263	_____
8. Saddleback	4120	1256	_____
9. Bigelow, Avery Peak	4090*	1247*	_____
10. Abraham	4050*	1234*	_____
11. South Crocker	4050*	1234*	_____
12. Saddleback, the Horn	4041	1232	_____
13. Redington	4010*	1222*	_____
14. Spaulding	4010*	1222*	_____

Four Thousand Footers in Vermont

Mountain	Elevation (feet)	(meters)	Date Climbed
1. Mansfield	4393	1339	_____
2. Killington	4235	1291	_____
3. Camel's Hump	4083	1244	_____
4. Ellen	4083	1244	_____
5. Abraham	4006	1221	_____

Appendix B
Accident Report

Your Name _____ Date _____ Time _____

DESCRIPTION OF LOST OR INJURED PERSON:

Name _____ Age/Sex _____

Address _____ Hair _____

_____ Fac. Hair _____

Phone _____

REPORTING PERSON:

Name _____ Phone _____

Address _____

WHAT HAPPENED:

_____

_____

_____

_____

_____

POINT LAST SEEN:

Car Description _____ Date _____

Car Location _____

Itinerary _____

WEARING (color/style/size):

Jacket _____ Shirt _____

Shorts/Pants _____ Hat/Gloves _____

Glasses _____ Pack _____

Footgear _____ Crampons _____

CARRYING (color/style/size/quantity):

Map _____ Sleeping Bag _____

Tent/Bivy _____ Rain/Windgear _____

Flashlight/Batts _____ Extra Clothing _____

Food/Water _____ Ski Poles/Ice Axe _____

Experience _____

Physical/Mental Conditions _____

ESSENTIAL PATIENT EXAMINATION

PROBLEM AREAS/INJURIES:

- ❏ Head
- ❏ Neck
- ❏ Shoulders
- ❏ Chest
- ❏ Abdomen
- ❏ Back
- ❏ Pelvis

- ❏ Left Upper Leg
- ❏ Left Lower Leg
- ❏ Left Foot
- ❏ Right Upper Leg
- ❏ Right Lower Leg
- ❏ Right Foot

- ❏ Left Arm
- ❏ Left Hand
- ❏ Right Arm
- ❏ Right Hand

Chief Complaint and Plan

_____
_____
_____

Problem 2 and Plan

_____
_____
_____

Problem 3 and Plan

_____
_____
_____

BACKGROUND INFORMATION

Allergies _____

Medication _____

Previous Injury/Illness _____

Last 24 hr food/water intake _____

Medical Conditions/Other _____

_____

FOR BACK, CHEST, OR ABDOMINAL PAIN, DETERMINE:

History _____

Duration _____

Intensity _____ **Changing +/-** _____

VITAL SIGNS

ESSENTIAL:				HELPFUL:		
TIME	LEVEL OF CONSCIOUSNESS	BREATHING RATE	PULSE	BLOOD PRESSURE	SKIN	PUPILS

NOTES

DATE/TIME:	WEATHER/LOCATION AND FINDINGS:	ACTION TAKEN:

Index

Note: **Boldface** type designates detailed description of trail.

Abbreviations, xxxv
Abenaki, 147
Accident report, 189–192
Adams, Mount (5799 ft.) [1:F9], viii,
    76, 78, 144
    trails on, 115–130
Adams, Mount Quincy (5410 ft.)
    [1:F9], 78
Adams, Mount Sam (5585 ft.)
    [1:F9], 78
Adams 4 (5355 ft.) [1:F9], 127
Air Line [1:E9–F9], 115–117
Air Line Cutoff [1E9], 116
Alpine Garden [1:F9], 11
Alpine Garden Trail [1:F9], 31–32
Alpine tundra, 10–11, 180–183
Ammonoosuc Ravine, 12
Ammonoosuc Ravine Trail
    [1:F8–F9], 44–45
Amphibrach [1:E9], 122
Animals, xviii–xx, 174–183

Ball Crag (6112 ft.) [1:F9], 27
Beechwood Way [1:E9], 141
Bemis Bridge, 56
Bemis Ridge [1:H9–H8], 15
Bigelow Lawn [1:F9], 12
Bluff, 142
Boots, xvi
Boott Spur (5502 ft.) [1:F9], viii, 12
Boott Spur Link [1:F9], 28–29
Boott Spur Trail [1:F9], 27–28
Boundary Line Trail [1:F8], 135
Brookbank [1:E9], 140
Brooks, crossing, xxi
Brookside, The [1:E9], 112
Bruin Rock [1:E9], 112
Bugle Cliff [1:G8], 47

Bumpus Basin [1:E9], 76
Burt Ravine, 12
Buttress Trail [1:F9], 103–104

Cabin-Cascades Trail [1:E9–F9],
    128
Camel Trail [1:F9], 33–34
Camping
    fire regulations, xxiv
    Forest Protection Areas (FPAs),
        xxiii, 19–20, 79–80
    Great Gulf Wilderness, 79–81
    low-impact, xxiv
    regulations, xxiii–xxiv, 19–21
    roadside campgrounds, xxv
    shelters and tentsites, xxii–xxiii,
        80–81
Caps, Ridge of the [1:F8–F9], 76, 77
Caps Ridge Trail [1:F8–F9],
    133–134
Cascade Ravine [1:F9–E9], 76
Castellated Ridge [1:F8–F9], 76, 77
Castle Ravine [1:E8–F9], 76, 77, 78
Castle Ravine Trail [1:E8–F9],
    130–131
Castle Trail [1:E8–F9], 132–133,
    144
Cave Mountain (Bartlett NH) (1439
    ft.) [3:H9], 15
Cave Mountain Path [3:H9], 66
Cell phones, use of, xxviii
Chandler Brook Trail [1:F9],
    100–101
Chandler Fall [1:E9], 124
Chandler Ridge [1:F9], 11
Chapel Rock [5:E10], 137
Chemin des Dames [1:F9],
    120–121

Clam Rock [1:F10], 96
Clay, Mount (5533 ft.) [1:F9], viii, 76, 77
    trails on, 90, 135–136
Cliffway [1:E9], 123
Clinton, Mount. *See* Pierce, Mount
Clothing, xv–xvi
Cold Brook Fall [1:E9], 122
Compass, how to use, xiii–xiv
Coosauk Fall [1:E9], 109
Cornice [1:F9], 91–92
Crag Camp (RMC) [1:E9], 80
Crawford, Ethan Allen and Lucy, 148–156
Crawford, Mount (3119 ft.) [1:H8–H9], viii, 15, 69
Crawford Cliff Spur [1:G8], 39
Crawford Connector [1:G8], 39, 42–43
Crawford Notch State Park [1:G8], 20
Crawford Path [1:G8–F9], 38–43
Crew-Cut Trail [1:F9–F10], 36–37
Crippies, 65–66
Crystal Cascade [1:F9], 11, 69
Cutler River [1:F9], 20

Daniel Webster–Scout Trail [1:F10–F9], 106–107
Davis, Mount (3819 ft.) [1:G9], viii, 15
Davis Path [1/3:H8–F9], 56–59
Devil's Kitchen [1:E9], 109
Direttissima [1:F9–G9], 31
Dome Rock [1:E9], 111, 112, 142
Dry River [1:G9–H8], 15
    trails on, 51–55
Dry River Cutoff [1:G8], 55
Dry River Shelter #3 [1:G9], 21, 52
Dry River Trail [1:H8–F9], 51–53
Duck Fall [1:E9], 113
Durand Ridge [1:E9–F9], 76, 78

Durand Scar [1:E9], 117

Edmands Col (4938 ft.) [1:F9], 77, 78, 82–84, 87–89
Edmands Col Cutoff [1:F9], 90–91
Edmands Path [1:G8], 45–46
Eisenhower, Mount (4760 ft.) [1:G8], viii, 14, 70
    trails on, 43, 45–46
Elephant Head [1:G8], 47, 69
Elephant Head Spur [1:G8], 47
Emerald Bluff [1:F9], 129, 130
Emerald Tongue [1:E8], 129
Emerald Trail [1:F9], 130
Equipment, xv–xvi

Fallsway [1:E9], 139–140, 142
Fan [1:F9], 25
Field, Darby, 8, 146, 147–148
Fire regulations, xxiv, 19–20, 79
Forest Protection Areas (FPAs), xxiii, 19–20, 79–80
Four Thousand Footer Club, 184–188
Franklin, Mount (5001 ft.) [1:G9], viii, 13–14

Gem Pool, 44, 45
Geology, 169–172
George's Gorge Trail [1:F9], 37
Giant Stairs [1:H9], 15–16
Gibbs Brook Scenic Area [1:G8], 39
Glen Boulder [1:G9], 29
Glen Boulder Trail [1:G9], 29–30, 69
Glen Ellis Falls [1:G9], 11–12
Gordon Fall (Mount Madison) [1:E9], 142
Gordon Ridge, 76
Gray Knob (RMC) [1:F9], 81
Gray Knob Trail [1:F9], 125–126
Great Gulf, 11, 78

Great Gulf Link Trail [1:F10], 97–98
Great Gulf Trail [1:F10–F9], 95–97
Great Gulf Wilderness [1:F9–F10], 74–76
  camping, 79
  trails in, 95–106
Great Gully Trail [1:F9], 121
Green Hill (2181 ft.), 16
Gulf of Slides Ski Trail [1:F9–G9], 9, 29
Gulf Peak (Slide Peak) [1:G9], 30
Gulfside Trail [1:F9], 81–89

Hanging Cliffs (Boott Spur) [1:F9], 28
Hart Ledge (2020 ft.) [1:H9], 15, 16
Hermit Lake [1:F9], 9, 69
Hermit Lake Campsites [1:F9], 20–21
Highland Center at Crawford Notch (AMC), 17–18
Hincks Trail [1:E9–F9], 125
Hitchcock Fall [1:E9], 109
Hope, Mount (2505 ft.) [1:H8], 15, 16
Hotels, era of the grand, 156–161
Howker Ridge [1:E9–F9], 76, 109
Howker Ridge Trail [1:E9–F9], 109–111, 142
Huntington Ravine, 11
Huntington Ravine Fire Road [1:F9], 25
Huntington Ravine Trail [1:F9], 25–26
Huts, 16–19, 79
Hypothermia, xvi–xviii, 4

Ice storm of 1998, impact of, xxxi–xxxii
Inlook Trail [1:E9], 111–112
Insects, xx

Iron Mountain (2726 ft.) [3:H10], 16, 69
Iron Mountain Trail [3:H10], 67–68
Isolation, Mount (4003 ft.) [1:G9], viii, 15
Isolation Trail [1:G9–G8], 61–62
Israel Ridge (Emerald Tongue) [1:F9], 76
Israel Ridge Path [1:E8–F9], 128–129
Israel River [1:F9], 77

Jackson, Mount (4052 ft.) [1:G8], viii, 14, 70
  trails on, 47–48, 66–68
Jacob's Ladder (4800 ft.) [1:F8–F9], 8
Jefferson, Mount (5716 ft.) [1:F9], viii, 77, 144
  trails on, 90, 130–135
Jefferson Ravine [1:F9], 76, 77
Jefferson's Knees [1:F9], 77
Jewell Trail [1:F8–F9], 135–136
John Sherburne Ski Trail [1:F9], 8, 9

Kelton Crag [1:E9], 111
Kelton Trail [1:E9], 111
King Cliff [1:E9], 123
King Ravine [1:F9–E9], 76, 78, 119, 143
King Ravine Trail [1:E9–F9], 119–120
Knife-edge (Mount Adams) [1:E9–F9], 116
Knight's Castle [1:E9], 124

Ladderback Trail [1:E9], 123
Lakes of the Clouds [1:F9], 13
Lakes of the Clouds Hut (AMC) [1:F9], 18, 21

Langdon, Mount (2390 ft.) [1:H9], 15
Mount Langdon Trail [3:I9–H9], 63
Langdon Shelter, Mount, 21
Lawn Cutoff [1:F9], 33
Leave No Trace, xxvii–xxviii
Ledge Trail (Pine Mountain) [1:E10], 138
Liebeskind's Loop [1:F9–F10], 37–38, 69
Lightning, xviii
Link, the (Northern Peaks) [1:E9–F8], 94–95
Lion Head [1:F9], 11
Lion Head Trail [1:F9], 24–25
Little Monroe (5225 ft.) [1:F9], 13
Log Cabin (RMC) [1:E9] 80
Log Cabin Cutoff, 93
Logging, 161–163
Lower Bruin [1:E9], 115
Lowe's Bald Spot (2884 ft.) [1:F9], 69, 99
Lowe's Path [1:E9–F9], 126–127

Madison, Mount (5366 ft.) [1:F9], viii, 78, 143
  trails on, 106–115
Madison Gulf [1:F9], 76, 78
Madison Gulf Trail [1:F9], 98–100
Madison Hut (AMC) [1:F9], 79, 82–84, 88–89
Madison Spring [1:F9], 79
Maple Walk [1:E9], 140
Maps, xiii, xxxiii–xxxiv
Marshfield [1:F8], 8
Memorial Bridge [1:E9], 94
Mizpah Cutoff [1:G8], 49–50
Mizpah Spring Hut (AMC) [1:G8], 18–19, 70
Monaway [1:E9], 124
Monroe, Mount (5372 ft.) [1:F9], viii, 13, 70
  trails on, 44
Montalban Ridge [1:F9–H10], 12, 15
  trails on, 56–66
Monticello Lawn [1:F9], 77
Mossy Fall [1:E9], 118, 119
Mount Clay Loop [1:F9], 90
Mount Clinton Trail [1:G8], 53–54
Mount Eisenhower Loop [1:G8], 43
Mount Eisenhower Trail [1:G8], 54–55
Mount Jefferson Loop [1:F9], 90
Mount Langdon Shelter, 21, 63
Mount Langdon Trail [3:I9–H9], 63
Mount Monroe Loop [1:F9], 44
Mount Parker Trail [3:H9], 64
Mount Stanton Trail [3:H10–H9], 65–66

Nauman Tentsite, 21
Needle Rock [1:E9], 116
Nelson Crag (5620 ft.) [1:F9], 11
Nelson Crag Trail [1:F9], 26–27
Northern Peaks (Presidential Range) [1:F9–E9]
  camping, 79–81
  geography, 76–78
  huts, 79
  safety issues, 74–76
  trails, 81–141
Nowell Ridge [1:E9–F9], 76, 78

Oakes Gulf [1:F9–G9], 12
Oak Ridge (2140 ft.) [1:H9], 63
Old Jackson Road [1:F9], 35–36
  skiing, 9
Osgood Campsite [1:F9], 81
Osgood Cutoff [1:F9], 106
Osgood Ridge [1:F9–F10], 76
Osgood Trail [1:F10–F9], 104–106

Parapet, the [1:F9], 78
Parapet Trail [1:F9], 107
Parker, Mount (3004 ft.) [1:H9], viii, 15
Peabody River, West Branch [1:F9–F10], 76
Pentadoi [1:E9], 122
Perch (RMC) [1:F9], 80
Perch Path [1:F9], 126
Pickering, Mount (1930 ft.) [1:H10], viii, 15, 16, 69
Pierce, Mount (Mount Clinton) (4312 ft.) [1:G8], viii, 14, 70
Pine Link [1:E10–F9], 108–109
Pine Mountain (2405 ft.) [1:E10], 78, 142
    trails on, 136–138
Pine Mountain Road [1:E10], 137–138
Pine Mountain Trail [5:E10], 136–137
Pinkham Notch Visitor Center (AMC) [1:F9], 16–17
    trails from, to Mount Washington, 21
    trails North of, 35–38
Pinnacle, the (Huntington Ravine) [1:F9], 25
Plants, 9–10, 174–183
Pleasant, Mount. *See* Eisenhower, Mount
Presidential Range
    animals and plants, xviii–xx, 9–10, 174–183
    geology, 169–172
    peaks in, viii
Presidential Range–Dry River Wilderness [1:G8–G9–H9], 15, 19

Quay, the [1:F9], 127

Randolph Path [1:E9–F9], 92–94
Ravine of Raymond Cataract [1:F9], 11
Raymond Cataract [1:F9], 11
Raymond Path [1:F9], 35
Resolution, Mount (3415 ft.), viii, 15
Resolution Shelter, 21
Ridge of the Caps [1:F8–F9], 76, 77
Rivers, crossing, xxi
Rocky Branch Ridge [1:G9–H10], 12, 16
Rocky Branch Shelter #1 and Tentsite [1:H9], 21
Rocky Branch Shelter #2 [1:G9], 21
Rocky Branch Trail [3:G10–H9], 59–61
Roof Rock [1:F9], 131

Saco Lake [1:G8], 51
Saco Lake Trail [1:G8], 51
Saco River [1:G8–H8], 51
Saco River Trail [1:G8–H8], 50–51
Safety, 2–5, 74–75
Salmacis Fall [1:E9], 112
Salroc Falls [1:E9], 142
Sam Willey Trail [1:G8], 50
Scar Loop [1:E9], 117
Scar Trail [1:E9], 117
Sherburne Ski Trail, John [1:F9], 8, 9
Short Line [1:E9], 118–119
Six Husbands Trail [1:F9], 102–103
Snow Arch (Tuckerman Ravine) [1:F9], 22–23
Snyder Brook, 76
Snyder Glen (Snyder Brook ravine) [1:F9–E9], 116
Society for the Protection of New Hampshire Forests (SPNHF), 163

Southern Peaks (Presidential Range) [1:G8–F9], 12
    trails on main ridge of, 38–44
    trails to, from the west and south, 44–51
Southside Trail [1:F9], 32
Spaulding Lake [1:F9], 79, 144
Sphinx Col (4959 ft.) [1:F9], 78, 84–85, 86–88
Sphinx Trail [1:F9], 101–102
Spur Brook Fall [1:E9], 122, 123
Spur Trail [1:E9–F9], 124–125
Stairs Col [1:H9], 57
Stairs Col Trail [1:H9], 59
Stairs Fall (Mount Madison) [1:E9], 109
Stairs Mountain (3463 ft.) [1:H9], viii, 15, 69
Stanton, Mount (1716 ft.) [1:H10], viii, 15, 16
    Mount Stanton Trail [3:H10–H9], 65–66
Star Lake [1:F9], 78
Star Lake Trail [1:F9], 118
Sylvan Cascade [1:F9], 99
Sylvan Way [1:E9], 139

Tama Fall [1:E9], 114, 142
Thunderstorm Junction [1:F9], 82, 129
Town Line Brook Trail [1:E10], 139
Trail(s)
    descriptions, xxxi–xxxii
    distances, times, and elevation gains, xxxii–xxxiii
    following, xiii–xv
    lost on, what to do, xiv–xv
    markings, xiv
Trinity Heights Connector [1:F9], 34
Triple Falls [1:E10], 139, 142
Trip planning, xii–xiii

Tuckerman Crossover [1:F9], 32–33
Tuckerman Junction [1:F9], 23
Tuckerman Ravine [1:F9], 11
    skiing, 8–9
Tuckerman Ravine Trail [1:F9], 21–23
    camping restrictions, 20
    skiing, 9
Tunnel Rock [1:F9], 121

Upper Bruin [1:F9], 115

Valley Way [1:E9–F9], 113–114
Valley Way Campsite [1:E9], 81, 114
Vespers Falls [1:F9], 35

Wamsutta Trail [1:F9], 101
Washington, Mount (6288 ft.) [1:F9]
    Auto Road [1:F10–F9], 6–7
    books on, 10–11
    Cog Railway [1:F8–F9], 7–8
    first recorded ascent, 10, 146
    geography, 10–16
    Glen House site, 6–7
    Halfway House site [1:F9], 7
    hikes, suggested, 69–71
    history of, 145–168
    observatory, 6
    origin of name, 147
    safety, 2–5
    skiing, 8–9, 165–166
    summit buildings, 5
    trails from Northern Peaks, 81–89
    trails from Pinkham Notch, 21–31
    trails on Upper Cone, 31–34
    water, 45
Water, drinking, xxi–xxii, 5
Waterfall hikes, 142, 143
Watson Path [1:E9–F9], 113
Weather, xii, 2–4, 173–174

Webster, Mount (3910 ft.) [1:G8],
viii, 14
trails, 46–49, 70
weather, xii, 2–4
Webster Cliff Trail [1:G8], 48–49
Webster-Jackson Trail [1:G8],
46–48
Weeks Act (1911), 163–164, 167
Weetamoo Falls [1:F9], 97
Westside Trail [1:F9], 34
White Mountain National Forest
(WMNF), ix–xi
Forest Protection Areas (FPAs),
xxiii, 19–20
formation of, 166–167
scenic areas, x
trailhead parking fees, x–xi
wilderness areas, ix–x
White Mountains, history of,
145–168
White's Ledge (1410 ft.) [1:H10], 65
White Trail (Mount Sam Adams)
[1:F9], 82–83
Winniweta Falls [1:G10], 66
Winniweta Falls Trail [1:G10],
66–67
Winter climbing, xxv–xxvii

ABOUT THE AMC

Since 1876, the Appalachian Mountain Club has helped people experience the majesty and solitude of the Northeast outdoors. We offer outdoor skills workshops, guided trips, and lodging options for all levels of outdoor adventuring. Our conservation programs include trail maintenance, air and water quality research, and advocacy work to preserve the special outdoor places we love and enjoy for future generations.

Join the Adventure!

Take a hike, ride a bike, paddle a canoe. We believe that people who enjoy breathing fresh air, climbing mountains, splashing in streams, and walking on trails have more fun and take better care of the outdoors. Join the fun today. Call 617-523-0636 for membership information.

Outdoor Adventures

From beginner backpacking to advanced backcountry skiing, we teach outdoor skills workshops to suit your interest and experience. If you prefer the company of others and skilled leaders, we also offer guided hiking and paddling trips. Our five outdoor education centers guarantee year-round adventures.

Huts, Lodges, and Visitor Centers

With accommodations throughout the Northeast, you don't have to travel to the ends of the earth to see nature's beauty and experience unique wilderness lodging. Accessible by car or on foot, our lodges and huts are perfect for families, couples, groups, and individuals.

Books and Maps

We can lead you to the best hiking, biking, skiing, and paddling destinations from Maine to North Carolina. With more than 50 books and maps published, we're your definitive resource for discovering wonderful outdoor places. For ordering information call 1-800-262-4455.

Check us out online at **www.outdoors.org**, where there's lots going on.

Appalachian Mountain Club
5 Joy Street
Boston, MA 02108-1490
617-523-0636

LEAVE NO TRACE

The Appalachian Mountain Club is a national educational partner of Leave No Trace, Inc., a nonprofit organization dedicated to promoting and inspiring responsible outdoor recreation through education, research, and partnerships. The Leave No Trace Program seeks to develop wildland ethics—ways in which people think and act in the outdoors to minimize their impacts on the areas they visit and to protect our natural resources for future enjoyment. Leave No Trace unites four federal land management services—the U.S. Forest Service, National Park Service, Bureau of Land Management, and U.S. Fish and Wildlife Service—with manufacturers, outdoor retailers, user groups, educators, organizations like the AMC and the National Outdoor Leadership School (NOLS), and individuals.

The Leave No Trace ethic is guided by these seven principles:

- Plan ahead and prepare.
- Travel and camp on durable surfaces.
- Dispose of waste properly.
- Leave what you find.
- Minimize campfire impacts.
- Respect wildlife.
- Be considerate of other visitors.

The AMC has joined NOLS—a recognized leader in wilderness education and a founding partner of Leave No Trace—as the sole national providers of the Leave No Trace Master Educator course through 2004. The AMC offers this five-day course, designed especially for outdoor professionals and land managers, as well as the shorter two-day Leave No Trace Trainer course at locations throughout the Northeast.

For Leave No Trace information and materials, contact:

Leave No Trace, Inc.
P.O. Box 997
Boulder, CO 80306
800-332-4100
www.LNT.org

Notes

Notes

APPALACHIAN MOUNTAIN CLUB BOOKS

EXPLORE THE POSSIBILITIES

Don't get caught in the rain!
Waterproof *Presidential Range* Map

- Tear-resistant
- GPS-plotted
- Full-color

Includes an inset of the Mt. Washington summit area and tips on gear, safety, and low-impact camping.

ISBN 1-929173-26-1 $7.95

White Mountain Guide, 27th ed.
EDITED BY GENE DANIELL & STEVEN D. SMITH

ISBN 1-929173-22-9 $22.95

Discover the White Mountains of New Hampshire
BY JERRY & MARCY MONKMAN

ISBN 1-878239-88-0 $15.95

Nature Hikes in the White Mountains, 2nd ed.
BY ROBERT BUCHSBAUM

ISBN 1-878239-72-4 $14.95

Backcountry Skiing Adventures: New Hampshire & Maine
BY DAVID GOODMAN

ISBN 1-878239-64-3 $14.95

Sales of AMC Books support our mission of protecting the Northeast outdoors.

AMC Books · 5 Joy Street Boston, MA 02108 · 800-262-4455
SHOP ONLINE: WWW.OUTDOORS.ORG